A
COMPREHENSIVE
FAITH

An International *Festschrift*

for

Rousas John Rushdoony

Edited by
Andrew Sandlin

Friends of Chalcedon
San Jose, CA

Published by
Friends of Chalcedon
4960 Almaden Expressway, #172
San Jose, CA 95118
United States of America

Library of Congress Catalog Card Number 95-083815
ISBN 1-879998-09-2

Printed in the United States of America

To Sharon Lynn Sandlin
Covenant partner, wife of my youth, and
the love of my life

This volume was made possible by the generous contributions of the following individuals or organizations:

Elario N. Baldini

Stacy, Stephanie, and Alexander Baldree

Ivan R. Bierly

Claud and Betty Boyd

J. Robert Brame

Clyde Clapp

Robert and Martha Coie

Christine, Jennifer, Mary, and Glenn Coie

Church of the Word (of Painesville, Ohio)

Dr. Anne Davis

Dr. and Mrs. Truman Davis

Richard G. Deemer

Rev. Jefferson G. Duckett

Nick and Janie Edwards

Mr. and Mrs. David R. Estler

Paul and Sheryl Ferroni in memory of
Thomas H. Shiffler and the former
Sovereign Grace Reformed Church of
Ashland, Ohio

Craig and Grayce Flanagan

Gary T. Gorski

Grace Community Day Care(s) and Schools

Great Christian Books, Inc.

Bob and Mary Helen Green

Catherine Harnish

Keith and Antha Harnish

Bernice Howell

Nathan E. Johnson

Theron Johnson

Wayne and Jennifer Johnson

Dr. and Mrs. Edwin D. Johnston, Jr.

W. Daniel Jordan, M.D.

William and Susan Kellogg

Douglas F. Kelly

Don Krumm

Dr. and Mrs. J. H. Lawson

Michael and Jill Leake

Walter Lindsay

Niels and Suzanne Linschoten

Joe and Cindy LoGiudice

Mark and Patricia Ludwig

Bob and Joanna Manesajian

Rachel and Daniel Manesajian

Thomas E. Mansfield, M.D.

Hugh and Kaye Martin

Scotty, Nancy, and Shawn McEachern

Kim and Dorenda Melton

Norm and T. A. Milbank

Clint and Elizabeth Miller

Walter Miller and Linda Nard

Mr. and Mrs. Lee R. Musgrave

Dr. and Mrs. Richard Nichols

Mike and Debbie Nylin

Don and Pam Patterson

Lowell and Pam Peterson

Byron and Jean Phelps

Howard and Margaret Phillips

Steven and Linda Phillips

Robert and Barbara Piacentini

Thomas B. and Claire T. Pollard

E. and Joan Poumakis

Ardath and Edward Rhoads

Dwayne Riendeau

Mr. and Mrs. Donald Roberts

Rebecca, Jill, Sarah, Levi, and Emily Rouse

Mark and Darlene Rushdoony

Isaac, April, and Marie Rushdoony

George and Margaret Sapora

Steve and Jeanne Schlissel

Ford and Andrea Schwartz

Leah Settlemyre

Shiloh Christian Church

David and Connie Souther

William and Jane Staudenbaur

Darl and Emily Stern

Rev. and Mrs. C. L. Stover

Don Thompson

Takeshi Tomii

Michael and Rosemary Tuuri

Ellen Vasbinder

Dr. Richard Vest

Gary and Christa Wagner

Billie Welch

Allan Withington

Paul M. Wright

Mr. and Mrs. Jeffrey Zylstra

TABLE OF CONTENTS

Theology

Culture

Application

Afterword

Preface

The impetus behind the essays comprising this *Festschrift* constitutes not merely profound gratitude for the unparalleled godly influence of R. J. Rushdoony, but also the endeavor to elucidate and employ Rushdoony's foundational thinking in numerous spheres. This is, after all, one aspect of Rushdoony's genius (see my introductory essay in this volume). The essayists are convinced that it is only by an application of Rushdoony's thought to all spheres of human existence that Christians can expect to "reconstruct" modern life on an explicitly Biblical basis.

Rushdoony's epochal work has been routinely ignored or opposed, not only by theological and political liberals, who are the frequent objects of his incisive critiques, but also by evangelicals and other "conservatives," many of whose truncated theological orientation is shamed and overshadowed by Rushdoony's comprehensive, courageous, and cerebral approach to the Christian Faith.

The present volume testifies that the staggering theological and philosophical work of Rushdoony will, by the grace of God, continue into the next millennium. Not only will his ground-breaking writings stand permanently in their own right, but they will continue to inspire younger scholars and workers dedicated to the advancement of a world-conquering Faith under the Crown Rights of Jesus Christ pressed ineluctably in every sphere.

I wish to thank all the patrons whose gifts made this project possible and whose names appear elsewhere in this volume. Special thanks is due Friends of Chalcedon, under whose aegis this work has been published. Walter Lindsay was a capable and tireless proofreader. Joanna Manesajian furnished the photographs. Finally, I must thank Andrea Schwartz, without whose patient and unflagging work this project from beginning to end would have been impossible.

Andrew Sandlin

January 1996

1

Foreword

John M. Frame

If readers are surprised to find me writing in this volume, I am at least equally surprised to have been invited. Over some years, I have been known, not as an advocate for the Christian Reconstruction Movement, but as a sympathetic critic. This is, however, not the time for critical analysis, but for a tribute. And as Rousas John Rushdoony reaches age 80, I find that I earnestly want to bring such a tribute. Indeed, I want him to know that his work has been profoundly appreciated, even by many of us who agree with his distinctive ideas only 80% of the time rather than, say, 95%.

First, I am profoundly grateful to God that Rushdoony introduced so many of us to Cornelius Van Til. When I was a philosophy major at Princeton University, a representative of Westminster Seminary gave me a copy of Rushdoony's *By What Standard*, which I have used and recommended to others many times since. It was a wonderful eye-opener. Van Til's own writings are for the most part technical, somewhat disordered, and rather daunting in their style. Rushdoony put Van Til's thoughts in good order, added some great illustrations (I'll never forget "The Emperor's New Clothes"), and made Van Til available to a great many people that Van Til himself could not have reached. I still hear of people in communions far removed from conservative Reformed and Presbyterian circles who are ardent Van Tillians because of Rushdoony's work.

Not only did Rushdoony introduce Van Til to a wider audience; he also applied Van Til's thought to a number of subjects that Van Til himself ignored. Van Til's "one and many" became the key to politics and economics, not only theology and metaphysics. In society, too, Rushdoony taught us, the one tends to eat up the many (totalitarianism) or vice-versa (anarchy), when that society is given over to false gods. Only the word of the true God, the Trinitarian Lord, can provide both order and freedom.

And so, *second*, as Rushdoony would say, I am also grateful to him for teaching us the law of God. At Westminster Seminary, I received good teaching in many areas of Biblical content: Old Testament history, poetic and prophetic books, gospels, Acts, epistles, and Revelation. There was one utter vacancy in the curriculum: the Mosaic law. This was a very serious omission. The Torah is central to the Old Covenant, and no part of the Bible can be well understood without a good knowledge of it. Rushdoony filled that gap, for many of us. For all my disagreements in detail with Rushdoony's *Institutes of Biblical Law*, the overall thrust of it left me amazed at the wisdom of God's statutes. It again became possible to understand why the Psalmist would meditate in that law day and night (Ps. 1:2). And it was certainly Rushdoony's book which provoked all of our more recent discussions of the law at

3

Westminster. Without Rushdoony's *Institutes*, for example, Poythress's *Shadow of Christ in the Law of Moses* could not have been written.

We are, I think, still a long way from understanding in detail how the law of God is now to be applied to church and state. But Rushdoony's work has been a giant step in the right direction. That direction is a direction of *love* for God's law, a passion for God's holiness and righteousness, a heart desire that God's will be done on earth as it is in heaven. I am convinced that no "view of the law" will prove Scriptural unless it motivates us to that *praise* of God's law which fills Ps. 119.

Third, I am grateful to Rushdoony for giving us the courage to resist the evil trends of our time. In my early years as a Reformed Christian, I was never taught that there was anything wrong with public schools, or the welfare state, or the dishonor shown to parents and families in the public media. But Rushdoony has shown us that the antithesis between belief and unbelief takes some very concrete forms in our society and that as Christians we cannot be content to practice our faith on Sunday and then melt into the crowd for the rest of the week. And his testimony in court on behalf of harassed and persecuted Christians has been a great encouragement.

My wife and I are home schoolers today; I doubt if we would even have considered that option if it were not for Rushdoony's work and for the work of others inspired by him. There is no doubt that the growing resistance of Christians to the tyrannical secularism of the cultural and political establishment owes a great deal to Rushdoony. He has taught us that in this area also, the emperor has no clothes.

Which leads to my *fourth* and final observation, that Rushdoony has taught us not to accept defeat in the spiritual warfare. It has sometimes been assumed as a matter of course that Christians are doomed to failure in any attempt they may make to influence society. But if God has elected a vast multitude from every nation to glorify Jesus, and if he regenerates those to make them new creatures, is it conceivable that they should not make a large impact upon culture and upon history? A study of history itself (especially under Rushdoony's remarkably insightful guidance) shows us that Christians have in fact had a vast impact for good upon the culture and institutions of human society. Of course, Christians have been persecuted for their faith and have died for it — defeat of a sort, but only in the eyes of the unsaved world. In the long run, Jesus wins his battles — not only at the last judgment, but constantly through history.

Questions do remain, I think, about how those battles are to be fought, how we can love our enemies while defeating their aspirations. But surely we cannot go back to spiritual pacifism. God has used Rushdoony to awaken us from that slumber, and we return to it at our peril. To put it more positively, there are wonderful blessings which await the faithful and their children —

with persecutions, as Jesus says in the wonderful balance of Mk. 10:29-31—both in the present age and in the age to come.

These four emphases, and doubtless others, have profoundly influenced many of us who are not normally considered Christian Reconstructionists. There is a new spirit in the church universal today, a passion for learning God's word in detail and applying it seriously, without compromise, to the world in which we live. Rushdoony has been one of the earliest and most powerful voices motivating that spirit. For that we honor him and pray that God will give him many more years of effective witness.

John Frame is Professor of Apologetics and Systematic Theology at Westminster Seminary in California. He holds degrees from Princeton, Yale, and Westminster Seminary in Pennsylvania. He has written several books and numerous articles.

The Genius of the Thought of Rousas John Rushdoony

Andrew Sandlin

Just as all genuine Calvinists agree with Benjamin Warfield that "[i]n Calvinism ... objectively speaking, theism comes to its rights,"[1] so do the disciples of Rousas John Rushdoony believe that Christian Reconstructionism is the purest and most consistent expression of historic Calvinism. All reconstructionists are Calvinists, and they perceive in Rushdoony a refined Calvinism — interpreted through the grid of the epistemology and apologetics of Cornelius Van Til[2] — propelling Reformed convictions[3] to their most consistent and logical conclusions. Rushdoony, few would deny, represents theological and historical *development* in traditional Calvinism,[4] bearing as he does the accouterments of historic Calvinism fashioned to quell Enlightenment and post-Enlightenment barrages against the Faith.

While the sheer depth and extensiveness of Rushdoony's thought[5] preclude a comprehensive elucidation of the spheres in which he has posited consistent extrapolations of historic Calvinism, I intend to note five specific areas of legitimate development of traditional Calvinism in his work: first, the repudiation of all forms of dualism; second, opposition to the eternalization of any dimension of the temporal; third, the solidification of the historic Reformed view of the law; fourth, the inherent historical progressiveness of the success of the Christian Faith; and fifth, the reordering of all areas of human endeavor in terms of the Christian Faith as revealed in the Bible.

[1.] Benjamin Warfield, *Calvin and Augustine* (Philadelphia, 1956), 289.

[2.] Cornelius Van Til, *The Defense of the Faith* (Phillipsburg, NJ [1955], 1967).

[3.] Eugene Osterhaven, *The Spirit of the Reformed Tradition* (Grand Rapids, 1971).

[4.] The *locus classicus* on the issue of theological development is John Henry Newman's *An Essay on the Development of Christian Doctrine* (Notre Dame, 1989). For a more consistently Protestant perspective, see Jaroslav Pelikan, *Development of Christian Doctrine: Some Historical Prolegomena* (New Haven, 1969).

[5.] I can here allude to merely several works I cannot consider in detail. For Rushdoony's views of education, see *The Messianic Character of American Education* (Vallecito, CA [1963], 1995), *Intellectual Schizophrenia* (Phillipsburg, NJ, 1961), and *The Philosophy of the Christian Curriculum* (Vallecito, CA [1981], 1985); on American history, see *This Independent Republic* (Fairfax, VA [1964], 1978) and *The Nature of the American System* (Fairfax, VA [1965], 1978); on anthropology and psychology, see *Revolt Against Maturity* (Fairfax, VA, 1977); on science, see *The Mythology of Science* (Nutley, NJ, 1967); on textual criticism and translations, see "The Problems of the Received Text" and "Translation and Subversion," *Journal of Christian Reconstruction*, Vol. 12, No. 2 [1989], 7-18. For a veritable compendium of Rushdoony's views, consult *The Roots of Reconstruction* (Vallecito, CA, 1991).

Repudiation of All Forms of Dualism

A prime tenet of the Reformation was its insistence on the sacredness of calling — its objection to the sacerdotal caste that had developed in the Western church included dissent from the Roman Catholic practice of separating the faithful into two classes, the truly "spiritual" believers and the ordinary believers, a sequestering spurred by the idea of "holiness as a special vocation."[6] To the reformers, and especially the Reformed, all of life is sacred, the vocation of Monday no less than the worship of Sunday. Most notable are the Puritans, whose "work ethic" presupposed the sacredness of all of life: "[The] secular-sacred dichotomy was exactly what the Puritans rejected as the starting point of their theory of work."[7] More broadly, the reformers saw the affairs of this "mundane" life as significant.

Rushdoony equally denies this secular-sacred distinction. In fact, he carries the denial to its logical conclusion: the Faith must apply to *all* spheres of life (see section 5 of this essay). Rushdoony's opposition to the secular-sacred distinction, however, is somewhat more reflective and philosophically based than that of the older Reformed tradition. The foil of his insistence on a full-orbed Faith is, as is so with Van Til, Hellenic philosophy. He has a dim view of much of the Hellenic influence in early Christianity, a conviction emerging in his very first work, *By What Standard? An Analysis of the Philosophy of Cornelius Van Til.*[8] Rushdoony finds especially offensive the Greek propensity to *dualism,* a radical separation of ideas and matter, soul and body, forms and expressions, abstract and concrete, and so forth. Rushdoony embraces what may be termed a "Biblical monism." One must not be lead to conclude, however, that he swallows up differentiation in a single unifying and monistic principle. Rushdoony follows Van Til in arguing that the ontological Trinity constitutes the only solution to the age-old philosophical problem of the One and the Many.[9] That God is both and equally One and Many and that all facets of the universe derive from him as the absolute Creator means that unity does not destroy true diversity and diversity does not eliminate true unity. There can be true unity and diversity only because God is both unity and diversity.

[6.] D. Martyn Lloyd-Jones, *Expository Sermons on Second Peter* (Edinburgh, 1983), 234.

[7.] Leland Ryken, *Worldly Saints: The Puritans as They Really Were* (Grand Rapids, 1986), 24. As North notes, "Calvinism took the Roman Catholic ideal of the ascetic monk — a special layman or cleric removed from the affairs of the world — and placed it as the standard for Christians in their daily activities. The man who lives a religiously rational life fulfills his spiritual duty," in Gary North, "The 'Protestant Ethic' Hypothesis," *Journal of Christian Reconstruction,* Vol. 3, No. 1 [summer, 1976], 191.

[8.] Vallecito, CA [1958], 1995. In this essay, unless otherwise noted, all italics appearing in citations are original.

[9.] *ibid.,* 32, 33. See also Rushdoony, *The One and the Many* (Fairfax, VA, 1971), 1-20.

Nevertheless, Rushdoony perceives and excoriates the fragmenting effects dualism poses to the Faith;[10] his aversion to dualism works itself out in various ways. The first is in an intense interest in history. Rushdoony holds to the orthodox Christian view of the direct creation of the universe by God as the first step in understanding history.[11] The corollary to the creation doctrine is predestination: the universe is what it is because God determines that it shall be so; there is no meaning apart from God. Man's sin and God's redemption of man by the atoning work of Christ occurring on the plane of history are the visible exhibition of the divine determination to thwart and vanquish the rebellion of Satan: the defeat of Satan is not postponed until eternity. Crucial to history is the infallible word of God, inscripturated revelation speaking predictively and authoritatively to man. History is a personal affair because God is a personal God — man is everywhere confronted by God. Man cannot escape God at any point. While dualism posits true reality as beyond history, Rushdoony draws attention to the intense interest of true Christianity in history, a central stage of God's dealings.

This view of history presupposes a unified view of man himself. Rushdoony sees man as a unified — not a tripartite or bipartite — being.[12] The frequent dualistic attempt by man to escape his creaturehood is often equally an attempt to become God.[13] Man seeks to transcend the limitations of his humanity in order to play God. Thus Rushdoony gives quite a different cast to the popular "deeper-life" theology that parades as the supreme expression of submission to God — according to Rushdoony, it is quite the opposite.

A prime aspect of Rushdoony's repudiation of dualism is his aversion — like the Puritans' — to the isolation of the so-called "spiritual" tasks from the mundane, "carnal" callings of man in this life. This is a recurrent theme in Rushdoony's writings.[14] He notes characteristically:

> A radical deformation of the gospel and of the redeemed man's calling crept into the church as a result of neo-platonism. Dominion was renounced, the earth regarded as the devil's realm, the body despised, and a false humility and meekness cultivated.[15]

Dualism is pernicious not merely because it skews sound theology and philosophy, but also because it saps the proper dominion impulse, diverting man into a retreat mode and therefore away from his task of the exercise of godly dominion. Man is as "this-worldly" as "other-worldly"; to squelch the

[10.] Rushdoony, *Flight from Humanity* (no location: Thoburn Press, 1978).

[11.] *idem., The Biblical Philosophy of History* (Phillipsburg, NJ, 1979), 3.

[12.] *idem., Systematic Theology* (Vallecito, CA, 1994), 1:46.

[13.] *idem., The Flight from Humanity*, 3.

[14.] *idem., Law and Society: The Institutes of Biblical Law, Vol. II* (Vallecito, CA, 1982), 227-230.

[15.] *idem., The Institutes of Biblical Law* (Phillipsburg, 1973), 449.

eternal in favor of the temporal as in theological liberalism or the temporal in favor of the eternal as in fundamentalism and evangelicalism is equally erroneous.

Rushdoony, then, extends the traditional Reformed distaste for the secular-sacred distinction to a biblico-philosophical critique of Hellenic dualism and its key manifestations in the past and today.

Opposition to the Eternalization of Any Dimension of the Temporal

The ministry statement of Chalcedon, the foundation Rushdoony instituted in 1965, contains the following illuminating description of the purpose and justification for existence:

> Chalcedon derives its name from the great ecclesiastical Council of Chalcedon (A. D. 451), which produced the crucial Christological definition: "Therefore, following the holy Fathers, we all with one accord teach men to acknowledge one and the same Son, our Lord Jesus Christ, at once complete in Godhead and complete in manhood, truly God and truly man ...." This formula challenges directly every false claim of divinity by any human institution: state, church, cult, school or human assembly.

Rushdoony's extrapolation of what he later calls in the ministry statement "the foundation of Western liberty" from Chalcedonian Christology and his elicitation of equally notable social application from the other early creeds and councils[16] engenders perhaps the principal element of Rushdoony's thought and contribution to historic Calvinism: the dictum of individual freedom under God and His law-word as a specifically theological and creedal tenet. Of course, Calvinist theology has historically been noted for its inclination to assail and subvert civic and ecclesiastical tyranny,[17] but, as in the case of opposition to dualism, Rushdoony offers a profundity and sophistication beyond the traditional Calvinist insistence on the relation between divine sovereignty and individual liberty.

For one thing, Rushdoony prefers to cast this issue, as noted above, in creedal — and specifically Chalcedonian — terms. Much of the dazzling volume *The One and the Many* elucidates the frequency with which authority that inheres in Christ alone has historically been arrogated by or vested in a human institution: "Lacking the transcendental standard which Scripture provides, other systems inevitably turn to an immanent one and absolutize the state, the individual, or some other aspect of life."[18] Note that Rushdoony's concept of opposition to tyranny and defense of freedom is neither instrumental ("We need freedom so we can preach the gospel and train our

---

16. *idem., The Foundations of Social Order* (Fairfax, VA [1968], 1978).
17. N. S. McFetridge, *Calvinism in History* (Edmonton, Alberta, Canada [1882], 1989).
18. Rushdoony, *Intellectual Schizophrenia* (Phillipsburg, NJ, 1961), 52.

children properly") nor anthropological ("Man is made in God's image so nobody may tyrannize him"). Rather, Rushdoony's view is Christological — God in Christ alone is irrevocably authoritative and to ascribe this authority to any human or human institution is blatantly idolatrous and leads ultimately to tyranny. Only God possesses ultimate and irrevocable authority, and all valid human authority rests on divine authority:

> Only God has absolute authority, and only God can require absolute obedience. Where God's authority is acknowledged, all other legitimate authorities are obeyed as part of man's obedience to God and His order. However, where God's authority is denied, the logic of that denial when developed in all its implications, undercuts all other authorities.[19]

Historically, various institutions have vested themselves or been vested with ultimate authority. In ancient societies, the family was often eternalized.[20] As a reaction to statism, the individual is eternalized, a condition known socially as anarchy. Two spheres that come in for the severest criticisms, though, are the church and the state, not because anarchy and familialism are less evil but because in Western culture statist and ecclesiastical tyranny are most routine.

Rushdoony sees the institutional church as an impediment to godly Christianity if vested with authority God never intended it possess, nor does he spare Protestantism the criticism usually reserved for the medieval tyranny of the Papacy. The extension of the kingdom is paramount to Rushdoony, and if the church precludes that extension, it is no less culpable than a tyrannical state: "To limit this [Christ's] *church* to an institution or to history is to limit Christ's kingship."[21] Rushdoony does not limit the meaning of church to its institutional expression, nor identify the visible covenant community with the institutional church. The church must not become an end in itself, but must work to extend the kingdom of God on the earth.

No less than the institutional church has the state from almost the earliest times been guilty of temporalizing the eternal, *viz.*, depicting itself as God walking the earth. Unlike the typical conservative or libertarian critique of state tyranny, Rushdoony sees the latter in exclusively theological terms.[22] The state cut loose from Biblical Faith develops a "Messiah complex." Rushdoony therefore opposes socialism and other interventionist state policies not mainly because they curb individual freedom but because they constitute evidence of the state's playing God. Nor is Rushdoony an uncritical conservative. Libertarianism, he asserts, "overlooks the basic matter of faith

---

[19.] *idem.*, *Salvation and Godly Rule* (Vallecito, CA, 1983), 37.

[20.] *idem.*, *The Biblical Philosophy of History*, 58-59.

[21.] *idem.*, *Law and Society*, 342. Note pp. 335-342 for a summary of Rushdoony's ecclesiology. For a fuller expression, see *Systematic Theology*, 2:669-783.

[22.] *idem.*, *The One and the Many* (Fairfax, VA, 1978), *passim*. See also his *Christianity and the State* (Vallecito, CA, 1986), 157-168.

and fails to recognize that the liberty it looks back to was a youthful *accident* of the humanistic dialectic, of which *statism* was the essence,"[23] and is therefore a "failure."

As one might expect, this message does not endear Rushdoony to ecclesiocentric Protestants or to centralist statists. However, this message captures the purest note of historic Calvinism's war against every idol and against every attempt by man or his institutions to play God.

Solidification of the Historic Reformed View of the Law

Rushdoony is a modern-day champion of Biblical law. And since no sector of the Christian church has held the inscripturated law in such high esteem as the Reformed Faith, it is not surprising that his dedication to inscripturated law has endeared historic Calvinism to him. While unambiguously denying any role of the sinner's law-keeping in his justification, the Reformed nonetheless exalt the law in both their theological system and life practice. The Ten Commandments, for example, are inscribed in both the Heidelberg Catechism and the Larger and Shorter Catechisms of the Westminster Confession of Faith (WCF).[24] The WCF describes the inscripturated law of God as "a perfect rule of righteousness," valid for mankind both before and after the Fall.[25] The Reformed, following Calvin,[26] support what is ordinarily termed the "three uses of the law." Its first use is political and social: it inhibits external sinfulness and thus maintains social order. (The Reformed are careful to point out that the outward conformity this use of the law induces in no way contributes to salvation.[27]) Its second use is to convict the sinner of his iniquity, and thereby motivate him to trust in Christ, whose impeccable conformity to the law is imputed (credited) to the account of those exercising faith in him. The third use of the law is in sanctifying the Christian: it spurs him to greater obedience, serving as the absolute standard toward which he, empowered by the Holy Spirit, strives.

It is with the first and third uses of the law that Rushdoony is principally occupied, and he perceives certain weaknesses among the traditionally Reformed and the broader Christian community in expressions and

---

[23.] *idem., The One and the Many,* 29.

[24.] Confessional Lutheranism too holds the law in high regard, though its unique accent on the law-gospel distinction leads it to something of an ambivalent view of the law. See David P. Scaer, "The Law and the Gospel in Lutheran Theology," *Logia,* Vol. III, No. 1 [January, 1994], 27-34.

[25.] It is important to note that Rushdoony dissents from the common Reformed notion of the pre-Fall covenant of works. See Rushdoony, *Systematic Theology,* 1:376-379.

[26.] John Calvin, *Institutes of the Christian Religion* (Grand Rapids, 1949), 376-395 [Bk. 2, Ch. 7].

[27.] Thus Calvin: "And they [the wicked] are restrained, not because it internally influences or affects their minds, but because, being chained, as it were, they refrain from external acts, and repress their depravity within them, which otherwise they would have wantonly discharged," *ibid.,* 386 [Sec.10].

applications of both of these uses. In the case of the first, or political use, Rushdoony is disturbed that "natural law," universally recognizable regulation inhering in man *qua* man and in the structure of the universe, has traditionally supplanted Biblical law as the foundational regulation of the civic order:

> Roman Catholic scholars offer *natural law.* The origins of this concept are in Roman law and religion. For the Bible, there is no law in nature, because nature is fallen and cannot be normative. Moreover, the source of law is not nature but God.

> ... Neither positive law nor natural law can reflect more than the sin and apostasy of man: *revealed law* is the need and privilege of Christian society. It is the *only* means whereby man can fulfill his creation mandate of exercising dominion under God.[28]

For Rushdoony, the attempt to ground societal order in an amorphous natural law undercuts the possibility of a truly Biblically based and therefore Christian civilization.

Another aspect of the first use of the law as articulated in the traditional Reformed understanding to which Rushdoony takes exception is the inclination to divide the inscripturated law into three classifications (moral, judicial, and ceremonial) and limit the permanence of its application to the first, *i.e.,* moral.[29] He observes:

> It is a serious error to say that the *civil* [judicial] *law* was also abolished, but the moral law retained. What is the distinction between them? At most points, they cannot be distinguished. Murder, theft, and false witness are clearly civil offenses as well as moral offenses. In almost every civil order, adultery and dishonoring parents have also been civil crimes. Do these people mean, by declaring the end of civil law, that the Old Testament theocracy is no more? But the kingship of God and of His Christ is emphatically asserted by the New Testament and especially by the book of Revelation. The state is no less called to be under Christ than is the church. It is clearly only the sacrificial and ceremonial law which is ended because it is replaced by Christ and His work.[30]

Rushdoony perceives considerable continuity between the testaments in the role of the law. Our presumption should favor not the expiration of any law but its eternal validity, unless we have evidence to believe otherwise:

> The law is done away with only as an indictment against us; it stands as the righteousness of God which we must uphold. Every aspect of the Old Testament law still stands, except those aspects of the ceremonial

---

[28.] Rushdoony, *The Institutes of Biblical Law,* 10; cf. 503 and 606-611. The normativeness of Biblical law in contrast to natural law is not merely a key theme in a number of Rushdoony's works but an axis on which his thought depends.

[29.] This was Calvin's view, *op. cit.,* 788 [Bk. 4, Ch. 20, Sec. 14, 15].

[30.] Rushdoony, *The Institutes of Biblical Law*, 304, 305.

and priestly law specifically fulfilled by the coming of Christ, and those laws specifically re-interpreted in the New Testament.[31]

That the judicial no less than the so-called moral law is binding on man and his society leads naturally, for Rushdoony, to the conviction that *all* the law,[32] not merely certain well-known parts like the Ten Commandments, is eternally binding and applicable: "Without case law ['the illustration of the basic principle in terms of specific cases'], God's law would soon be reduced to an extremely limited area of meaning. This, of course, is precisely what has happened. Those who deny the present validity of the law apart from the Ten Commandments have as a consequence a very limited definition of theft."[33] Refusing to observe the applicability of the case laws limits not merely divine authority but also Biblical signification: to know what the Ten Commandments mean and how they are to be applied, we must consult the authoritative case laws.[34]

Rushdoony, in addition, laments the neglect of the third — or sanctifying — use of the law in the modern church. He assails lawless Christianity, or *antinomianism.* He notes that while "[m]an's *justification* is by the *grace* of God in Jesus Christ[,] man's *sanctification* is by means of the *law* of God."[35] The rampant sin in the modern church derives from its rampant antinomianism. For Rushdoony, there are no legitimate excuses for antinomianism, and pious or "spiritual" excuses are the worst of all.

Rushdoony's criticisms of both the inconsistencies in the traditional Reformed notions of the nature and function of the law and of the pervasive neglect of the law among the evangelicals have created perhaps the most refined conception of the law in historic Calvinism to date. Supporting the viability of the judicial or civil dimensions of the law as well as the case laws, in addition to reviving the traditionally Reformed stress on the sanctifying use of the law, Rushdoony propels historic Calvinism to new heights.

Inherent Historical Progressiveness of the Christian Faith

Rushdoony is unabashedly postmillennial.[36] His postmillennialism, however, is distinguishable from the classical approach, if not content, of postmillennialism.[37] He espouses what I term *dynamic* or *progressive*

---

[31] *idem., The Roots of Reconstruction*, 553.

[32] That is, all the law not specifically altered in the New Testament, unlike the sacrificial portions.

[33] Rushdoony, *The Institutes of Biblical Law*, 11, 12.

[34] For an expansion of this theme by one of Rushdoony's early disciples, see Greg Bahnsen, *Theonomy in Christian Ethics* (Phillipsburg, NJ, 1984 ed.).

[35] Rushdoony, *The Institutes of Biblical Law*, 4.

[36] *e.g., God's Plan For Victory: The Meaning of Post Millennialism* (Fairfax, VA [1977], 1980).

[37] By classical postmillennialism, I refer to eschatological conceptions like those of Jonathan Edwards, *A History of the Work of Redemption*, in *The Works of Jonathan Edwards* (Edinburgh [1834], 1974), 532-619, especially 604-611.

postmillennialism. It seems on the surface that any notion of postmillennialism must necessarily be progressive, for the very nature of that eschatological view entails the progress of the salvific and societal work of God in history. By *dynamic* or *progressive* postmillennialism, though, I mean the endorsement of godly improvement by means of *change* in all areas of life and the social order. Rushdoony is no enemy of change, and for this reason cannot be classified as what is usually termed a "conservative."[38] Rushdoony values the past, but unlike many modern conservatives, Rushdoony perceives the past not as an Archimedean point against which the present and future must be judged, and thus as in some sense normative; rather, all reality is relative and alterable in terms of God speaking in Scripture:

> During the many years of my life, I have more than a few times been disappointed in men whose knowledge at first glance made them notable. Their problem was a past-bound vision. Their focus was on the early church, or the medieval church, or the Reformation church, and so on and on. If their interest was political they often looked backward to a particular era in history.
>
> Now such interests can be good, but too often such people idealize the past and want a return to something no longer tenable. The modernist, on the other hand, wants a continual revision of the content of the Faith in terms of the spirit of the age. Those of us who hold that it is God's enscripturated word that is alone authoritative must recognize that it must transform and govern our todays and tomorrows.[39]

Bullock furnishes a suitable context for understanding Rushdoony's dynamic postmillennialism in explaining the different way in which the Renaissance perceived ancient history:

> There was ... a crucial difference between the way the ancient world was viewed in earlier centuries and the way it came to be viewed, first of all in Italy, in the fourteenth and fifteenth centuries. The Middle Ages had been able to appropriate what they wanted from classical antiquity precisely because they felt no sense of separateness from the ancient world. But whatever they borrowed from antiquity, whether in art, mythology, literature or philosophy, they incorporated into their own an entirely different Christian system of belief and altered its original significance to fit this without any sense of anachronism. It was only with Petrarch and the Italian humanists of the fourteenth and fifteenth centuries that the worlds of antiquity came to be seen no longer as a storehouse to be plundered, but as a separate civilization in its own right.
>
> Instead of the sense of casual familiarity with the ancient world which the Middle Ages had felt, the renaissance saw it for the first time in an historical perspective, as remote, unfamiliar, fascinating.[40]

[38.] See Michael Oakshott, "On Being Conservative," in *Rationalism in Politics and Other Essays* (Indianapolis, 1991 ed.), 407-437.

[39.] Rushdoony, "Unconstructive Religion," *Chalcedon Report*, No. 362, September, 1995, 2.

[40.] Alan Bullock, *The Humanist Tradition in the West* (New York), 14.

The recrudescence of Reformed orthodoxy too includes an inclination to see the Reformation and the period of High Calvinism "as remote, unfamiliar, fascinating." Its supporters, like the eighteenth-century neo-classicists in literature and the nineteenth-century Pre-Raphaelites in painting, posses the historical perspective to judge today's theological and moral declension against the purity of an earlier "Golden Age." Like any who exercise such historical perspective, they are tempted to romanticize earlier ages. As a result, this former age develops to the mind something of normative status, a criterion against which the depraved present is mercilessly judged. By contrast, Rushdoony employs historical perspective to "relativize" the past, relativize, that is, in the sense that every human era must be judged in terms of the inscripturated word of God. Therefore, he is not such a strict subscriptionist that he believes the great Reformed confessions can never be amended, and is unafraid to criticize them for precisely the same reason.[41] His unwillingness to absolutize the past distinguishes him not merely from political conservatives but also Reformed confessionalists, who are more past-bound than forward-looking. He opposes the absolutization of the past on the part of conservatives no less than the obsession with incessant change on the part of liberals. Rushdoony thus takes on both the Greek view of *"perfection as self-sufficiency and permanence"* as well as the modern fascination with "change for the sake of change."[42] Since only God speaking in Scripture, and not the past, is normative, any change that more closely conforms to the revealed will of God is desirable and necessary. In fact, "For man to resist change means to resist growth and progress. It means that man has frozen into a virtue an aspect of the fallen order and has thereby precluded its correction."[43] In application, this means we must constantly support godly change.

For example, in education, change is natural: "Precisely because a sound curriculum has as its foundation an unchanging faith in the sovereign and triune God and His infallible word, it will therefore recognize that man and his problems will change and develop."[44] To hold that the curriculum cannot change is to absolutize the curriculum. To say that it must change in terms of the word of God is to say that only Holy Scripture is ultimate. And what is true of the curriculum is true equally of all areas of human existence.

Rushdoony does not perceive the indicia of kingdom advancement merely in increasing conversions, or even in the gradual Christianization of the social order, desirable and predicted though these phenomena are. In addition, he supports the incremental revision of all spheres of life by conformity to the Scriptures and thus the progress of the Faith and even the progress of progress

---

[41.] Rushdoony, *Institutes of Biblical Law*, 550, 551.
[42.] *idem., Salvation and Godly Rule*, 144, 145.
[43.] *ibid.*, 145.
[44.] *idem., The Philosophy of the Christian Curriculum*, 13.

itself. Rushdoony's, then, is not merely a static postmillennialism embraced by many Calvinists, but faith in an actual inherent progressiveness of redemptive history.

The Reordering of All Areas of Human Endeavor in Terms of the Christian Faith as Revealed in the Bible

To the contemporary conservative church, the mindset of Rousas John Rushdoony must represent something of an enigma. Rushdoony is blessed of God by what Lecerf calls an "exceptionally synthetic mind":

> Divine grace prepared the way of the Lord by endowing exceptionally synthetic minds, like those of Zwingli, Calvin, and Beza, with an extensive classical culture, which caused them to connect closely their dogmatic constructions with the premises laid down by divine revelation. The distinguishing principle of the *auctoritas normae* in Scripture is evidently one which does not lead us to deny that which has been previously acknowledged as true and that which one continues to acknowledge as true.[45]

Precisely because of Rushdoony's affirmation of the all-controlling providence of God in creation, and its original goodness, he can — and insists we must — harness any and every field of human endeavor to the Christian Faith. We dishonor God by limiting knowledge and its application to theology proper. I recall in my first reading of Rushdoony's *Institutes of Biblical Law* a puzzlement at the staggering array of disciplines and topics he introduced in his discussion of the Ten Commandments. Later, I had a conversation with Rushdoony in which he stated of a certain magazine, "This may sound strange for a theologian to say, but I think the magazine is *too theological.*" What he meant was that it was interested only in "pure theology," that is, theology abstracted from life and history, theology as nothing more than an academic exercise. This approach to theology Rushdoony abhors with all his being. In the introduction to his *Systematic Theology,* he declares:

> It is a serious mistake to see theology as an academic exercise. The word *theology* means *God's word*; it begins with the presupposition that Scripture is the word of God, and it is the duty of the theologian to understand it *and* to apply it to every area of thought and life.[46]

Religion, to employ one of Rushdoony's favorite expressions, is an *inescapable concept.* In this conviction, Rushdoony follows Kuyper,[47] Dooyeweerd,[48] and others in the Calvinistic (and especially the Dutch

---

45. Auguste Lecerf, *An Introduction to Reformed Dogmatics* (Grand Rapids, trans. [1949], 1981), 381.
46. Rushdoony, *Systematic Theology,* xv.
47. Abraham Kuyper, *Lectures on Calvinism* (Grand Rapids, 1931).
48. Herman Dooyeweerd, *A New Critique of Theoretical Thought,* trans. David H. Freeman and H. De Jongste (Jordan Station, Ontario, Canada [1969], 1984).

Calvinistic) tradition in recognizing in the Christian Faith the fundamental shaping of culture. Rushdoony agrees with the distinctively Calvinistic sentiment expressed by Meeter regarding the cultural obligation of the godly man:

> Man was made in the image of God. Just as God is King over the universe and has brought to pass many and noble things in the creation which He made, so he has given to man His image bearer control over nature as his dominion and charged him: "Subdue creation, and bring out the many possibilities in it and in your own nature." Culture is the execution of this divinely imposed mandate. In his cultural task man is to take the raw materials of this universe and subdue them, make them serve his purpose and bring them to nobler and higher levels, thus bringing out the possibilities which are hidden in nature. When thus developed man is to lay his entire cultural product, the whole of creation, at the feet of Him Who is King of man and of nature, in Whose image and for Whom man and all things are created.[49]

Of particular interest is Rushdoony's view of the Faith as it applies to the state. In a democratic age of political and cultural pluralism, Rushdoony's notion of the inescapably religious character of the state seems quite controversial:

> Not only is every church a religious institution, but every state or social order is a religious establishment. Every state is a law order, and every law order represents an enacted morality, with procedures for the enforcement of that morality. Every morality represents a form of theological order, *i.e.*, is an aspect and expression of a religion. The church thus is not the only religious institution; the state also is a religious institution. More often than the church, the state has been the central religious institution of most civilizations through the centuries. The war between the Roman Empire and the early church was a religious warfare, a struggle between two claimants who represented rival religions and wanted to order society in terms of their faith. The claims of each faith were total claims, as all religious claims are.[50]

Rushdoony denies the idea of the religious neutrality of the state, and therefore opens the door for the Christianization of the political order: *some* religion will inevitably prevail in every political order, and that religion *should be* orthodox Christianity. To those imbibing the myth of political neutrality, such sentiment smacks of religious intolerance. They fail to realize, however, the intolerance of their own secularism, undergirded by a religion at war with the sovereign God. It is only the politics shaped by orthodox Christianity that furnishes a tolerance tempered by order.

But political neutrality is only one myth Rushdoony exposes. He denies, in fact, the neutrality of any area of life. Men are either covenant-keepers or

---

49. H. Henry Meeter, *The Basic Ideas of Calvinism* (Grand Rapids, fifth ed., 1960), 80, 81.
50. Rushdoony, *Christianity and the State* (Vallecito, CA, 1986), 7.

covenant-breakers, and their beliefs and actions will directly reflect their faith, whatever it may be. Rushdoony endorses Van Til's conviction that there are no "brute facts": all facts are interpreted either from the presupposition of Christian theism or from the presupposition of an anti-Christian religion.[51] The idea of the possibility of a zone of epistemological neutrality is simply misguided.[52] The Faith, therefore, applies no less to, say, science or music than it does to church and prayer:

> Our goal is to bring every area of life and thought into captivity to Jesus Christ. We believe that the whole word of God must be applied to all of life.
>
> It is not only our duty as persons, families, and churches, to be Christian, but it is also the duty of the state, the school, our callings, the arts and sciences, economics, and every other sphere to be under Christ our King. Nothing is exempt from His dominion. Like the Puritans, we seek to assert the "Crown Rights of Christ the King" over all of life.[53]

In this determination to reshape all areas and disciplines in terms of the Christian Faith, Rushdoony's program does not diverge from the full-orbed scheme of the Reformed tradition. Unlike his predecessors, however, Rushdoony is quite explicit about the source and criterion of that program. He contends for an *overtly Biblical* framework in which the reconstructive task must occur. Abjuring all deference to natural theology and abstractionist Biblical "principles," Rushdoony declares that the blueprint of godly man's dominion is the Bible:

> The issue is the word of God, or the word of man. Whose word shall prevail? If we limit the word of God to the realm of faith, we have denied it. The word of God is His infallible word and law for the whole of creation, for every man. His word is the binding word for every realm, and his law governs all things.[54]

These lines conclude Rushdoony's masterly *Infallibility: An Inescapable Concept* and constitute the core of his thinking. All areas of thought and life are subject to the Bible and, because of the entrance of sin, must be reordered in terms of the infallible word. While the Bible does not furnish specific data about all conceivable topics, it does furnish the knowledge of the matrix in which all topics must be understood. To begin the reconstruction of any area of reality apart from the Bible is to renew the original sin — determining for oneself what is good and evil (Gen. 3:15).

[51.] *idem.*, *By What Standard?*, 50-56.
[52.] *idem.*, "The Quest for Common Ground," in ed., Gary North, *Foundations of Christian Scholarship* (Vallecito, CA [1976], 1979), 27-38.
[53.] Rushdoony, "The Vision of Chalcedon," *Journal of Christian Reconstruction*, Vol. 9, Nos. 1, 2 [1982-1983], 129.
[54.] *idem.*, *Systematic Theology*, 1:56.

For Rushdoony, therefore, the Christian Faith is for all of life. The Gospel is comprehensive in its totality:

> [T]he gospel is for all of life: the good news is precisely that the whole of life is restored and fulfilled through Jesus Christ, that, in the counsel of God, the kingdom is destined to triumph in every sphere of life. This gospel cannot be proclaimed and the dominion of the kingdom extended except on Christian presuppositions. The answer to the question, how wide a gospel do we have, is simply this: as wide as life and creation, as wide as time and eternity.[55]

Absolutely every area of life must be brought under the rule of God by means of his law-word:

> If God is God, if he truly is the Lord or Sovereign, everything must serve Him and be under His dominion, the state, schools, arts, sciences, the church, and all things else. To limit the jurisdiction of the God of the Scripture to the soul of man and to the church is to deny Him.[56]

Conclusion

These dazzling contributions — first, the repudiation of all forms of dualism; second, opposition to the eternalization of any dimension of the temporal; third, the solidification of the historic Reformed view of the law; fourth, the inherent historical progressiveness of the success of the Christian Faith; and fifth, the reordering of all areas of human endeavor in terms of the Christian Faith as revealed in the Bible — represent genuine development in historic Calvinism, working out its inner principles to their logical conclusions and therefore bringing Calvinism to a more consistent plane.

If Warfield's assertion "that the future, as the past, of Christianity itself is bound up with the fortunes of Calvinism,"[57] is accurate, then we may contend with equal conviction that the future of Christianity will be shaped by the extent to which Calvinism and the wider church takes Rushdoony's thought seriously. The church ignores Rushdoony's thought to its own peril.

Andrew Sandlin, an ordained minister, is editor of Chalcedon Report *and the* Journal of Christian Reconstruction; *assistant editor of* Christianity and Society; *and president of the National Reform Association. An interdisciplinary scholar, he holds academic degrees or concentrations in English, history, and political science. His essays have appeared in numerous scholarly and popular publications.*

---

[55] *idem., By What Standard?*, 176.
[56] *idem., The Roots of Reconstruction*, 182.
[57] Warfield, *op. cit.*, 300.

A Biographical Sketch of My Father

Mark Rousas Rushdoony

My father was born Rousas John Rushdoony at Sloan Hospital in New York City on April 25, 1916. It is customary in a biographical sketch such as this, of course, briefly to note parentage. But I believe brevity would do injustice to an understanding of my father, his faith, and his thinking, for his roots and early life are tied to the Old World and a generation of immigrants who survived persecution and genocide because they were Christians in a non-Christian political order.

Family Heritage

My father's parents were natives of the state of Van in Armenia. Armenians as a people are descended from numerous ethnic groups from as far away as Scandinavia, Western Europe, and China. Their origins as a political entity go back at least to the kingdom of Urartu (from Ararat, the resting place of Noah's ark) which challenged the power of ancient Assyria in Biblical times. What set the Armenians apart and crystallized their culture was their official conversion to Christianity early in the fourth century. The Rushdoonys trace their ancestry to several Urartan kings. The bronze shield of one of those, Rusas III, c. 629-615 BC, is now in the possession of the British Museum.

The ancestral house of the Rushdoonys was in the Kavash district southwest of Lake Van. "Rush" refers to the royal name Rusas (or Rousas), "doon" means town, house, or fortress, and "y" means belonging to. Hence the family name means the house, town, or fortress belonging to Rusas. Historically, not all Armenian names ended in "yan" or "ian," although Turkish authorities tried to standardize them so Armenians could be identified easily on official documents. My paternal grandfather's name was thus automatically changed to Rushdoonian when he applied for a passport, but he never adopted the name.

When Islam spread throughout Asia Minor, Syria, and Mesopotamia, Armenians clung to their Christian Faith. Armenians under Turkish rule were resented not only because they were considered "infidels," but also because they tended to be prosperous merchants and traders and skilled artisans and craftsmen. There were several periods of persecution and atrocities in the years just prior to the genocide of 1915-16.

It was traditional for the leading families of Armenia to support a priest from their number in the Armenian Orthodox Church (not to be confused with the Eastern Orthodox Church). My father's great grandfather was a priest and his grandfather was studying to succeed him when he was blinded by Turkish soldiers in an altercation. His father Yeghiazar Khachadour Rushdoony was

21

left an orphan not long thereafter at the age of eleven. He was raised by members of the extended family until he went to live with a relative in the city of Van so he could attend the parish school there. A wave of massacres in 1896, however, left him homeless in Van at the age of fourteen. Dr. George C. Raynolds, an American missionary, took him into his new orphanage. Before long he was one of 500 orphans. This tragedy drew my grandfather into Protestantism and caused him to devote himself in gratitude to the American mission and Dr. Raynolds. He finished his education there while assisting Dr. Raynolds and teaching in outlying villages. He was sent to college and returned to teach at the mission high school. He became what he described as a "collector of the facts" about Turkish atrocities and a translator for the British consul. Because of this and his close association with the American missionaries, his arrest and death were ordered by Turkish authorities, from which he was saved by a general amnesty provision in the Turkish Constitution of 1908. Still, he was arrested four times and three attempts were made on his life.

Through Dr. Raynolds, Y. K. Rushdoony was sent to Edinburgh University and New Mound College for his masters and seminary degrees. He was, upon graduation in 1912, offered a position in the Armenian church in Fresno, California but wished to return to help Dr. Raynolds in Van. There he was married by Dr. Raynolds to Vartanoush (Rose) Gazarian, daughter of a prominent merchant. Their first child, Rousas George, was born in 1914 at the mission hospital.

Within a year the threats of the Young Turks to eliminate non-Turkish elements within their empire found an opportunity in the disruption of World War I. In most of Armenia this took the form of "deportations," which were really forced marches. Armenians were forced to leave behind all property and were marched for weeks. Many were murdered, raped, or sold into slavery. In the state of Van there was not even the pretense of marches. There, the Turks conducted systematic massacres of one village after another. The ancestral home of the Rushdoonys was one of those areas so decimated that none of a large extended family survived. In the city of Van, however, the large population was able to put up an armed resistance which kept the Turkish authorities at bay for a month. The advance of a Russian army with a large force of Armenian volunteers forced the Turks to give up the siege and retreat. Three days before the siege ended, Rousas George Rushdoony died. He was eleven months old.

For a few weeks that spring and summer, the Armenians in the city of Van governed themselves. There was hope that with Russian and perhaps other Allied help, Armenians could begin to rebuild, and a just resolution would come with victory. But the war went badly for the Russians, and by the end of July, they had begun a retreat back into their borders. With only a few hours notice, the Armenians in the region were warned to escape toward the

Russian frontier, over a hundred miles to the northeast. By this time Rose Rushdoony was pregnant with my father. They were more fortunate than many, however, for they did have a brief opportunity and an avenue of escape. At the Bendimahu River they were the last to make safety before a group of Turks massacred those preparing to cross.

With the aid of Rose Rushdoony's dowry, my grandparents and several other relatives were able to travel to Archangel and book passage on a Russian steamer to New York. They arrived in October, 1915, and my father was born the following April. Soon thereafter they boarded a train for California where my father was baptized Rousas John Rushdoony in the First Congregational Church in Los Angeles by Dr. Charles C. Tracey, another of the American missionaries to Armenia for whom my grandfather had such a love and respect.

Early Life

The Rushdoonys then moved to Kingsburg, California where Y. K. Rushdoony started the Armenian Martyrs' Presbyterian Church. My father's first language was Armenian. Bible reading and prayer were part of the daily activities on the farm. Though a small child, my father still remembers the procession of Armenian friends and relatives, some recently arrived from the old country. Always the questions about lost friends and relatives were asked. A stream of Armenians came by the farm whenever such guests arrived to ask, "Did you see...?", or "Have you any word of...?" Fasts and prayers during the Russian famine of 1922 made an impression on my father since family members still remained in Russia at the time. He had an early knowledge that many Armenians had and were dying because they were Christians and held in contempt by a non-Christian empire.

My father did not really speak fluent English until after he began school. He read voraciously from a very early age. By his teens he had read the Bible half a dozen times or more. He loved it and he learned to love both Armenian and American history. At an early age he felt his roots were very deep in both cultures because of their conscious attachment to the Christian Faith.

In 1925, when he was nine years old, my father went with his mother, seven-year-old sister Rose, and newborn brother Haig, to Detroit where his father had been called earlier to aid a struggling Congregational church. There the family lived until 1931 when my father was a freshman in high school. He became a fan of the Detroit Tigers and saw the likes of Babe Ruth and Lou Gehrig play the national pastime.

In 1931, Y. K. Rushdoony's ill health necessitated the family's return to the farm in Kingsburg. There my father attended Kingsburg High School. When his father answered a call to organize Bethel Presbyterian Church in San Francisco, my father remained on the farm with the new pastor of the

Kingsburg church to finish his senior year. He was class president and editor of the yearbook. But the Depression was deepening, and when the local bank failed, the class yearbook funds were lost. Not to be deterred, the yearbook was printed without pictures which were then glued in individually and the book was covered in course yardage. Little did my father realize that sixty years later he would still be struggling with budgets to get books into print.

University Years

After graduation in 1934, my father joined the family in San Francisco, where he got a highly coveted job in the Crystal Palace Market, working fifty-nine hours a week for fourteen dollars. It ended with the general strike organized by the Marxist Harry Bridges. He attended Santa Monica Junior College his freshman year and San Francisco Junior College his sophomore year before transferring to the University of California in Berkeley. It was not until his university days that his thinking switched over entirely to English.

It was also in the university that his Faith was seriously challenged. The 1930's were the high watermark of Marxism in the United States. The Soviet Union was still being viewed as a noble and progressive experiment and the Depression opened the door to socialist ideology in many circles. It was sometimes churchmen who steered him in the wrong direction. He began systematically to read the classics which were regarded with reverence by many in the church. He looked to them for the wisdom of the ages. He began with the Greeks and Romans and read the European writers as well. He has said it was one of the ugliest experiences of his life, because he was too naive to dismiss much of what he read as humanism. He was reading garbage and looking for its wisdom. He reacted against the university and came to distrust it as a degenerate institution. He would eventually graduate with honors but has said he doesn't know how, because he took so rebellious an attitude. Frequently, he would take a course for something that interested him and then drop it. I can remember him saying of the "hippies" of the 1960s that, although he had no use for them, at least they were intelligent enough to see the meaninglessness and futility of modern thought — even if their reaction was also meaningless.

Basis of Thought

My father's days at the university were not without great benefit, however. He has frequently cited two men who greatly aided the development of his thinking. One was Edwin Strong who taught philosophy. He once warned his class never to let themselves be trapped into a discussion of origins, since evolution posits as great a miracle as God. From Strong he learned that the key to philosophy was the "given." Strong's "given" that day was the existence of the universe. Later my father picked up the term "presupposition" from Cornelius Van Til. From Ernst H. Kantorowicz my father saw the centrality of theology to politics and the state. Kantarowicz was discussing the iconoclastic controversy in Byzantine history when he pointed out that neo-platonic thought caused both church and state to believe that God is continually incarnated. The question in their minds was, who represented that power — did the church or the state represent the kingdom of God? In the iconoclastic controversy, the state emerged as the victor. The state still sees itself as the primary sphere of authority. At that time the question was framed in theological terms — *i.e.,* the state or the church advancing the kingdom of God? In more modern times, the question is in purely political terms. The state is the center of sovereignty, change, and progress, and the church is boxed into the role of a social appendage. The idea of humanism (the worship of man) as the antecedent of statism was beginning to form in my father's mind. He graduated with his bachelor's degree in 1938.

The Christian Ministry

While working on his master's degree (also at the University of California at Berkeley), my father spent one summer working at Sunset Presbyterian Church and some time at the Presbyterian Church in Chinatown, both in San Francisco. He received his M.A. in English Literature in 1940, though he continued his studies there while attending the modernist Pacific School of Religion in Berkeley. It was in the modernist seminary that he first affirmed his belief in the total applicability of the Bible and Biblical law. The alternative he saw was the "basics" of the Faith, a reductionist and regressive view of the kingdom of God. The response was livid. He later said he "got clobbered." He was no longer in the university where even a rebel was tolerated if he stimulated discussion. The seminary as an extension of the church sees its duty as squelching "dangerous" teachings — such as the applicability of Scripture. So my father waited and read and studied. He did not begin speaking on Biblical law until the late '60s, as he was writing *The Institutes of Biblical Law.* On finishing his seminary studies in 1944, he was ordained by the San Francisco Presbytery of the Presbyterian Church, USA. He became the eighth generation of father and son in the ministry. His father had left his San Francisco church earlier in the same year to take a Congregational church in Providence, Rhode Island.

While still in school my father had the idea of teaching somewhere and starting a small mission church on the side or perhaps filling empty pulpits on a volunteer basis. Even then he wanted to maintain a degree of independence from the organized church which, like the state, tended all too often to act like it represented God on earth. No such situation presented itself, so he chose to go where no one wished to go — the Western Shoshone Indian Reservation at Owyhee, Nevada. He ministered to the Paiute and Shoshone Indians there for two reasons. He felt compassion on this neglected and mistreated people, and he also felt that he needed to know how to communicate the Faith effectively to a people unfamiliar with it. He stayed there for eight-and-a-half years. Owyhee was snowed in for the duration of the long winters. He was the only missionary for a hundred miles in any direction.

It was in 1946 that R. J. Rushdoony first picked up a book by Cornelius Van Til (*The New Modernism*). It immediately commanded his attention. Van Til talked about the "given," though he used the term "presupposition." Modern thought is rooted in humanism and thus centers on man. Arminian theology centers the Christian Faith in man's will and therefore is powerless to stop such a trend. Public education accelerated the trend toward humanism because it forced a complete separation of God and knowledge. Theology as a basis of philosophy, knowledge, and social action was virtually dead. Van Til saw all knowledge and meaning as presuppositonal — based on the "given" of the sovereign Creator and Lord, who reveals himself in his word. He was a philosopher of religion, but my father saw him as one leading Christian thinking away from humanistic rationalism to a foundation in God's word.

In 1953 my father left the reservation and took the pastorate of Trinity Presbyterian Church (also Presbyterian Church, USA) in Santa Cruz, a retirement community on the California coast about seventy miles south of San Francisco. Because of its demographics, he was frequently called to the bedsides of the sick and dying. In 1980 he estimated that he had held over 500 funerals — many of them in Santa Cruz. He was also present at many deathbeds. He had believed in predestination even while in seminary but it was the constant questions of the dying that forced the subject. Mostly they asked "Why?" In order to answer honestly, he had to speak in terms of predestination by God as the only alternative to chance. The alternative to total meaninglessness is total meaning. What churchmen argued about, the dying wanted to hear. My father saw that the dying knew they were not sovereign, and were comforted in hearing of a God who was. He also came to the conclusion that it was fruitless to debate the matter since predestination was a doctrine given to comfort believers, not divide them.

My father's eschatology also crystallized by the mid 1950s. He had very early studied premillenialism as it was so widely espoused, but was horrified at what he thought resembled fantastic fairy-tale exegesis. He then turned to amillennial writers but never felt comfortable with that position, either. By the end of the '40's he had read Hendricksen's *More Than Conquerors*. He was encouraged by the optimism he found in that book but was disappointed in that Hendricksen ended as an amillennialist. He was encouraged by reading Warfield and later Boettner, but definitely considered himself a post-millennialist after reading Roderick Campbell's *Israel and the New Covenant* (1954).

My father stepped down as pastor of Trinity in 1957 and organized the Santa Cruz Orthodox Presbyterian Church. He was received by the presbytery of that denomination in May of 1958 and continued as pastor of the Santa Cruz congregation until 1962.

Writings

It was during this time my father's involvement in the Christian school movement began. In the 1950s he had given a series of lectures at Christian school conferences. These were compiled into a book and published in 1961 under the title *Intellectual Schizophrenia*. A grant from the Volker Fund, an educational and charitable foundation, allowed him to do a great deal of study at the Stanford University Library. This resulted in the publication of *The Messianic Character of American Education* in 1963. Many people became interested in Christian schools because of these books, and many Christian schools were started as a result.

In 1962 my father resigned from the pastorate of the Santa Cruz church to join the William Volker Fund full-time. Volker then created the Center for American Studies which he joined before leaving to work on a research grant. While still in Santa Cruz he had been given a grant which led to *The Messianic Character of American Education*; the later grant led to the eventual publication of *The One and the Many*.

The Formation of Chalcedon

In 1965 my father incorporated Chalcedon. He had been invited to speak several times in Southern California that spring. A group said that they would pledge their support to him if he would come down and hold Bible studies, so that summer he moved the family to Woodland Hills.

In October of 1965 my father wrote a single-page report to those who had pledged to support him as well as to all others who were interested. That mimeographed letter was the beginning of the *Chalcedon Report*. It grew to four or five pages which were collated and stapled on the dining room table. In the early '70s, it changed to a professionally printed format. In 1987 the *Chalcedon Report* became a magazine.

When my father moved to Southern California he did not join the local presbytery of the Orthodox Presbyterian Church (OPC). Instead, he remained with the northern presbytery and attended their meetings. A minister in the southern presbytery brought charges against him for teaching Scripture outside the church on the Lord's day! The northern presbytery, not too surprisingly, said there was nothing in Scripture or the OPC "black book" that made such activity an offense. But church government at its worst can devolve into legalistic bureaucracy, and my father knew his acquittal would be appealed and debated endlessly. He therefore resigned from the OPC on October 1, 1970. His ministry now was in his writings, and he chose not to be distracted by those who wished to use the church to regulate and control his work. Had he allowed himself to be placed in such a position there were (and still are) numerous individuals who would have sought to suppress or altogether stop his work.

Biblical Law

Meanwhile, my father had begun to study and write extensively on Biblical law. Having read the Bible omnivorously in his youth, he had a predisposition to take it seriously. He had affirmed his belief in Biblical law as early as seminary, but had learned to remain reticent until he was ready to defend it. Van Til's thinking had only reinforced the Biblical law view because he said man's thoughts must begin with God's word. But the weight of the modern church was against a return to Biblical law; thus my father held his peace on the subject while he continued to study it. By the late '60s he was speaking in his weekly Bible studies and writing in the *Chalcedon Report* on Biblical law. The result was *The Institutes of Biblical Law* (1973). Biblical law as a means of personal sanctification and self-government became a major tenet of his teachings. But, as opposed to a purely personal piety, my father also saw Biblical law as the revealed will of God for society as a whole. His Calvinistic belief in the sovereignty of God and his postmillennial belief in the victory of God in history caused his teaching on Biblical law to take the approach of two options — judgment for the rebels or rewards for those obedient and faithful to the King of Kings. In his second *Chalcedon Report* (October 31, 1965) he had urged his readers to take up "the task of reconstruction." The term "Christian Reconstruction" would eventually attach itself to my father's teachings.

Growing Ministry in the '70s

The rising property taxes in Southern California in the 1970s and the more widespread distribution of Chalcedon's supporters caused my father to look for land or facilities that could become his and Chalcedon's permanent home. In 1975 he found a 100-acre ranch with a home and an abandoned gold mine in Vallecito, California, in the heart of the Mother Lode region of the western Sierra Nevada foothills. He subdivided the property and purchased a portion for himself and one for Chalcedon. He moved there in the fall of 1975, though he continued his meetings in Southern California for several years thereafter.

My father traveled extensively in these years. Often he spoke at conferences or churches. Beginning in the late 1970's, however, a new reason for extensive travel kept him busy. Christians were increasingly being tried on various charges stemming from the exercise of their Faith. Most cases revolved around the attempt to license, regulate, or close Christian schools. Often it was the individual parents who were placed on trial for contributing to a child's delinquency or truancy by placing him in a non-government controlled school or home schooling him. Sometimes the schools, their administrators, or even the churches which sponsored them, were accused of criminal activity for not allowing the state to have jurisdiction over the education of children. Occasionally, it was child welfare services or any number of county or state agencies which tried to claim jurisdiction. Sometimes, especially during the Jimmy Carter administration, the regulatory pressure came from Washington, D.C. My father's knowledge of the history of religious freedom contributed to his frequent call as an expert witness in many such trials. But the Christian education movement successfully held off this concerted onslaught of statist attack and emerged independent and vigorous.

After the 1980 Republican landslide, the "Religious Right" gained much attention for its role in bringing down an incumbent President and electing a Republican majority in the Senate. *Newsweek* had a feature article about the Religious Right soon after the election. Under "Who's Who in the Religious Right" they listed only one "think tank" — Chalcedon. This was an appropriate designation. R. J. Rushdoony's and Chalcedon's contribution have been in the area of ideas — teaching men how to exercise dominion in terms of God's word over every area of life. This is not to say these ideas can be divorced from practice but rather that the most effective practice of the Christian life requires an understanding of the presuppositions, or the "givens," of the Christian faith.

My father has continued to speak and write in recent years. *Systematic Theology* was published in 1994. Several commentaries are being prepared for publication.

Y. K. Rushdoony lived to be 80, despite precarious health. Rose Rushdoony lived to be 90. My father will be 80 on April 25, 1996. His health is as good as many men twenty years younger and his mind sharper than most at any age. Lord willing, he has a number of productive years ahead of him.

Mark Rushdoony is vice president of Chalcedon and director and a teacher at Chalcedon Christian School.

Vartanoush (Rose) and Yeghiazar Khachadour Rushdoony with their children, Rousas (age 5) and Rose, in Kingsburg, California about 1921. Rev. and Mrs. Rushdoony arrived in Kingsburg just weeks after Rush's birth where the senior Rushdoony organized the Armenian Martyrs Presbyterian Church. The family kept a farm there until just prior to Y. K. Rushdoony's death in 1961.

Rev. and Mrs. Rushdoony and family in Detroit in 1924. Haig, their third child, was born the following year. Y. K. Rushdoony was the pastor of the Armenian Congregational Church in Detroit from 1923 until 1931 when his ill health necessitated the family's return to the farm in Kingsburg.

Rush with his younger brother, Haig, and father in Y. K. Rushdoony's study in their San Francisco home about 1941. Y. K. Rushdoony was then the minister of Bethel Presbyterian Church and Rush was in seminary (Pacific School of Religion).

Rush in the late 1940s while still on the Western Shoshone Indian Reservation at Owyhee in northeastern Nevada, where he served as a missionary to the Paiutes and Shoshones from 1944 - 1953.

Rush and Dorothy (Ross) Rushdoony in 1991. Dorothy played a crucial role in Chalcedon's formative years. She stuffed thousands of newsletters into envelopes each month for over twenty years before the Chalcedon Report *was turned over to a professional mailing house. In addition, she proofread and typed Rush's handwritten manuscripts until 1994 when she lost much of her eyesight. Rush named Ross House Books in honor of her labors.*

How Rushdoony Changed My Family

Andrea Schwartz

The teacher who does not grow in his knowledge of his subject, in methodology and content, is a very limited teacher, and his pupils are "under-privileged" learners.

The teacher as student is, above all else, a student of God's word. To be a student means to advance and grow.

Our growth in teaching requires our growth through and under the teaching of the Holy Spirit. We must become good learners as a step towards becoming good teachers. Our profession is a very great one in Scripture: our Lord was a Teacher, and the Holy Spirit is our continuing Teacher. We cannot treat our calling lightly, nor grieve the Spirit by abusing our calling.

R. J. Rushdoony, *The Philosophy of the Christian Curriculum*

The Bible accurately identifies the fact that without vision, the people perish. For many of us, our original reasons for home schooling pale in comparison to the strong motivations we now cling to. Too few of us really knew what was at stake. We began with the Spirit's prompting — in many cases living quite above our stated theology. Without a strong theological, intellectual base, though, well-meaning friends and family, an intrusive school board, or political legislators answering to strong and well-funded lobbies would have knocked us down and in many cases out.

The writings of R. J. Rushdoony (specifically his books on public education, Christian education, and the struggle between Christianity and humanism) provided the necessary guidelines to keep us on track. I can remember that often when my son was young, I would threaten him with sending him to "public school" when he repeatedly failed to adhere to my instruction. However, as a result of Rushdoony's influence, I came to understand the extent of the assault on Christianity and God's law in state schools, and I never threatened again. I realized that my threats would be comparable to telling him that if he failed to listen to me I would abandon him along the side of the road to the care of robbers and thieves.

But Rush's works do more than sound a warning. His *Institutes of Biblical Law* and recent *Systematic Theology* give home schooling parents the "seminary-like" education to allow them the grounding to teach every subject from a godly, orthodox perspective. His experience and expertise have often led me along paths that would reap tremendous rewards for me and my children. Thanks to his influence and perspective that *every area of life and thought is subject to the law of God,* from the time my children were very little, discussions on daily problems or situations were viewed from the perspective of where (not if) God's law addressed it. Many times our dinner table has been the place of important theological discussions that were undergirded by a solid orthodox base.

But these are personal encounters with a writer and his work. The groundwork Rush laid with his spearheading the Christian and home school movements, and his participation in landmark cases involving the rights of Christians to educate their children as directed by God, helped me even before I had the blessing to know him. For the work he and those who worked with him did paved the way for me to be able to home school without significant incident or opposition. Additionally, there were the many people who had read his work and heard him speak and began to take dominion in the area of home schooling support groups, magazines, legal assistance, and writing and designing curriculums, etc. In other words, others built on his work; as a result, there are myriads of good resources available to home schoolers around the country and world.

But Rush didn't stop there. He continues to write and challenge Christians to *cast their bread upon the waters*. He is not interested in becoming a celebrity-guru who has followers who follow him blindly. Far from it. He lives humbly, takes the time to answer questions (even from children), and challenges people to begin a work in their own area and re-take ground for the kingdom of God. The quality of the people he has drawn to him over the years is astounding. Their books fill my bookshelves as do the works of many great men he often references and on whose work he expands.

There are many home educators to whom I've spoken over the years that have known Rushdoony, the work of Chalcedon Foundation, and read his books. They agree with me that he has served as a prophet and mentor in the arena of home schooling. Often, when our family meets another that has had the benefit of Rush's teachings, there is an instant comraderie and depth of understanding that is not always present with those who don't have the same grounding.

R. J. Rushdoony, the Christian, the man, the theologian, the advocate, has had an impact that is growing yearly. God has been gracious to us by giving us one who could help us understand our times and be prepared to apply his law-word to every area of life and thought. This good and faithful servant, we believe, will be remembered alongside other greats of our Faith such as Augustine, Calvin, and Knox. How blessed we are to be given a chance to walk alongside him as he does the work God has called him to do!

Andrea Schwartz is co-director of Friends of Chalcedon. She has been home schooling her own children since 1983 and has had a number of articles on home schooling published in various magazines. She continues to advise other home schooling families in areas of philosophy and curriculum.

The Ecclesiastical Text *Redivivus?*

Theodore P. Letis

The English New Testament text critic, F. C. Burkitt, once said of the Christian Religion, "we do not know why it lived and lives, any more than we know why we ourselves are alive."[1] Since E. J. Epp announced fifteen years ago the mystifying fact that there was a revival underway of the views of J. W. Burgon, text critics have been saying the same thing about the Ecclesiastical Text.[2] Two recent assessments of this phenomenon are those by Professor Daniel B. Wallace, of Dallas Seminary and the late Professor Kurt Aland, of the *Institut für neutestamentliche Textforschung.* Both essays are windows to how scholars are responding to this development.

Daniel Wallace

Daniel Wallace's brief essay, "Some Second Thoughts on the Majority Text," *Bibliotheca Sacra* (July-September 1989), is primarily an in-house discussion directed to the Dallas Seminary constituency. Wallace points out, as I have,[3] "in the last several years some if not most of the leading advocates of the majority text view have received their theological training at Dallas Seminary."[4] This is an important point.

Why did Dallas interest so many in the textual views of a nineteenth century, High Church, Anglican divine (John William Burgon), with whom they hold next to nothing in common theologically? Strangely, Wallace raises the point but never attempts to address it. I believe, to do so, would call attention to his own "Dallas theology."

To those of us outside of American fundamentalism the connection between Dallas' theology and the rise of Majority Text advocates at Dallas is all too obvious. Dallas's doctrine of inerrant autographs has largely informed the Majority Text project of Hodges and those influenced by him over the years. His scheme of statistical probability, which Wallace has done a fine job in criticizing, seems to offer, on *a prima facia* basis, a more objectified, scientific approach. This is in keeping with the post-Enlightenment desire on

---

[1] F. C. Burkitt, *The Gospel History and its Transmission* (Edinburgh, 1911, 3rd ed.), 75.

[2] E. J. Epp, "New Testament Textual Criticism in America: Requiem for a Discipline," *Journal of Biblical Literature* 98 (1979), 94-98.

[3] "For some years now a small group of conservative evangelicals, affiliated mostly with the American dispensational institutions of Dallas Seminary and Moody Bible Institute, has sought to circumvent all detracting criticisms lodged against the *Textus Receptus,* or the King James Version, by producing a 'critical' edition of the majority Greek text." T. P. Letis, *The Majority Text: Essays and Reviews in the Continuing Debate* (Ft. Wayne, IN, 1987), 1.

[4] D. B. Wallace, "Some Second Thoughts on the Majority Text," *Bibliotheca Sacra* 143 (July-September 1989), 271.

the part of some to give Scripture a scientific aura, claiming it was *inerrant* in the original autographs.[5] In truth, it is ultimately a more simplistic means[6] for claiming a closer approximation to these autographs, rather than the more demanding, and at times more subjective, approach of the eclectics.[7] Wallace omits this neglected influence of the inerrant autographs theory, I believe, simply because on this point there is complete agreement between himself and the Majority Text advocates from Dallas. Nevertheless, I think it offers one explanation for why this school has produced an abundance of Majority Text defenders.

That there is a larger world of scholarship, outside of Dallas Seminary, which does not hold to the doctrine of inerrant autographs, and yet sees value in retaining the received texts for canonical purposes, is ignored.[8]

It is important for Wallace to continue stressing that Hodges's Majority Text is *not* the *Textus Receptus*. By making this point he claims that scholars like the Alands and others have misunderstood Hodges. As I have stated elsewhere,[9] I simply do not believe this to be the case. Hodges' critics see his project as an attempt to produce a *critical* edition of the text-type represented

---

[5.] For a survey of the development from the view of the continental Protestant dogmaticians, to the mostly American view of inerrant autographs, seeT. P. Letis, "The Protestant Dogmaticians and the Late Princeton School on the status of the Sacred *Apographa*," *Scottish Bulletin of Evangelical Theology*, Vol. 8, No. 1 (Spring 1980), 16-42.

[6.] One Majority Text advocate recently seemed to suggest that certain data on textual variants do not merit a place in the textual apparatus because such data are irrelevant to the Majority Text theory: "Both groups of critical [Greek text] editions contain a good number of notes which ought to be considered irrelevant because they are readings found in only one, or some very few MSS." W. G. Pierpont, "Modern Critical Editions of the Greek New Testament and Their Critical Notes," a paper distributed by the Majority Text Society, n.d., n.p. Also, another member of the Majority Text Society, Dr. Maurice A. Robinson, has remarked in response to another essay distributed by the Society, "Such continues to make it appear as though a preference for the Byzantine (or Majority/Traditional) textform is somehow tied to a severe inerrantist harmonization of differences among parallel passages. Such a hermeneutic could thus use the Majority Text issue as a convenient vehicle for a wider-ranging agenda." "Majority Affirmations and Peter's Denials: On Keeping Critical Issues Distinct," an unpublished lecture presented before a regional meeting of the Evangelical Theological Society, 1990.

[7.] It should be pointed out that many of the American reasoned eclectics — namely, those involved with the Evangelical Theological Society — are also interested in inerrant autographs. They find a high degree of satisfaction in the Codex Vaticanus/p[75] witness, believing it to be the closest link to the objective certainty they are striving after. On the other hand, the British, who generally seem never to have been affected by this doctrine of inerrant autographs, have developed a more rigorous eclecticism. Unconcerned by such theological considerations they are not as confident of the near exclusive quality of the B/p[75] witness. I. A. Moir expresses this when he judges, "there were probably several 'Ur-texts' of the NT derived from oral tradition and thus we are no nearer the autographs than we were a century ago," "Can We Risk Another 'Textus Receptus'?," *The Journal of Biblical Literature* 100 (1981), 618 .

[8.] See the works of B. Childs. Also, recall the position of M. M. Parvis, "The *textus receptus* is not *the* 'true' text of the New Testament but it is one text. It was the Scripture of many centuries of the Church's life. It cannot today displace our so-called critical texts, but it is worthy of a place, a very special place, beside them," "The Goals of New Testament Textual Studies," *Studia Evangelica* 6 (1973):406.

[9.] Letis, *The Majority Text*, 11, l2, 14, 19.

for the last four hundred years in the Protestant *Textus Receptus.* The *Textus Receptus* is simply the generic term used to refer to this ecclesiastical text-type and tradition.[10] It is only Wallace and other Dallas folk who think the *Majority Text* edited by Hodges, *et al.,* has made a dramatic break with this ecclesiastical tradition. No one else seems impressed by their claims.

There are a few other points Wallace should have considered. He will have to reevaluate the generality that the Byzantine text is overly harmonistic[11] in light of Dr. W. F. Wisselink's recently published research on this subject.[12]

Furthermore, Wallace needs to qualify his statement, "Hoskier's work [*Concerning the Text of the Apocalypse*] stands out as the only complete collation of the Greek witnesses for any New Testament book."[13] Dr. J. K. Elliott has pointed out that Hoskier did not consult all available MS. evidence in his project.[14]

Regarding Wallace's critique of Hodges proper, it is here that their common theological tradition helps. Wallace is the rare critic who perhaps alone truly understands Hodges' position — Wallace studied under him at Dallas. He addresses the specifics of Hodges' method and demonstrates its failure, point by point. Wallace has done a good job here and has performed an important service in his analysis of the *Dallas* Majority Text School.

Nevertheless, in this essay my own position is seriously misrepresented as a pre-critical advocacy of the *textus receptus.* This also served Wallace's purposes of wanting to conveniently dismiss alternatives to his own highly selective American fundamentalist approach to text critical theory and method. Almost to the man American fundamentalists who engage text criticism do so searching for that method which will provide the most

---

[10.] Wallace, *op. cit.,* 275. Parvis's is typical of a score of examples that could be cited. I give his quotation without context merely to illustrate his usage of the phrase: "A third option which we may mention is to edit a late Koine text, to reproduce, in fact, the *textus receptus,* if we may use that phrase to designate the 'received text' of the Greek Church as opposed to the Stephanus and Elzevir texts derived from it," *op. cit.,* 405.

[11.] *ibid.,* 279, n. 39.

[12.] *Assimilation as a Criterion for the Establishment of the Text: A Comparative Study on the Basis of Passages from Matthew, Mark and Luke,* Ph. D. dissertation, The Reformed Theological College, Kampen, 1989. I was happy to be invited to participate in the defense of this dissertation and to provide some editing assistance on the English translation. For a brief abstract see *The Bulletin of the Institute for Reformation Biblical Studies I* (Fall 1989):11. The published form of this dissertation can be purchased from Kok Publisher BV, P.O. Box 130, 8360 AC Kampen, the Netherlands.

[13.] Wallace, *op. cit.,* 284, n. 61.

[14.] Dr. Elliott's recent study of Hoskier's work on the MSS. of the Apocalypse led him to point out, "It is to be noted that Hoskier did not collate every manuscript of Revelation available to him." "Manuscripts of the Book of Revelation Collated By H. C. Hoskier," *Journal of Theological Studies* 40 (1989), 111, n. 2.

satisfying sense of objective certainty.[15]

This as a goal is commendable enough but when this desire for certainty leads to the distorting of other options that do not confirm the presuppositional *a priori* belief in the "inerrant autographs" theory held to by Wallace, then it becomes a problem. Even after personally communicating with Wallace and citing journal publications by me that made clear mine was not a pre-critical advocacy of the *textus receptus* he ignored such data and in a more recent incarnation of this same essay by him he continues to erroneously class me in this category.[16]

Here Wallace's claim that I do not accept the Majority Text theory "precisely because their resultant text is not the TR"[17] could not be more misleading. In this introduction by me which he cites I compiled a general consensus of misgivings about the Hodges/Farstad *The Greek New Testament According to the Majority Text* (1982), from every major journal review article written by American and British text critics and New Testament scholars at the time, and demonstrated that on purely technical grounds the Majority Text theory could not stand.

Finally, how ironic it is that Wallace is keen to highlight the fact that there are few text critics among advocates of the Ecclesiastical Text (a point I first brought out in 1987 regarding the Dallas Majority text advocates specifically) when I know of no substantial text critical work produced by Wallace, who

---

[15.] This always results in advocating the "reasoned eclectic" approach which canonizes the fourth-century Egyptian recension. This approach provides American fundamentalists with the same sense of certainty that pre-critical advocates of the *textus receptus* find in excluding text criticism altogether in favour of the Ecclesiastical text. On the source of this fundamentalist approach to text criticism see my "B. B. Warfield, Common-Sense Philosophy and Biblical Criticism," *American Presbyterians* 69:3 *(Fall* 1991), 175-190. Wallace is just more selective in which aspects of text criticism and Biblical criticism in general, that he disallows. I have also dealt with the pre-critical advocates of the *textus receptus* but Wallace again conveniently leaves this material unacknowledged, *i.e.*, my *The Revival of the Ecclesiastical Text and the Claims of the Anabaptists* (Fort Wayne, IN, 1992).

[16.] Daniel B. Wallace "The Majority Text Theory: History, Methods, and Critique," in Bart D. Ehrman and Michael W. Holmes, eds., *The Text of the New Testament in Contemporary Research: Essays on the* Status Quaestionis (Grand Rapids: William B. Eerdmans, 1995). Furthermore, Wallace has — and I can say this only in disbelief — even misrepresented specific statements, twisting them in directions that are nearly preposterous. Here he claims I "erroneously assumed Dallas Theological Seminary's confessional stance ... include[d] a belief in the traditional text," 301-302, n.25. What I actually said was that "Dallas Seminary (and Moody Bible Institute) held very rigorously to *the old Baconian position of Warfield, although they rejected his Calvinism"* (emphasis mine), and that "a new hybrid arose *within* some fundamentalist-dispensational institutions, mixing Warfield's inerrancy position with Hills's advocacy of the Byzantine text" (emphasis mine), Letis, *Edward Freer Hills' Contribution to the Revival of the Ecclesiastical Text,* 167-168. Pertinent literature is then cited in a footnote to document this movement *within* these institutions. Even cited is a review by a Dallas Seminary journal reviewer denouncing the Byzantine text theory. At no point can my language be used to bear the meaning given it by Wallace.

[17.] Wallace, "The Majority Text Theory," 304.

had, in fact, required the assistance of a British text critic to produce a book review of a text critical treatise.[18]

In short, Wallace's own unacknowledged predispositions as an American fundamentalist leave him less than capable of accurately assessing the various schools advocating the Ecclesiastical Text. What is required is someone trained more in the scientific study of religion and with a genuine pedigree as a text critic and less oriented by one's own unacknowledged sense of advocacy.

Kurt Aland

The translation of Kurt Aland's important essay, "The Text of the Church?"[19] is yet another response to the revival of the Ecclesiastical Text. Several of Professor Aland's remarks are exceedingly helpful in focusing the issues as understood by some of us outside of the Dallas orbit.

Professor Aland admits forthrightly that,

> it is undisputed that from the 16th to the 18th century orthodoxy's doctrine of verbal inspiration assumed ... [the] Textus Receptus. It was the only Greek text they knew, and they regarded it as the "original text."[20]

Furthermore, he asks the question "who in the German-speaking countries today would seek to revive the arguments of 18th century orthodoxy? ... and yet in the United States Burgon is enjoying a considerable revival."[21]

In response to this development, Aland, like Wallace, goes after Hodges, the most visible, but perhaps the easiest target (passing by Edward F. Hills, the scholar who truly initiated this revival.)[22]

[18.] In reality a post-critical advocacy of the Ecclesiastical Text is a theological decision, not a text critical one, though, as with the canonical approach as advocated by Brevard Childs, it is clearly predicated upon the historical circumstances of actual ecclesiastical use as opposed to attempting to reconstruct either a theoretical *ur* text, or "inerrant" autographs.

[19.] K. Aland, "The Text of the Church?," *Trinity Journal* 8 (Fall 1987),131-144.

[20.] Aland, *op. cit.*, 131. One could certainly challenge Professor Aland's assertion that the T. R "was the only Greek text they knew." I have highlighted T. H. L. Parker's study of Calvin's N. T. commentaries, where Parker admits, "there existed even in the sixteenth century an alternative to the *textus receptus* which already ruled" but it "was largely disregarded as an eccentricity." Letis, *Majority Text*, 136.

[21.] *ibid.*,135.

[22.] *ibid.*, 136. Professor Aland has, perhaps unkindly, pointed out a typographical error in the first edition of Hills' *The King James Version Defended* (1956). This, however, was corrected in subsequent editions, *e.g.*, *The King James Version Defended* (Des Moines, 1984, 4th ed.), 115, 116, actually making reference to Professor Aland's own excellent essay, "The Greek New Testament: Its Present and Future Editions," *The Journal of Biblical Literature* 87 (1968).

In his criticism of Hodges, Aland actually wants to go so far as to suggest we have no real evidence for the Egyptian origin of Codices Vaticanus and Sinaiticus.[23]

Elsewhere though, Aland puts the state of the debate in very helpful terms, noting,

> Hodges asserts for the Egyptian text that "its existence in early times outside of Egypt is unproved." But this statement can easily be turned about to read: the existence of the Majority Text in early times is unproved.[24]

Ironically, for Aland, the way out of this impasse is to invoke the data of patristic citations: this was the decisive argument for Burgon in the nineteenth century, used to get around the absence of hard data for the Ecclesiastical Text in Greek MSS. before the fourth century. Now, one presumes, Aland invokes statistics from *critical* editions of the fathers which seem to overturn the patristic evidence compiled by Burgon and employed by Miller.[25] Who will arbitrate the conflict between these two interpretations of patristic data? Is it really necessary to await an arbitration before one comes to a conclusion on this issue?

For those who find the received texts of the Jewish/Christian ecclesiastical traditions sufficient for religious, canonical purposes, it is enough to know that by the sixth century,

> Every church had a Gospels manuscript on its altar .... Their use of the Majority text indicates clearly that it was the choice of those in authority as the text to be recognized officially and propagated .... In the age of Justinian as in the 9th century the Majority text consolidated the position it had clearly claimed in the 4th century as the official, proper, and correct text of the developing Byzantine Church.[26]

Aland continues,

> This Byzantine text was regarded as "the text of the church" — to return to the title of this essay. It was the text of the official Byzantine church, and the church in its striving for uniformity did all that it could to make it the common text.[27]

[23.] On the clear connection of these uncials with Egypt see the references to Hoskier as they appear in, "The Gnostic Influences On the Text of The Fourth Gospel: John 1:18 In the Egyptian Manuscripts," *The Bulletin of the Institute for Reformation Biblical Studies* (Fall 1989), 4-7.

[24.] Aland, *op. cit.*,139. Historically speaking, among the Greek witnesses, Professor Aland's assessment is certainly correct.

[25.] J. W. Burgon, *The Traditional Text of the Holy Gospels Vindicated and Established,* Arranged, Completed, and Edited by Edward Miller (London, 1896), 90-122. To see how this data can be mishandled at times, consult Pickering's response to Gordon Fee, Letis, *Majority Text,* 33-41.

[26.] Aland, *op. cit.,* 140-141.

[27.] *ibid.,* 143.

Aland concludes, saying the claim for the Majority Text as the "text of the Church," is "the most impressive and effective claim of its proponents."[28]

Aland, however, personally opts for an earlier MS. tradition: B/p[75]. Believing it comes closest to the autographic exemplar(s), Aland seems to echo Hort's old belief that B/Aleph represented a "Neutral text."[29] Aland prefers *this* "church text" to that of the Byzantine Church.

Contrary to the Alands' sanguine view of the Egyptian textual tradition (B/p[75]), Dr. Johnston, an authority on the Syriac text, has demonstrated that the alleged agreement in these two witnesses, supposedly linking the second century with the fourth century, is anything but certain.[30]

Furthermore, Professor J. C. O'Neill has shown that Codex Vaticanus probably does not represent a pure line of careful, Alexandrian transmission from the second century. Instead, it is probably a fourth century recension, the project of an Egyptian scriptorium.[31] In fact, there seems to be no criteria that would qualify the Egyptian recension as an *ecclesiastical* text, with any hint of catholicity. Note the words of Parvis in the early seventies regarding the state of the current critical text, "When we reconstruct the 'original' text, we are not reconstructing but rather we are constructing something that never before existed in heaven and earth."[32] J. K. Elliott made a similar assessment in 1988,

> The recent printed editions of the Greek New Testament, which we can buy give a text which never existed as a manuscript of the New Testament. They are all reconstructions based on their editor's choice of readings from Manuscripts they had at their disposal, or which they elected to concentrate on.[33]

The *Textus Receptus* at least has the continuity and sanction of catholic usage to commend it to faith communities.

Was there development on the way to Ecclesiastical Text? No doubt there was, although to what extent is still greatly debated. There simply is not

---

[28] *ibid.*, 144.

[29] Aland seems to have merely substituted the less emotive word "strict" for neutral, his protestations to the contrary notwithstanding, cf. K. Aland and B. Aland, *The Text of the New Testament* trans. by E. F. Rhodes (Grand Rapids, 1987), 14. If strict means a text which transmits "the text of an exemplar with meticulous care (*e.g.*, p[75]) and depart[s] from it only rarely," (*ibid.*, 64) surely this is what Hort meant by *neutral* — a good copy of an exemplar resembling the autographic text, not seriously contaminated by either extant or original depravations. Certainly Hort also acknowledged that Codex Vaticanus was a "living text" when he rejected certain of its singular readings.

[30] See his essay, "Codex Vaticanus (B) plus P[75] — The 'Best' Text of the New Testament?," *The Bulletin of the Institute for Reformation Biblical Studies"* I (Fall 1989), 2-4.

[31] J. C. O'Neill, "The Rules Followed by the Editors of the Text Found in the Codex Vaticanus," *New Testament Studies* 35 (April 1989), 219-228.

[32] Parvis, *op. cit.*, 397.

[33] J. K. Elliott, "The Original Text of the Greek New Testament," *Fax Theologica* 8 (1988), 6.

always a clear-cut distinction in the relationship between source criticism, redaction criticism, and textual criticism.[34]

Analogously, we know there was *canonical* development which terminated in the fourth century. There was also *christological* development, beginning in the fourth century and culminating at the seventh century, Council of Constantinople (680-1). Is it so surprising, therefore, if the shape of the text developed as well?[35]

A contemporary example of how various pericopes could have been present in an early form of the text, then were omitted during a period of controversy, and then were reinserted at a later canonical stage, can be seen in the recent history of the debate surrounding the long ending of Mark's Gospel. Kurt and Barbara Aland have observed that,

> The practice of concluding the gospel of Mark at 16:8 ... continued to be observed in some Greek manuscripts as well as in versional manuscripts for centuries, although the "longer ending" of Mark 16:9-20 was recognized as canonical ....[36]

From the Reformation to the late nineteenth century this ending retained its canonical status. With the discovery/collation of the early Alexandrian uncials it was then thought to be a late interpolation, and on this basis it was therefore considered to be non-canonical (recall the first edition of the R.S.V. relegated these verses to very small, italicized print at the foot of the page). Recently, however, Bruce Metzger has acknowledged that while the ending may not be Mark's, nevertheless, because of its very early appearance in the second century, "the passage ought to be accepted as part of the canonical text of Mark."[37]

Furthermore, the lesson learned only this century about so-called *late* interpolations, found in third century papyri, has not yet had its full effect on some.

We are indebted to Kurt and Barbara Aland for the crucial work they have done while directors of the *Institut für neutestamentliche Textforschung*. In the present essay, however, we are particularly indebted to Kurt Aland's rare command of church history. It is this that informs his analysis of the *Majority* Text as the *Ecclesiastical* Text, first of the Eastern Orthodox Church and then of the Protestant Reformers and their heirs in the seventeenth and eighteenth centuries. Both Burgon and Parvis made this their argument. Parvis summarizes,

---

[34.] Cf. John Wenham, "Why Do You Ask Me About the Good? A Study of the Relation Between Text and Source Criticism," *New Testament Studies* 28 (January 1982), 116-125.

[35.] Regarding the hermeneutical and theological significance of this, again, consult the works of Childs.

[36.] Aland/Aland *op. cit.*, 69.

[37.] B.M. Metzger, *The Canon of the New Testament: Its Origin, Development, and Significance* (Oxford, 1987), 270.

We may recall the reliance which Dean Burgon placed on what he styled the "traditional text." "Speaking generally," he wrote, "the Traditional Text of the New Testament Scriptures, equally with the New Testament Canon, rests on the authority of the Church Catholic." This text is, in fact, "neither more nor less than the probate of the orthodox Greek Christian bishops, and those, if not as we maintain of the first and second, or third, yet unquestionably of the fourth and fifth, and even subsequent centuries."[38]

Parvis then offered his concurring sentiment,

> The *textus receptus* is the text of the Church. It is that form of text which represents the sum total and the end product of all the textual decisions which were made by the Church and her Fathers over a period of more than a thousand years.[39]

Currently we are experiencing a renewal of both pre-critical and a post-critical interest in reviving the Ecclesiastical Text. But perhaps it is closer to the truth to say the Ecclesiastical Text never really died. Certainly in light of the unbroken usage within the Greek Church one cannot properly speak of a *return* to the Ecclesiastical Text. Furthermore, the Alands' attempt to project the impression that there is now but one *Standard Text* (what others are calling the new *Textus Receptus*) will not make a horizon filled with a multiplicity of theoretical *original* texts go away. Parvis observed,

> Each one of these critical texts differ quite markedly from all of the others. This fact certainly suggests that it is very difficult, if not impossible to recover the original text of the New Testament.[40]

One of the reasons no agreed upon original text has emerged — the recent harmony between NA[26] and UBS[3] notwithstanding — has been addressed by many studies suggesting there never was one original, in the strict sense. It can be unsettling for those who have invested these *originals* with the quality of inerrancy when someone as safe as F. F. Bruce claims,

> If we appeal to the "autographic" texts, we should consider the implications of the fact that for some of the most important books of the Bible autographs never existed. There was no autograph of the Epistle to the Romans in the proper sense — that is, no copy written by Paul himself. Paul dictated, and Tertius copied. Indeed, the early textual history of the epistle suggests that more copies than one may have been made at Paul's direction — not only the primary one, naturally lacking the personal greetings at the end, for other churches that would be glad to have this definitive exposition of the gospel. When a letter was intended to go to a number of different places, it is conceivable that

---

[38.] Parvis, *op. cit.*, 406.
[39.] *ibid.*
[40.] *ibid.*, 397.

several simultaneous copies were made by as many amanuenses at one dictation.[41]

This no doubt explains in a large measure why the elusive original still haunts us. Still short of such objective certainty, Parvis recognized that the various attempts at approximation,

> further suggests that that which we look upon as Scripture may be determined by our own theology — by whether or not we are Protestants or Roman Catholics, for example. Why do we have so many critical texts, that is, so many "original" texts? Which one of them is my Scripture? Which one of them is your Scripture?[42]

It was in the face of this same development in the early Church, no doubt, that the Greek Ecclesiastical Text emerged in the fourth century for the Eastern Church. Certainly we know from Jerome that this was the case in the fourth century for the Western Church, which resulted in thc *Vulgata Latina*. [43] That same climate, as it currently exists, probably offers some explanation for why the Ecclesiastical Text lived, and lives today.

Theodore Letis, director of the Institute for Reformation Biblical Studies, holds a Ph. D. in ecclesiastical history from New College, the University of Edinburgh. He is the world's preeminent scholarly advocate of the Received Text of Holy Scripture and a revival of catholic orthodoxy, particularly in the sphere of textual studies and Biblical translations. He has written or edited several books and written numerous scholarly articles. He is a member of a number of prestigious scholarly organizations.

[41.] F. F. Bruce, *Foreword*, 8- 9, in Dewey M. Beegle, *Scripture, Tradition, and Infallibility* (Grand Rapids, 1973). Furthermore, W. A. Strange, *The Problem of the Text of Acts*, unpublished D. Phil., Oxford University, 1988, has given new life to an old thesis, namely, that Luke produced two separate recensions of the book of Acts which accounts for the differences between the Western text and other text-types of this book.

[42.] Parvis, *op. cit.*, 397.

[43.] The same holds true for the Greek Old Testament text, as summed up by P. Kahle in his Schweich Lectures: "We may try to edit the Jewish standard text of the Greek Tora. But can we possibly regard such a text as an 'Urtext' — a text from which all existing texts have to be derived? A standard text of the Targum of the Pentateuch, the Targum Onkelos, was preceded by different forms of the old Palestinian Targum of the Pentateuch, of which some valuable fragments have been found in the Cairo Geniza. The standard text of the Latin Bible, the Vulgate, was preceded by different forms of the *Vetus Latina*.... It is always so, and there can be no doubt that the standard text of the Greek Tora was preceded by divergent forms of earlier translations." *The Cairo Geniza* (London, 1947), 175.

The Covenant of Grace and Law:
Rushdoony and the Doctrine of the Covenant

Brian Abshire

In a world man never made, God's covenant is grace, life and peace.

R. J. Rushdoony, *Systematic Theology, Volume I,* "The Covenant"

Rushdoony's Place in History

In later ages of God's grace, when the fallacy of humanism will have been fully rejected, and Neopaganism will have scurried back to its dank corners, when Christian civilization will have been rebuilt and the glory of God will have filled the earth, church historians will undoubtedly place two names above the rest as the most important of the twentieth century. Van Til's work in philosophy and apologetics cleared out the stumps, broke up the ground and prepared the soil. But R. J. Rushdoony was the one who planted the seeds that would generate genuine Christian reconstruction. At this end of the history, we do not know whether we or our far descendants will see that harvest. It may be in God's sovereignty, that Rushdoony, like Jan Huss, may go down as a forerunner of the Great Reformation. But his place in the history of the church is secure, because he not only critiqued the empire of Man, but offered a fully developed concept of the kingdom of God in its place.

Rushdoony and the Doctrine of the Covenant

Part of Rushdoony's genius is to examine well-established theological premises, and then bring his vast understanding of ancient cultures, church history and incredible knowledge of the Scriptures to bear, shedding light on what has been often poorly understood or inadequately communicated. The doctrine of the covenant is the backbone of the Reformed Faith. But as in every other area of study to which Rushdoony has turned his attention, he offers insights into this doctrine that eludes lesser men. Furthermore, he manages to communicate his wisdom in simple, elegant language, quite unlike the stultifying ponderings of theologians who bury the truths of Scripture underneath heavy verbiage, convoluted syntax and muddled thinking. A mark of Rushdoony's writing is "... an abstract definition leads to problems whereas to say 'We do what the Lord commands ...,' does not."[1] Rushdoony preeminently teaches the commandments of faithful covenantal living.

---

[1]. R. J. Rushdoony, *Systematic Theology* (Vallecito, CA 1994), I: 416.

Though his development of the covenant unfolds throughout his writings, the culmination of his work is found in his *Systematic Theology* (all page numbers in parentheses refer to this work). Rushdoony begins his definition of the covenant very traditionally *i.e.*, the original word (*berith*) may mean fetter, a bond or imposed treaty (420). He demonstrates that covenants in antiquity and Scripture were seen as the most important and governing fact in a man's life (426). A covenant could be one of two possible types of treaties, contracts or legal relationships. The first is between two parties of relative or comparable strength (*i.e.*, marriage, treaties between two nations, etc.). The second is between two radically unequal parties, a relationship where all the benefits are one sided. Rushdoony sees such a covenant as an act of grace, the greater giving grace to the lesser. Yet a covenant of grace is also a law relationship. Rushdoony notes that in a covenant of grace, the terms are set, not by negotiation, but exclusively by the word of the bestower of grace. God's word is law (374).

Rushdoony identifies the Bible as a covenant book; the text of God's treaty with man and therefore a legal document (373). There is no understanding of Biblical Faith apart from the doctrine of the covenant (384) and its legal implications. For Rushdoony, man can approach God only on his terms as covenant Lord (384). Furthermore, the covenant law governs our relationship with all men, without exception. Thus God's covenant does not allow us to exempt any area of life from his government (385). All of man's life is covenantal, *i.e.*, bound to a law treaty with God; man is tied to a contract that is given to him by God and which man has no choice but to obey or be judged a rebel (403). The Bible does not conceive of life or any aspect of life, apart from God's covenant. All of man's life is to be governed by God's covenant and by covenant law (423).

The covenant does two things to a covenant people; it marks their election by sovereign grace and it declares them to be holy because God separates them to himself. This judicial holiness must be followed by our personal holiness and this means obedience, keeping God's commands or laws (412). There is thus a vital relationship between the covenant, covenant law and holiness.

Rushdoony emphasizes that though the covenant is a legal fact, a treaty made by sovereign grace (413), it is also a highly personal fact (citing Dt. 7:7-8). God's covenant of election and grace is inseparable from his love. Hence, violations of the covenant result in more than legal penalties; they precipitate his wrath. God repeatedly compares covenant-breaking with adultery and whoredom to make clear his intense and personal anger at man's faithlessness. An offense against God is a personal affront, at the very least an act of carelessness for his love and contempt of his person.

Denial of Covenant of Works

Rushdoony does not find the Westminster Confession's two-covenant scheme as the best expression of the Biblical doctrine. He rejects the idea of "the covenant of works." The idea of a mutual or jointly made contract is never present in Scripture. The covenant is always an act of grace on God's part; man receives the covenant as God's gift and requirement (436). Any covenant between God and man must be initiated and executed by God. While it requires works, the works are the response of gratitude for the grace of God's covenant. Man cannot terminate God's covenant, since he does not institute it. Man's works of the law are a legal requirement of the covenant, not a condition of it; they do not make a covenant, though they are required by it. This is a covenant of grace, because it is made entirely on God's initiative (376). He does not think that the Westminster Divines intended the covenant of works to be seen as a covenant of merit. It is a covenant of law, because covenants are a form of law and always require works. This, however, does not make it a covenant of works.

Man's incapacity in a relationship to God did not come into being through the fall. Man does not have any capacity to render anything to God in the way of works or accrued benefits; whether in the state of innocence, or the fall, or of grace, or of glory. The very life of Adam and Eve enjoyed in Eden was of God's grace, not a product of their obedience prior to the fall, since life itself is a gift of God's grace (1 Pt. 3:7), whether to the redeemed or the reprobate.

Thus, Adam's breach of the covenant was not a breach of a covenant of works but a breach of God's grace, a personal affront to and revolt against the grace of the person of God. Therefore God's curse for the violation of his covenant is personal and specific; it affects all creation and all men, but each in a different way. They suffer alike from sin and death, but within that framework, specific differences occur. Their judgment is particular and personal. Thus the covenant is always and only instituted by God's grace.

The Inescapability of the Covenant

The covenant with God is inescapable for all the sons of Adam; they are judged by it and it is the condition of their lives (375). All men are under the blessings and the curses of God's covenant. Man cannot walk away from the covenant; he is pursued relentlessly with God's curses and judgment of death. The covenant creates all the conditions of life so that whether a man is faithful or faithless to the covenant Lord, his life is determined by his relationship to the Lord and to the covenant. God's covenant with Noah embraces all men and every living creature. It is an everlasting covenant and a sovereign act of grace and government.

The New Covenant is simply the broken covenant, reestablished with a new people. With man's sin and the sentence of death, the covenant initiated by God in the garden was in effect rendered null and void. Man had despised the grace of the covenant and broken its law. God, however, remained faithful to the covenant. He sent his only begotten Son, to become not only truly God but also to become truly man, the new Adam (384). He is on familiar ground here; Calvin would have approved (cf. "The new covenant does not destroy the old in substance, but only in form," *Calvin, Moses 1:463*). Rushdoony notes that after the Babylonian captivity, God reestablished his covenant with a remnant of the people, and after the coming of Jesus Christ, God again reestablished his covenant with a remnant (386).

Thus Rushdoony sees the Scriptures as teaching that all men, without exception, are bound by the covenant with Adam. All men are covenant-breakers apart from Christ. Yet God who made the covenant by his sovereign grace, creates and calls unto himself a faithful people in every age and elects them to a covenant status. Precisely because such a covenant involves so great a difference between the two parties, a judge, ruler, umpire, arbiter, or mediator between the two parties is required (429). Rushdoony details the Old Testament history of types, of men who as forerunners of Jesus Christ mediated between God and man. The purpose of the covenant is to reveal God's grace and salvation. The purpose of the Messiah is to save God's covenant partner, man, to restore man in God's grace and calling and to empower man to fulfill his calling (432). Jesus Christ thus came in terms of the covenant, not to replace the covenant but to become the new covenant man and to create by regeneration a new covenant people to replace the old humanity (433). Christ's atonement releases us from the curse of the law, its penalties before God. Thus the covenant is not only of grace and law, but a covenant of salvation. God binds himself to redeem his people out of all their troubles, if they are faithful to him (434).

Covenant and Sovereignty

The covenant in Christ is thus the manifestation of Christ's sovereignty on earth. There are political implications of Christ's coming because the sovereign has come to claim his realm. No realm can be withheld from Christ's reign. The covenant is a total treaty (434) and therefore takes priority over us and over every relationship. Covenant man cannot have any unmediated relationships to anything. Furthermore, the blessing of covenantal faithfulness is harmony with God, harmony within man, between man, between men and animals and between men and the inanimate world (431). When man makes peace with God in the person of the God-man mediator, Jesus Christ, and when in faithfulness he establishes dominion in terms of God's law-word, God will extend his covenant of peace to include every aspect of life (430). With the triumph of the Messiah, the curse will recede and man shall live in peace with God's creation (Is. 11:6-9, 65:25).

Covenant and Land

Rushdoony also demonstrates the strong connection in Scripture between the covenant established with man in the garden and the promises of the land. He notes that by its very nature, a covenant is concerned with land. A covenant is a law treaty, the law of the covenant is the law of the land (379). He shows that the first example of a covenant grant of land is the Garden of Eden. God declared in Gen. 1:26-28 that the whole earth and all things therein were given to man as God's covenant vassal. The Garden of Eden was a "pilot project" wherein man was to learn to apply his covenant responsibilities. Man's violation of the covenant meant the revocation of the grant — the land would now be hostile to man. Yet, God renewed the land promise to Noah (Gen. 9:1-7) and to Abraham (Gen. 12:1-7, 13:14-17). However, even as God gave a limited sphere of earth to Adam as a test area, so now the chosen line is given a limited sphere, the general area of Palestine. The covenant grant is renewed to Isaac (Gen. 26:3-4) and Jacob (Gen. 28:4, 13-15, 35:10-12, 48:4). Later it is repeated to Moses (Ex. 3:8) and the whole of the law is given as the condition of blessing in the possession of the land grant (Lev. 26, Dt. 28).

Rushdoony notes that certain covenant facts about the land are clearly set forth in the commission of Joshua (Josh. 1:1-9). God is the lord of the land, not the Canaanite inhabitants who are to be evicted on God's orders as lawless and rebellious tenants who are abusing the Lord's law and property. Success and prosperity in the land are dependent on faithfulness to the covenant. The earth itself will become a curse to those who violate the covenant. The covenant earth will fulfill or put into force God's covenant purposes. Only faithfulness can ensure victory (380).

This commission to Joshua is given again in briefer form in the Great Commission of our Lord to his people, the New Israel of God (Mt. 28:18-20). The covenant land grant is renewed, this time to include all nations and all the earth. The last Adam, Jesus Christ (1 Cor. 15:45-50) restates the original dominion mandate of Gen. 1:26-28. The land grant is again total, but with a difference. The new Adam, who is both man of very man and God of very God, has total power and authority (381). Thus what the sin of one man ruined for his posterity, the righteousness of another man, guarantees for his.

Covenant Obligations

There are, of course, covenant obligations on the part of redeemed man. Because the earth is the Lord's, he is therefore strictly entitled to all the first-fruits and the tithes; his sabbaths of the land must be kept. We cannot defile the land, it must be kept holy, separated unto God and his law. In the same way, wilderness means unsown, uncultivated land, land which men have not yet brought under dominion in terms of God's law-word (382).

Rushdoony sees vivid validation of the continuity of the Testaments when our Lord called out twelve apostles to replace the twelve patriarchs of Israel, seventy disciples to replace the council of the elders and established a covenant in his own blood with this new Israel. He then sent them out to bring all the earth under his domain (382).

The doctrine of the covenant requires the presupposition of God's sovereignty and his law. When God gave his law (Ex. 20:1-23, 33). He immediately established publicly the covenant bond and demanded acceptance thereof by Israel (403). The covenant requires that we who by grace are made members of the covenant community and given God's law, give our total allegiance to the Lord of the covenant. The whole of our life must belong to the covenant Lord, all our possessions, and we must be ready to die for the covenant Lord (409). This requires the civil order to be subject to God's judgment if it violates his covenant (405).

Thus there are blessings and cursings for faithfulness or faithlessness. Rushdoony demonstrates that the penalties for offenses against God's covenant law differ in terms of their relationship to God and man. There are a variety of penalties for offenses against men, *i.e.*, penalties that can be enforced by either church or state. However, all offenses against God have a common penalty, death (Gen. 2:17), because all sin is treason against the covenant Lord and all sin is therefore deserving of and subject to the death penalty (386). Blood is therefore central to the doctrine of the covenant (Lev. 17:11) (387).

Covenant— Equally Grace and Law

The curse of the law, *i.e.*, its penalties, fall on all who despise the Lord of the covenant and his law-word. The first curse pronounced is death (Gen. 2:16-17). Although death is the ultimate, basic and final curse, there are other curses on man for his contempt of God's law; *i.e.*, sickness, plagues and epidemics (Dt. 28:21-22, 27-29, 59-61). Because salvation means the health of a man in all his being, the converse is that sin means that man in all his being is sick. The curse of the law also includes war, invasion, defeat and conquest, even captivity (Dt. 28:25-26, 36-38), drought and the destruction of urban and farm life (Dt. 28:15-19, 23-24) and poverty and disaster (Dt. 28:15-19, 38-46) (388). Rushdoony is careful to note, however, that poverty, like sickness, is a fact which besets an apostate nation. Because the enemies of God's covenant are usually in power in such nations, it is often the saints that suffer the most. Antinomianism is a denial of the covenant and we dare not forget that our God is a consuming fire. Rushdoony writes tellingly, "I find it startling and frightening that people can read these words and discount them because we are supposedly no longer under law, only in grace; surely this is at least in part a grim fulfillment of the curse of blindness that is basic to all sin..." (389).

Because Biblical law is covenant law, it is also grace simultaneously. Biblical faith was and is covenant faith. Rushdoony sees the blessings of faithfulness to the covenant add up to the grace of life: "I am come that they might have life, and that they might have it more abundantly" (Jn. 10:10). Jesus Christ is life (Jn. 14:6) and men cannot live apart from him. Thus the counterpole of the curses of the covenant is God's providential oversight of his beloved; the principle of health, an earth which is rich towards us and skies which give us the weather that blesses, wealth and providential care, prosperity, protection against our enemies, fulfillment, and wisdom and insight. The blessing of the law includes our total life surrounded by God's care and blessing.

Covenantal Faithfulness

Faithfulness to the covenant is not ritual obedience. God found the sacrifices of the Old Testament offensive because they were not backed up with heartfelt obedience. Today, instead of costly sacrifices, Rushdoony notes that churchman have an even cheaper substitute for covenant faithfulness. They indulge in pious gush, singing "'Oh, How I love Jesus': and then do as they please." They then wonder why they and the land are not blessed. To set aside the covenant law is to set aside the covenant God and his blessing and to choose his curse (390). Man's liberty within the covenant is simply the freedom to be blessed or be cursed (435).

Covenant and the Future

Rushdoony sees God's covenant looking to a glorious consummation in which all things are made new (Rev. 21:5). The false heirs of the land are to be dispossessed and the true heirs to occupy the whole earth. The joyful proclamation is sounded, "The kingdoms of this world are become the kingdoms of our Lord and of his Christ; and he shall reign for ever and ever" (Rev. 11:15).

Rushdoony, in his analysis of the covenant, offers a fully Biblical interpretation of one of the most often used, and confused, doctrines of the Reformed Faith. Rejecting dispensationalism, Rushdoony aptly demonstrates that the Bible speaks with one message from Genesis to Revelation: one covenant, seminal, organic, and blossoming as God reveals more of his glorious nature and being progressively through Scripture, yet still retaining the same substance. Thus all of Scripture fits in Rushdoony's view into a coherent whole. The result is a consistent Biblical worldview, that ties every area of man's life in humble submission to God's plan. The sovereignty, holiness, majesty and glory of God are maintained, while his gracious love, compassionate care and infinite mercy are declared.

Thus within Rushdoony's concept of the covenant, the wonderful, all encompassing revelation of God in Scripture is made clear. The neo-platonic, saccharine coated spirituality of pietism is rejected, and a full-orbed Biblical Faith offered in its place. The Lord God is magnified, his people are edified, and the kingdom advanced. This is Rushdoony's legacy and the seed from which genuine Christian reconstruction will spring.

The Rev. Brian M. Abshire graduated from Bethel College (magna cum laude) in two years, with a double major in Psychology and Biblical and Theological Studies. He attended Bethel, Talbot, International and Covenant Seminaries, earning an MA (summa cum laude) in Apologetics and Contemporary Culture and a Th.M. (magna cum laude) in Presuppositional Apologetics. Brian is presently a Teaching Elder in the Presbyterian Church of America, pastoring Lakeside Church-PCA, Milwaukee, Wisconsin and serves as the vice moderator of the Northern Illinois Presbytery.

The Synagogue of Christ

Steve M. Schlissel

The point is that the church itself in the New Testament was more a school than a temple.

R. J. Rushdoony — *Chalcedon Position Paper #1*

The training of ... mature men is the function of the church. The purpose of the church should not be to bring men into subjection to the church, but rather to train them into a royal priesthood capable of bringing the world into subjection to Christ the King.

R. J. Rushdoony —*The Institutes of Biblical Law*

What happens when a caricature of Jesus is presented, when obedience is constantly demanded without the God-ordained goal of obedience being mentioned, and when man is continually summoned to prepare himself in the Lord, but for no purpose? The ministry of the church then becomes trifling, and the life of the believer, frustrating.

R. J. Rushdoony —*The Institutes of Biblical Law*

The church wasn't born at Pentecost. It was Bar Mitzvah'd. No small matter, this. The church had a long, albeit dotted, history by the time the Spirit in Christ's fullness fell, and a glorious, albeit difficult, future. By Pentecost, the church, because of its history, its providentially-ordained organization and the Holy Spirit's promised guidance, was well-prepared to fulfill its function in the world.

The Belgic Confession, in Article XXVII, states, "We believe and profess one catholic or universal Church .... This Church has been from the beginning of the world, and will be to the end thereof ...." It has not, however, always had the same form. In the Garden of Eden, God identified and separated the church (then consisting of two) using the essential elements, word and sacrament, promise and token, which would be present throughout the church's history, in some form or another. Our first parents were created to understand themselves and all things else in terms of a word. They had received the defining word of God; they had heard the anti-word of the serpent. Choosing the devil's definitions, they had broken covenant with their creator and entered into league with the destroyer, becoming co-pretenders with him to the throne.

God was not about to forsake his purposes, or to quickly formulate a "Plan B." He graciously and forcefully took back Adam and Eve — he redeemed them — by *placing hostility* between them and their new master (the antithesis), by *promising* in their hearing the incarnation of the conquering,

suffering Messiah (the *Protevangelium*, first proclamation of the Gospel),
and by *clothing* them with God-provided coverings (the "sacrament"),
indicating in the clearest terms that their fig leaves (their instinctive effort at
self-atonement/covering) were wholly inadequate and unacceptable. It is God
who saves. Calvinism did not originate in Geneva; it is found in Eden. God's
people, the covenant line, would henceforth be the people redeemed by him
to live, once again, in terms of *his* word.

From Eden to Isaac

This word would be developmentally revealed in accordance with God's
purposes and the circumstances — ordained by him — in which the church
found itself. It would reach its fullness after the promised Savior arrived, after
he had fully accomplished his work in the estate of humiliation, and firmly
inaugurated his work in the estate of exaltation. The full and final word in
terms of which God's people must, and all people ought to, live is "the Word
of God which is contained in the Scriptures of the Old and New Testaments,"
i.e., the whole Bible. The tokens identifying and comforting the people of
God would also admit of changes in history, until they reached their
normative and simple state in Christ's institutions of baptism and the Lord's
Supper.

After hearing his sentence pronounced, and after our first parents'
expulsion from the Garden, Satan seeks to undermine God's purposes and
God's people in an effort to forestall the arrival of the Promised One. He does
this by a twofold method which has not undergone categorical change since:
the devil endeavors to remove the church from the world (seeking its
destruction), or remove it from the word (through seduction). The hostility
predicated in the antithesis of Gen. 3:15 was very soon revealed in the
respective approaches to God of Cain (the covenant-breaker) and Abel (the
covenant-keeper). God, in the Garden, implicitly required blood, a
substitutionary death, as the *first step of faith* a sinner must take in drawing
near to the Holy One. Cain was apparently offended by the requirement of a
blood sacrifice, just as he was offended by God's counsel to him to "do the
right thing" (Gen. 4:1-7).[1] Rather than approach God as per God's
prescription, he sought to eliminate the competition (perhaps with the insane
thought that God would *have* to accept him now, in virtue of his "monopoly").
Of course, God's church, though briefly set back, is not defeated by this
persecution. Soon God would raise up another covenant-keeper in the
person of Seth. In his day, the church would *advance* as "men began to call
upon the name of the LORD" (Gen. 4:26). Many orthodox commentators

---

[1.] It is wholly unnecessary to debate, as theologians have been wont to do, whether
God found unacceptable Cain's actual offering *or* his apparent lack of faith. Hebrews
11:4, read with Genesis 4:5, makes it clear that it was both: God didn't like his gift *or*
his attitude.

have understood this to mean that God was now worshiped "in a more public and solemn manner; praying being here put for the whole worship of God"[2] Poole goes on, "The sense is this: Then when the world was universally corrupt, and had forsaken God and his service, good men grew more valiant and zealous for God, and did more publicly and avowedly own God, and began to distinguish themselves from the ungodly world, and to call themselves and one another by the name of God, *i.e.*, the sons, servants, or worshippers *of God* as they are expressly called ...."

For our purposes we will call attention only to the fact that this corporate calling upon the LORD seems to have arisen by divine "permission" or providence rather than by express divine instruction. It is obvious that blood sacrifice in faith continued to occupy first place in the approach to God throughout the patriarchal period. Consider Gen. 8:20-21; 12:7; 13:18; 22:8-13; 26:25 (*q.v.*, and cf. Gen. 4:26); 33:20; Job 1:1-5; etc. The worship of the church is performed in the light of the first promise in Eden, and in confidence that God will redeem those who come to him in faith in accordance with his will. The worship of the church is *decentralized* during this period. The remarkable incident with Melchizedek suggests that "in those times God had his remnant scattered here and there even in the worst places and nations."[3] Further, the lack of detailed prescriptions apart from these *general requirements* suggests latitude in form, given the presence of the requisite elements.

Of Tracks and Tiers

At the time of the giving of the law sharp differences appear, chief of which are the *centralization* of sacrificial worship and the provision of a corpus of *detailed* instruction regulating it. What is important to note — because nearly universally overlooked — is the fact that with the giving of the law, God instituted and maintained a two-tiered track governing the life and worship of the church. This two-tiered track would remain in force until the time of our Lord Jesus Christ (though each track would undergo respective changes during the waiting period). At the ascension, the "upper deck" would be lifted into heaven (to which it had always testified — Heb. 9), and from that fixed location, serve as the temple in terms of which the "lower deck," the synagogue of Christ, or, the church, derives its meaning.

Think of the movement of form like this: The Verrazano Bridge (the most beautiful in the world, of course) connects Brooklyn and Staten Island. The interstate leading to it from Brooklyn has several lanes but only one level. The Bridge, however, has an upper and lower deck. When you arrive in Staten

---

[2.] Matthew Poole, *Commentary on the Holy Bible*, 3-volume edition, (McLean, VA. n.d.).
[3.] *ibid.*, on Gen. 14:18.

Island you're back on a single level. Similarly, the decentralized worship of the pre-Mosaic period of the church (the interstate leading up to the bridge) focused on faith (in God's word), the presence of the requisite elements of worship (sacrifice) and prayer. When we get to the Mosaic period, the bridge which will take us to the Christian era breaks out into an upper and lower deck.

The institution of tabernacle/temple, which we'll call the upper deck, is clearly the more prominent track from Moses to Christ. It is characterized by *exclusivity* — sacrifices henceforth being acceptable only if offered at the place where God causes his name to specially dwell, ultimately the temple at Jerusalem. It is also characterized by rigorous *particularity* and punctiliousness, so much so that seemingly minor infractions of worship order were punishable by death (*e.g.*, using the incense ingredients for any another purpose, touching the ark or other holy things, casually approaching God, or approaching him in the Most Holy Place on any occasion or in any manner other than that which is prescribed by him in the law).[4]

Sacrifice would now be confined to one location in order that the entire sacrificial system, and the laws regulating it, may better serve as the tutor leading to Christ (Gal. 3:24; 4:2). But the worship, broadly considered, of the covenant community is by no means so confined or specialized. God makes provision for covenant instruction, covenant worship and covenant continuity in the areas *outside* Jerusalem by providing a *decentralized*, indeed a deliberately *scattered*, Levitical order. The Levites, qualified by God and given by him to assist the priests at the temple service in Jerusalem (Num. 3:9), were also charged with providing instruction in God's law throughout Israel (Dt. 33:8, 10; 2 Chr. 35:3; cf. Neh. 8:7 and Mal. 2:4-8). The priests could serve *as priests* only at the temple in Jerusalem, but the Levites could help the priests in Jerusalem or serve as ministers and teachers throughout the covenant realm. *Keep your eye on the lower deck.*

The Root of the Synagogue

In Lev. 23 we have the listing of the appointed feasts of Israel. Most of them involved special priestly services to be performed at the tabernacle/temple. But heading the list of sacred assemblies is the Lord's Sabbath: "There are six days when you may work, but the seventh day is a Sabbath of rest, a day of

---

[4.] It should be noted that under extraordinary circumstances, God allowed latitude even in matters pertaining to the temple and sacrifice. See, for example, the Lord honoring Hezekiah's prayer for toleration of deviation from ceremonial prescriptions in view of prevailing conditions and the sincerity of the seekers (2 Chr. 30:17-20). Furthermore, development in the lower deck (decentralized) elements of Passover observance (not to mention other feasts) is hardly appreciated by modern regulativists. The Seder observed by Christ was nearly entirely the product of covenant evolution. Where, *e.g.*, does the law call for cups of wine as the skeleton around which the seder is to be constructed? Yet, a technical name for a particular seder cup, the "cup of blessing," was directly imported into the Christian community (1 Cor. 10:16).

sacred assembly. You are not to do any work; wherever you live, it is a Sabbath to the LORD" (NIV).

It is of particular importance to note that, a) This day was to be observed throughout the land ("wherever you live" in the NIV, or, "in all your dwellings" in the KJV); b) it was to be honored by the cessation of all ordinary work; and c) it was to be a day of sacred assembly. No further instruction is to be found regarding the character of or elements involved in these sacred assemblies apart from the command that they are to occur. *This is the elusive root of the synagogue system:*[5] a decentralized, loosely regulated gathering of God's people for the express purpose of imitating him in ceasing from labor on the seventh day, and praising him in sacred assembly as creator (Ex. 20:8-11) and redeemer (Dt. 5:15).

If we disallow the claims of the Jews to the divine authenticity of the oral law, we are led to conclude that these decentralized sacred assemblies, while divinely *commanded*, were not divinely regulated in their particulars (other than that they be gatherings to worship *the true God*, presumably including instruction in his word and covenant dealings). If this is so, then the command of Dt. 12:32, "Whatever I command you, be careful to observe it; you shall not add to it nor take away from it," has primary and particular reference to the priestly system (the upper deck) and only *general, principled* reference to decentralized worship.

Dt. 12 is explicitly providing guidance for the upper deck, *centralized* sacrificial system: "You shall not at all do as we are doing here today — every man doing what is right in his own eyes — for as yet you have not come to the rest and the inheritance which the LORD your God is giving you. But when you cross the Jordan and dwell in the land ... then there will be the place where the LORD your God chooses to make his name abide. There you shall bring what I command you: your burnt offerings, your sacrifices, your tithes, the heave offerings of your hand, and all the choice offerings which you vow to the LORD" (12:8-11, NKJV).

Further commands in the context reveal God's concern that his people not be tempted to sacrifice — as they lived their everyday lives outside the city where his name would dwell — their daily victuals to another god (vss. 20-22), that they not seek their life in sacrificial or other blood, as the Canaanites

---

[5.] Bannerman, in *The Scripture Doctrine of the Church* (Edinburgh, 1887), 123-4 notes that the apostles understood the synagogue system to be of venerable antiquity: "'From generations of old,' one of the leaders of the Hebrew Christian Church at Jerusalem said .... How far back do these 'generations' go? Vitringa, in his first book of his great work, *De Synagoga Vetere*, considers with characteristic thoroughness all the references to worship in the Old Testament from the creation onwards ... but fails to find the synagogue anywhere before the exile." We do not quarrel with this so long as it be granted, as Bannerman seems to, that "We may recognise a preparation for the synagogue system before that date, that the same objects were sought and attained by other means in a partial and preliminary way ...." We are only concerned to demonstrate that God was worshiped *decentrally* and *without rigid regulation*, before Moses as well as during and after the establishment of the Levitical order.

did, but rather in him (vss. 23-25), and that holy things, vowed things and burnt offerings be brought and offered only at the *central* location designated by God (vss. 26-28). And the verses immediately preceding the command "not to add or take away" forbid even an inquiry into how these abominable nations worshiped their abominable false gods, as if it were permissible to follow them. For these nations went so far as to sacrifice their own sons and daughters (vss. 29-31), something which God would never require (Jer. 7:31; 19:5; 32:35).

The entire passage, then, deals with what will become the primary concern of the upper deck: the centralized, sacrificial system leading — through types, shadows, and explication — to the one efficacious sacrifice of Christ. Decentralized covenant worship had heretofore included sacrifice and prayer in light of the word of God. The sacrificial elements, which were divinely revealed earlier (Gen. 3-4), were now being relegated exclusively to the place God would choose for his name to dwell. The other prayerful assemblies responding to his word seem to have arisen less by express command than by a divinely-originating impulse in the hearts of worshipers to "call upon his name." Here, at Sinai, the course of covenant divides into upper and lower decks.

The employment of Dt. 12:32, then, to establish a so-called "regulative principle" for the non-sacrificing (though sacrifice-of-Christ-believing!) church of Christ — which, we shall see, is patterned after the lower deck, synagogue model — is misguided and untenable. In its worst forms, it has led to the monstrous arrogation by some of a supposed right to excommunicate Christians for, as it were, worshiping God without a license. In its best forms it has hindered the confessional unity of the church. Whatever *positive* norms are to guide the decentralized sacred assemblies will not be discovered here, for here we find only universally applicable prohibitions: No one, anywhere, at any time, may sacrifice children; no one is permitted to consume blood (so as to gain life); and no one anywhere may worship another god (do you hear anticipations of Acts 15:28, 29 here?).

It would seem that the local assemblies knew what *not* to do. But if, as regulativists claim, no one may "add" to the worship-regulating word of God as per Dt. 12:32, the decentralized sacred assemblies could not do *anything at all*, for the sacrifices and offerings (the only positive elements) now *had to* be made at Central. The local gatherings commanded in Lev. 23:3 would be utterly vacuous.

Lev. 23:3, then, implicitly endorses the use of sanctified covenant sense, first glimpsed in Gen. 4:26, to order *decentralized* worship. Sacrifice, not the word of God, was restricted to Jerusalem. Worship is the appropriate response to God's self-disclosure. What constituted right sacrifice and offering was revealed from above. The other elements of worship — prayer, praise, petition and pedigogy— seem to have arisen rather spontaneously through (yes, Spirit-prompted) men on earth. Covenant men gathered for simple prayer and praise, and to publicly show themselves to be God's people, believers in his covenant word, supplicators of his blessing, Sabbath obeyers according to the pattern revealed in Gen. 1 and 2. The only alternatives to this view, it seems to this author, are 1) Talmudism (the suggestion of a secondary divinely-inspired code apart from Scripture to justify the belief that decentralized services were strictly regulated), or 2) the suggestion that God, in fact, did not intend to be worshiped *at all* outside Jerusalem, after sacrifice was restricted to that place.

Solomon to Nehemiah

At the very time the tabernacle was absorbed into the temple service, however, Solomon makes quite clear that God was and would be sought, worshiped and adored outside the precincts of Jerusalem. Perhaps it should first be noted that at the dedication of the temple, Solomon was completely self-conscious regarding its typical character, publicly avowing that "heaven and the heaven of heavens cannot contain You. How much less this temple which I have built!" Though there would be a manifest presence of God among his people through the temple, Solomon asked that God would, when prayer was directed toward "this place," hear *in heaven* (1 Kin. 8:30, 34, 36, etc.).

Moreover, he was asked to be attentive to the prayers made in faith beyond Jerusalem's borders: "When an enemy besieges them in any of their cities [literally, 'in the land (in) its gates'] ... whatever prayer, whatever supplication is made by anyone, or by all Your people Israel, when each one knows the plague of his own heart, and spreads out his hands toward this temple: then hear in heaven Your dwelling place, and forgive, and act, and give to everyone according to all his ways, whose heart You know (for you alone know the hearts of all the sons of men), that they may fear You all the days that they live in the land which you gave to our fathers" (vss. 37-39).

Solomon also prayed that foreigners who would come and worship the true God would be answered and would then take back the knowledge of God to their (temple-less) lands (vss. 41-43). And he prayed that when God's people would go out to battle, "wherever You send them," and they pray to the Lord toward this city and temple, "then hear in heaven their prayer ...." And he also asked that God would hear the prayers of his people outside the land, when they "make supplication to You in the land of those who took them captive ... when they return to You with all their heart and with all their soul in the land of their enemies who led them away captive" (vss. 47, 48).

Sacrifice, not worship was restricted to Jerusalem. Thus we read the lament of Asaph in Psalm 74, mourning the devastation wrought by Babylon: "They burned Your sanctuary to the ground; they defiled the dwelling place of Your

name to the ground. They said in their hearts, 'Let us destroy them
altogether.' They have burned up all the meeting places of God in the land"
(vss. 7-8). The ancients were more self-conscious than we that war is
religious in nature, and thus the Babylonians sought to destroy not only the
temple, but all the meeting places where God was worshiped. The word
translated "meeting places" in the NKJV is a technical term for congregation
and, by extension, the place of meeting. Some scholars, embarrassed by this
apparent confirmation of synagogue-like places existing before the exile,
have tried various ways to dismiss it.[6] The NIV Study Bible boldly suggests
that there "may have been a number of (illegitimate)[7] places in Judah where
people went to worship God." But if these meeting places were "illegitimate,"
why would a divinely-inspired author lament their destruction? Josiah and
other reformers certainly never lamented the land being cleansed of false
worship! No. These were lower deck, decentralized gathering places. The
regulations concerning them dealt primarily with what they could not do. But
since prayer and instruction in the word are appropriate for all places at all
times, *it was inevitable that worship centers would arise wherever the
covenant Faith took up residence in the hearts of a few.*

Of course, by the time of the exile and the return, we do begin to see some
codification in the synagogue system. Again, it is vital to note that so far as
we know, none of the code was divinely and specially revealed. On the
contrary, it arose as the community of Faith identified a covenant need. Then,
according to circumstance and necessity, propriety and opportunity, reason
and debate,[8] a regimen developed around a solid core.

Bannerman correctly notes that in Nehemiah 8, "all the elements of a
synagogue service present themselves. We have public prayer and
thanksgiving 'in the congregation'.... We have the people themselves taking
earnest part in the service, and answering 'Amen' at the close of prayers. We
have the reading and explanation of Scriptures by Ezra and other teachers
from a raised pulpit or platform of wood, with marked impression and
spiritual results for the audience."[9]

One could suggest that the whole scene was, in fact, too smooth and easy
to have been occurring for the first time. And indeed, the *Jewish
Encyclopedia* under "Synagogue," says, "it can be assumed that the returned
exiles brought with them the rudiments of that institution." But whatever
similarities we discover in Neh. 8 with later synagogue — and eventually
church — worship, there are as many and more differences. A partial list: this
gathering took place on a Lev. 23 holy day, it was led by priests and Levites,

---

[6.] Curiously, Calvin is among them; but see Bannerman's note treating Calvin's "solution" in *The Scripture Doctrine of the Church*, 123.

[7.] Illegitimate is inserted in parentheses as per the source.

[8.] You know what they say: Two Jews, three opinions—and each one firmly held!

[9.] *ibid.*, 124.

it was presided over by at least fourteen leaders, the governor had a leading role in the worship service as governor, the reading service alone was three hours, the people bowed down with their noses to the ground, their *sole* "earnest" participation consisted of amen-ing the word, there was no congregational singing, and the whole service was conducted in the public square.

Of course, these differences present no problem if we remember that strictness of positive regulation belonged to the upper deck. As the *Jewish Encyclopedia* points out, "[I]t is germane to draw attention to the fact that the establishment of the synagogue implies the evolution of standard forms of service."

By the time of Ezra and Nehemiah, the synagogue had attained this much form: in a community where there lived 120 Jews, a synagogue could be established if there were ten "men of leisure" to insure that it was maintained. Devout Jews (in the exile) would gather in an upper room with an open window facing Jerusalem (cf. Dan. 6:10). Praise and prayer, reading from and instruction in the word, came to form the nucleus of the service.

Synagogues quickly multiplied into every area where the Jews were scattered. The worship of God, the teaching of his word, and extending mercy toward his people was the threefold *raison d'être* of the synagogue. Education was (and continues to be) vitally important, essential, indispensable.[10]

With the establishment and early codification of the synagogue system, the office of scribe (expert in the law, lawyer) flourished. It was not long, however, before the so-called "wall around the Torah," the additional laws and customs invented by this new expert-class, began to push the law of God itself from center stage.

In the Time of Our Lord

Four hundred years later, by the time of our Lord's sojourn, the synagogue — and the traditions of men — were both firmly established. Jesus had no objection to the former, for it did not void or replace the temple but constructively supplemented it. But he had scathing, holy contempt for the latter because tampering with the word did have the effect of voiding it, displacing it (see Mk. 7:9-13). "Form" on the lower deck was of far less concern to our Lord than content and function.

[10.] An alternate name for synagogue, and the one commonly used by my Jewish community, is *shul* (Yiddish for school, though there are equivalent pedagogical titles in Hebrew). While I was growing up in Brooklyn, our custom was not to say, "We are going to synagogue," but always "to shul."

It was Jesus' custom to attend synagogue services on Shabbos (Lk. 4:16).[11] It was in the synagogue at Nazareth that he first (dramatically!) announced his Messiahship at the head of his sermon (Lk. 4:14-27).[12] And at the end of his earthly ministry he told the inquisitorial High Priest, "I have spoken openly to the world. I always taught in synagogues or at the temple, where all the Jews come together" (Jn. 18:20).

Jesus' ubiquitous presence among the Jews made inevitable a severe clash. As a group (praise the Lord, there were many exceptions), the teachers of the law, rather than fulfilling the Levitical *function* of teaching the people and showing mercy, had come to despise them for their "ignorance." Their collective attitude is made transparent in Jn. 7 where the chief priests and Pharisees are upbraiding the temple guards for being taken in by Jesus' speech: "You mean he has deceived you also? Has any of the rulers or of the Pharisees believed in him? No! But this mob that knows nothing of the law — there is a curse on them" (vss. 47-49). If that "mob" knew nothing of the law, it was the fault of the teachers. They were condemning themselves.

Jesus is not only *the* Prophet, *the* Priest and *the* King; he is also *the* Levite. Luke summarizes his first book as having recorded "all that Jesus began to do and to teach" (Ac. 1:1). Teaching the people and doing mercy — healing, caring for, loving the people — were the twin Levitical functions. By Jesus' day, the leaders had become experts, not in the law of God, but in caring for themselves (cf. Ez. 34). But Jesus would not use his divine power to fulfill his own most basic human needs (Lk. 4: 3,4). He used it to *minister.*

Behold *the* Levite: "Jesus went through all the towns and villages, teaching in their synagogues, preaching the good news of the kingdom, and healing every disease and sickness. When he saw the crowds, he had compassion on them, because they were harassed and helpless, like sheep without a shepherd" (Mt. 9:35-36). When the teachers of the law saw the crowds, they had contempt for them and starved them. When Jesus saw the crowds, he had compassion on them, taught them, healed them and prayed for them. Simply by doing the right thing, by doing what the leaders should have been doing, Jesus became the object of intense hatred.

Christ's Synagogue Founded

The synagogue had become the center of much essential covenant activity. The synagogue was to serve the covenant. The unbelieving leaders felt that

---

[11.] Perhaps Jesus saw in Lev. 23:3 justification for synagogues outside Jerusalem (though there were many *inside* Jerusalem, as well), or perhaps he did not endorse the "regulative principle" for the "lower deck," or perhaps both.

[12.] The sermon had been well-received (v. 22) until he mentioned God's prerogative to save Gentiles. The crowd didn't like that at all. This would be the *major issue* between Christ and his apostles on one side, and the Jews on the other, throughout the gospels and to the end of the book of Acts.

the covenant ought to serve the synagogue. Jesus, who is the covenant incarnate (Is. 42:6), was too great a threat to the ecclesiocrats who wanted nothing more than to maintain their power and position. If Jesus was a threat, Jesus would have to go. But first they agreed "that if anyone confessed that He was the Messiah, he would be put out of the synagogue" (Jn. 9:22).

The importance of this passage in understanding the church as Christ's synagogue cannot be emphasized too strongly. The Jewish leaders who had inherited all the graces of the covenant were being confronted by the very hope of that covenant. Rather than submit to what so many "unlearned" people could clearly see — even a *blind man* (Jn. 9) — they determined to cut off from the covenant any who acknowledged that Jesus was in fact the Messiah.

Shortly before this incident with the blind man, Jesus had made provision for him by establishing the synagogue of Christ. At Caeserea Philippi, Jesus asked the disciples, "Who do men say that I, the Son of Man, am?" After reporting various speculations then current as to Christ's identity, Jesus reiterated, "But who do you say that I am?"

Simon Peter answered, "You are the Messiah, the Son of the living God."

Jesus answered and said to him, "Blessed are you, Simon Bar-Jonah, for flesh and blood has not revealed this to you, but My Father who is in heaven. And I also say to you that you are Peter, and on this rock I will build my church, and the gates of Hades will not prevail against it. And I will give you the keys of the kingdom of heaven, and whatever you bind on earth will be bound in heaven, and whatever you loose on earth will be loosed in heaven" (Mt. 16:13-19).

It is neither Peter in himself, nor Peter's confession abstractly considered, which will constitute the foundation rock of Christ's church, but rather the *confessing Peter*, the Peter who represents all then present and all who would follow in *confessing, as per the personal disclosure by the Father to his elect child,* [13] the truth that Jesus is the Messiah, the Son of God.

The confession of Jesus as the Messiah became, at one and the same time, the basis for expulsion from the apostate synagogue and the basis of admission into Christ's synagogue. Thus we read in Jn. 9:35:

> "Jesus heard that they had thrown him out, and when He found him, He said, 'Do you believe in the Son of Man?' 'Who is He, Lord, that I may believe in Him?' And Jesus said to him, 'You have now seen Him; in fact, He is the one talking with you.' Then the man said, 'Lord, I believe,' and he worshiped Him."

Church growth. Synagogue of Christ growth.

[13.] Cf. 1 Cor. 12:3.

The Lord Jesus our Messiah, before his departure, made clear two things about our two decks: The upper deck would be taken up in him and raised to heaven. It was of him the upper deck had testified. Now that he had come, he "absorbed" all its truth into himself, took it into the grave, rose as the new temple, ascended and established this temple forever in heaven. It was to this that the old temple had always directed the eye of faith (Jn. 2:18-22. And cf. Epistle to the Hebrews).

Jesus also made clear that the lower deck — decentralized, loosely regulated worship performed in spirit and in truth — would rise to prominence. It would not longer be performed under the shadow of an upper deck, but would live in the light of the *realities* of that system, now settled in heaven. In short, it would enter into the liberty of maturity: "Believe me, the hour is coming when you will neither on this mountain, *nor in Jerusalem*, worship the Father. But the hour is coming, and now is, when the true worshipers will worship the Father in spirit and truth; for the Father is seeking such to worship him" (Jn. 4:21, 23; see also Mal. 1:11).

This became a core issue in New Testament polemics, some Jewish Christians insisting on keeping the lower deck in its former place, *under* the temple, *under* Jerusalem. The Holy Spirit made clear through the apostles that *that* was impossible for Christ's New Testament synagogue.

The synagogue would overtake the earthly temple, for the true temple would be fixed in heaven. If you want to know where the upper deck is, look up toward the New Jerusalem, where Messiah is seated at the right hand of God. The upper deck went to heaven and the "regulative principle" which governed worship at it, went to heaven with it. But the wonderfully flexible synagogue had been providentially born and sustained for such a time as this.

Christ's synagogue would be marked by this core of features: A gathering of people who confessed him as Messiah and Lord, who wanted to worship God in spirit and truth and be fed his word. So, in the book of Acts, we find 120 believers (Ac. 1:15; the number required for the establishment of a new synagogue) gathered in an upper room (1:13; the place where the first exilic worshipers would gather), earnestly engaged in prayer (1:14; a core activity of the synagogue), and present among them were the requisite ten men (plus one plus one) who were qualified by Christ to look after the new synagogue. All systems go.

"Today I Am a Fountain Pen"

The upper-deck worship of the Mosaic and post-Mosaic period were necessarily restricted to Jerusalem, as we have seen. There was a particular temple, a particular priesthood, a particular calendar, a particular set of prescribed offerings, etc., all localized and confined. When the decentralized synagogues arose, worshipers regarded them as outposts organically related to the temple at Jerusalem. In other words, synagogues were *self-consciously* the lower deck.

With the temple, the priesthood, the offerings, *et al.*, seen and taken up in Christ, we need a real and living link, an organic connection, between our savior in heaven and his synagogue on earth.[14] That is not just for the sake of *self-conscious* connection. We need *power*. The task of the church, the synagogue of Christ, is far more comprehensive and expansive than the task given to Israel. We are to preach Christ to all the world, baptize nations and teach them to obey everything our Lord has commanded.

In other words, the synagogue of Christ must go beyond the borders of Jerusalem, beyond the borders of Israel, to plant synagogues of Christ (worship/teaching centers) all over the world.[15] The church must be able to leave home and reproduce.

A Bar Mitzvah (which literally means *son of the commandment*) is a ceremony marking an objective, historical change in the life of a young man. It marks his pubescence, the stage of physical development when reproduction becomes possible.[16] It also marks the point at which he becomes responsible for *obeying* the principles and *applying* the laws he learned in his youth.

The church was not born at Pentecost. It was Bar Mitzvah'd. It was imbued with the Spirit of God sent from the Father and the Son. The church is to bring all its childhood instruction to fruitful realization in its calling. The church is henceforth equipped to fulfill its mandate, to baptize the nations and bring God's law-word to bear in every sphere. It may "leave home." It can preach the Gospel in Jerusalem (to full Jews), then Judea and Samaria (to half-Jews), then to the uttermost parts of the earth (to non-Jews). The church at Pentecost was enabled to reproduce. And it was empowered to train its members to flesh out the law in life.

The church is organized according to the decentralized synagogue pattern and is commissioned to establish lower-deck covenant centers universally. These centers are united in looking to the right hand of the Father for their salvation, united by a common Faith and spirit. The core elements which would characterize Christ's synagogues henceforth are present from the beginning: Baptized families gathering to devotedly attend upon the word of God, to fellowship with one another, to break bread and to pray (Ac. 2:42). The shape and form of the synagogue of Christ would, like its predecessor,

---

14. "There was an organic connection between the temple and synagogue during the period of the Second Temple....", *Jewish Encyclopedia* at "Synagogue."

15. Though we have a *long* way to go, Christianity is the only religion in the world today with adherents in every country.

16. This is euphemistically alluded to in the oft-heard Bar Mitzvah quip, "Today I am a fountain pen."

admit of development and change from time to time as circumstances demanded and the word warranted.[17]

The synagogues of Christ, as per Christ and the apostles, gathered at least weekly for prayer and praise, for blessed fellowship, and for instruction in the word, under the leadership of men who would divide the Levitical functions: Elders are ministers and rulers who *must be* apt to teach law and gospel; deacons are ministers of law-based mercy.

When the critical question arose about the standing of converted gentiles, it was answered decisively in terms of the upper and lower deck. While the temple remained standing, Jewish believers were not required to abandon every vestige of their upper deck tradition (Rom. 14, etc.).[18] But, the *ad hoc* council decided,[19] gentiles could not be forced to adopt the regulative principle of the upper deck, nor be compelled to undergo circumcision,[20] which had preceded it (and had obligated Abraham's flesh descendants to abide by it until Christ). Jewish particularities must give way to the universal. But, like Dt. 12, the apostles and elders warned the gentiles not to worship God in pagan ways.[21]

Let's Get Together

What has been said in this essay is by no means intended to be considered as the last word. Certainly much more needs to be added, and the writer herewith solicits correction. The concern has simply been to emphasize the freedom and elasticity of ecclesiastical form we have been given by our master and head. The genius and strength of the synagogue system has been widely recognized as residing in its *flexibility*, its plasticity. The core is strong, absolutely essential: the word of God complete. The "sacraments" are

---

[17.] For example, at first they met daily (Ac. 2:46). The community of goods was "as needed" and never became normative (Ac. 2:44). The ministry of just mercy was established out of need in Ac. 5.

[18.] Though, in Hebrews, they were sternly and severely warned about going back to it "whole hog" (heh!), or, as if it had *any* salvific merit apart from Christ.

[19.] The Jerusalem conference of churches was called to address a *specific* concern. It was not a "standing commission" or presbytery. It has more in common with the multi-denominational Westminster Assembly or Synod of Dordt than the church governments adopted by the sons of those two conventions. For they, like the leaders of Acts 15, convened to articulate the Biblical answers to particular problems, not to form a denomination. This is not to suggest that the synagogue system *forbids* confessional denominating, mind you, simply that it manifestly does not require it!

[20.] No doubt accounting for much of the joy with which the gentiles received the decision (Acts 15:31)!

[21.] Pagan worship included sacrificing food to idols, ingesting blood as a means to life (by eating strangled, not blood-drained, animals), and, notoriously, by sexual immorality. To suggest that this was a comprehensive condensed version of the law Gentiles must follow is ludicrous. It leaves them free to, among other things, steal and kill. No. The apostles and elders agreed: "We're not going to strictly regulate what you do (so long as the core elements of Christian synagogue worship are there), but we will tell you what you mustn't do in worshiping God in Christ."

simple, necessarily so, for they must be decentrally administered everywhere in the world.

Hence, there is a uniform recognition throughout the New Testament that the local church *is* the church. Compare it to the family. The "institution" of the family is intangible. Famil*ies*, however, can be found. And just as familyhood comes from God (Eph. 3:14-15) and is realized in households, so also the church is discovered, for good or ill, in *local* churches. The synagogue of Christ has no existence apart from local expressions, from Eden on. All local churches will answer to Christ. In the meantime, all local churches, *especially those in the same communities*, ought to cooperate with other local churches as much as they can (not as little as they can), without compromising their confession of and witness to the truth.

It is interesting to note that synagogues only recently began to form federations. Jewish scholars attribute this to the influence of Protestant denominations. However, denominationalism, whatever use it may have been to the synagogues of Christ for the past 400 years, is functionally dead. We are now at a time in history when we should realize that the *content* of what we confess must take precedence over the forms in which it is presented. It is not suggested that these are separable matters, only that each has its own priority. The insistence upon an outmoded and anachronistic allegiance to denominationalism — as opposed to free and particular confessional association, church with church and church — has led, and continues to lead with alarming frequency, to "Church A" being formally aligned with "Church B" while "Church B" espouses manifest heresies contrary to "Church A's" confession. But because they are in "the same denomination," Church A not only remains aligned, but helps further the spread of the errors.

Most everyone will agree that a Bible-believing Presbyterian from the PCUSA, *e.g.*, has more in common with a fundamentalist from the GARB, than he does with most of the leaders in his own denomination. Today, particular churches may be (in the words of the Westminster Confession of Faith), "more or less pure," but denominations are, nearly uniformly, very mixed — and mixed-up — bags. As a rule, they are sustained not to serve the covenant, but themselves. Like the church leaders in Jesus' time, they put form at the fore and function on a back burner. Their instruction often reveals a dangerous despite for God's people, being offered, not so much to nourish the sheep as to be heard by and to impress themselves and their peers. Someone once quipped that institutions are dedicated to destroy the principles for which they are founded. How tragically true of denominations at the end of the twentieth century!

The key to ecclesiastical progress in our day lies in recapturing the importance of the church's *function* in the world. To do this we must go back, but not to Geneva (that's not far back enough), and certainly not to Rome (for Rome is rooted, futilely and fatally, in the upper deck). We must go back to

Eden and from there follow the path on through to the end of Scripture. The upper deck led us to Christ and has gone into heaven with him. Let us humbly trace the lower deck and see how God intended it to function.

The New Testament synagogue model is designed to allow us to concentrate on what we must *believe* and what we must *do*. What's missing from the church today is certainly not form, but rather Biblical law and, consequently, Biblical love. The church is to serve the covenant and not vice versa. Let us stand together before our God and his word and ask what he would have us *do* and *teach*. Thus we will continue that work begun by our Messiah, thus we will not be sidetracked, but will rather fulfill his purposes in establishing the synagogue of Christ.

Steve Schlissel has served as the pastor of Messiah's Congregation in Brooklyn since 1979. He currently serves as the Overseer of Urban Nations and as the Administrative Director of Meantime, a ministry to women who were sexually abused as children.

Dominion and Sexuality

Joseph R. McAuliffe

My first encounter with sexual lust was when I was eight years old, and as I recall, I had a passionate infatuation for my third-grade teacher, Miss Brooks. That was the beginning of a problem that intensified as I got older to a point where it dominated my thoughts and actions. Prior to my conversion it was impossible for me not to relate lustfully to any fairly attractive member of the opposite sex. I never had a problem with homosexuality, but I was plagued with sexual fantasies for women. After my conversion to Christ, I continued to struggle with lust, but I'll deal with that later.

The Meaning of Lust

The term *lust* in and of itself is a neutral term and in the Scriptures it is used positively or negatively depending on the context and qualifying adjectives. The Hebrew (*nepes*) and Greek (*epithymia*) terms for lust mean a "craving to gratify a strong desire."[1] That desire may serve a positive end, such as God's intense desire for his people ["If the Lord *delights* in us" (Num. 14:8)]; or the desires of the righteous being granted (Pr. 10:24); and even of Jesus *"earnestly desiring* to eat this Passover with you" (Lk. 22:15). Certainly it is commendable to *"lust"* after or fervently desire the Lord and his purposes.

Of course, most today prefer other adjectives than lust to convey positive passions. Personally, I wouldn't be comfortable about singing, "I *lust* you Lord and I lift my voice" although I do have very intense feelings for God. However, my studies did indicate that the principal meaning for lust was neutral in its usage, at least through the mid-nineteenth century in America. For example, Webster's 1828 Dictionary defines lust first as "longing desire; eagerness to possess or enjoy" and then secondarily as it is commonly used today "concupiscence (unlawful or irregular desire of sexual pleasure.)"[2] The shift in principal meaning from the neutral to the sexual is reflected in most modern dictionaries. The 1984 Webster's II New Riverside University Dictionary cites the primary usage of lust as "intense or unrestrained sexual desire." And in terms of this article on the deadly sin of lust, my focus will be on the problems associated Scripturally with unrestrained sexual desire.

---

[1] Colin Brown, ed., *The New International Dictionary of New Testament Theology* (Grand Rapids, 1975), 1:456-458.

[2] Noah Webster, An *American Dictionary of the English Language* (New York, 1828, Reprinted, Anaheim, 1967).

Legitimate Sexual Acts

But before we address the improper manifestations of sexual behavior, I should note that the sin of sexual lust does not bear in any way on the nature of sexual relations in their proper context, that is, the marriage covenant. Sexual activity in marriage is positively endorsed by Scripture and prohibited outside that covenant.

"Marriage is honorable among all, and the bed undefiled; but fornicators and adulterers God will judge" (Heb. 13:4). Paul exhorts married couples to render sexual affection to one another, to defer to one another's sexual needs, and regularly to engage in sexual relations: "Let the husband render to his wife the affection due her, and likewise also the wife to her husband. The wife does not have authority over her own body, but the husband does. And likewise the husband does not have authority over his own body, but the wife does. Do not deprive one another except with consent for a time, that you may give yourselves to fasting and prayer; and come together again so that Satan does not tempt you because of your lack of self-control" (1 Cor. 7:3-5). The sixth and seventh chapters of Song of Solomon romantically highlight the beauty and joy of physical intimacy in marriage. This is affirmed by the advice of Solomon in Pr. 5:15-19: "Drink water from your own cistern, and running water from your own well. Should your fountains be dispersed abroad, streams of water in the streets? Let them be only your own, and not for strangers with you. Let your fountain be blessed, and rejoice with the wife of your youth. As a loving deer and a graceful doe, let her breasts satisfy you at all times; and always be enraptured with her love." And when we go back to the beginning and consider God's original intent for mankind, we see God instituting marriage in order for men and women to enjoy unabashedly one another sexually and to propagate the human race: "Therefore a man shall leave his father and mother and be joined to his wife, and they shall become one flesh. And they were both naked, the man and his wife, and were not ashamed" (Gen. 2:24-25). I stress the Biblically supportive view of sex in marriage because historically and presently the church has not consistently represented this position and has tended towards dualistic thinking which denigrates the physical order in general and sexual relations in particular.

History of the Issue

During the Patristic Age because of the influence of Hellenistic philosophy on the church through Gnosticism, Manicheanism, and neo-platonism, it was not uncommon for many of the church fathers to promote a sexual asceticism. Origen (185-254) taught that the serpent seduced Eve physically and he regarded all sexual activity as inherently wrong because it was the basis for all actual sins. But most of the Fathers acknowledged that marriage had been instituted and blessed by God and sanctified by Christ, though they regarded it more as a concession to the inordinate desires of fallen humanity and as a "refuge for those weaker souls who could not bear the discipline of celibacy."[3]

Tertullian (160-220), who probably never would have been a guest on James Dobson's "Focus on the Family" radio show, said, "We do not reject marriage, but simply refrain from it." The eloquent John Chrysostom (344-407) maintained that while marriage is not an obstacle to salvation or sanctification, it was less than the ideal because it hindered the freest possible service to God. Gregory of Nyssa (330-395) dismisses marriage as a "sad tragedy," and Ambrose (339-397) considered it a "galling burden."[4] A number of troubled marriages that I have counseled also hold to this perspective, but usually for different reasons.

Whereas today we are ridiculed for advocating sexual abstinence before matrimony, during both the Patristic period and Middle Ages it was occasionally recommended for even married folk. During the early centuries some "deeper-life" saints entered into "spiritual" marriages which were characterized by couples sharing the same house, room, and even bed, but not their bodies. Tertullian initially supported these kinds of marriages for the clergy for companionship and domestic purposes, and the anti-coitus arrangement was a forerunner to later celibacy requirements for clergy. But the "spiritual marriage movement" fizzled out during the fourth century when church councils enacted prohibitions against the custom because the marriages did not always remain spiritual and numerous sexual scandals occurred. The recent sexual downfalls of well-known Christian leaders have generated a great deal of lurid sensationalism by the media; but without condoning their transgressions, we should bear in mind that both Scripture and church history record a long trail of scandal and failure in this area.

Before leaving this era of church history we should consider Augustine's observations, because as C. W. Lloyd states "his writings have probably exerted more influence in the West on love and sexual practice than those of any other man. The clearest expression of the innate evil in sexual passion even within marriage is set forth. These teachings gave theological structure to feelings of guilt and shame in the biological drive."[5]

Augustine's (354-430) nine-year odyssey with dualistic Manichaeism appears to have influenced his thoughts on sexual relations. Augustine opposed the idea that intercourse in marriage was intended for pleasure as well as procreation, and insisted that to derive pleasure from the act is carnal and sinful. Augustine's remarkably candid confessions reveal "that he was particularly offended and embarrassed by the act of coitus, with its intensity

---

[3.] Dwight Small, *Christian, Celebrate Your Sexuality* (Old Tappan, NJ, 1974), 53.

[4.] Derrick Sherwin Bailey, *Sexual Relation in Christian Thought* (New York, 1959), 47-51.

[5.] C. W. Lloyd, *Human Reproduction and Sexual Behavior* (Philadelphia, 1964), 27.

of venereal emotion and its uncontrollable orgasm, and he blushed to think that even the good work of generation cannot be accomplished without 'a certain amount of bestial movement' and a 'violent acting of lust.' He believed that it could not have always been thus, and that the shameful copulations which men and women now endure in the discharge of their procreative functions are not natural to our kind, but result from the transgressions of our first parents."[6] This is a significant contrast from the perspective suggested in such popular contemporary Christian books like Dr. Ed Wheat's *Intended for Pleasure*, Dr. Herbert Miles' *Sexual Happiness in Marriage*, or Tim and Beverly LaHaye's *The Act of Marriage*.

Gregory the Great (540-604) modified Augustinan theory slightly by introducing the idea that the evil element in coitus is not in the act itself, nor in the lust which compels mating, but rather in the sensual pleasure that accompanies the act. It is the acquiescence of the will in such pleasure that is sinful. This kind of thinking helps me to understand H. L. Mencken's misguided indictment of a Puritan as "someone who lives in the constant dread that someone, somewhere, might be having a good time."

Middle Ages

By the Middle Ages the sexual ruminations of Augustine and Gregory were modified by medieval theologians like Peter Lombard (1095-1169), who repudiated the idea that intercourse and its accompanying pleasure is sinful. He did, however, say that coitus does contain an element of evil, but not sin[!]. Thomas Aquinas (1224-1274) developed this idea by denying that intercourse had been so corrupted by the fall as to contain no trace of goodness in arguing that since a good God created man's bodily nature, nothing pertaining to that nature can be wholly bad. Therefore it is possible that the sexual act might be conducive of some virtue and, indeed, even meritorious when performed by married couples in a state of grace.[7] However, because of Aristotle's influence on Aquinas, he, like Lombard, maintained that there was an element of evil in coitus because the intensity of sensual emotion culminating in orgasm tended to impede the exercise of the rational faculty which thereby deters one's pursuit of the good life.

During this period the Roman Catholic Church went to great legalistic lengths to circumscribe sexual activity in marriage. Roman Catholic writer Ernest Messenger has catalogued that the church required "complete abstinence from sexual relations on no less than five days out of seven: on Thursdays in memory of the arrest of our Lord, on Fridays in commemoration of his death, on Saturdays in honor of the Blessed Virgin, on Sundays in honor of the Resurrection, and on Mondays in honor of the faithful departed."

---

[6] Bailey, *op. cit.*, 53.
[7] Small, *op. cit.*, 72.

(This was probably the only time in history when married people got excited about mid-week... "Praise God, honey, it's almost Tuesday.") Messenger speculates as to the negative implication conveyed to newly married couples who "were enjoined to remain continent on their wedding night out of respect for the church's blessing" — a blessing granted by the celibate priest invoked to the ever-virgin Mary.[8]

A major concern addressed by Aquinas in his *Summa Theologica* bearing upon our study of sexual lust was that of responsibility for sexual offenses. As mentioned above, for Aquinas, sin is that which contravenes reason by which everything is directed to its proper end. Therefore lust was adjudged not only as a deadly sin but the chief of all sins because its focus was principally with sensual pleasure and more than any other sin, it debauches the mind and obstructs reason. Aquinas lists a minute classification of sexual transgressions and their appropriate penances. For example, kissing and caressing may be innocent acts without inciting lust, but when the motive is to enjoy forbidden pleasure, they became mortal sins. Aquinas viewed masturbation (self-abuse) as a vice against nature and thus, an act contrary to right reason. Because sexual activity was designed only for procreation, any contrary act or motive was a sin. Small remarks that masturbation was held an offense "more serious than incest, adultery, or violent seduction because the act invoked an ejaculation of semen (which many believed contained the entire embryo) furthest removed from the possibility of procreation."[9]

Despite the exhaustive sexual prescriptions by the church during the medieval era, the society then, not unlike ours now, was highly promiscuous. Pope Bonifare (d. 625) lamented that the English "utterly refuse to have legitimate wives and continue to live in lechery and adultery." Alcuin of York (d. 804), the influential scholar of Charlemagne's court, declared "the land has become absolutely submerged under a flood of fornication, adultery, and incest, so that the very semblance of modesty is absent." Because of these conditions, the church developed an uneasy acquiescence to prostitution, accepting it as a necessary evil. The church from Augustine to Aquinas never admitted prostitutes into its fellowship, but held that they served the well-being of the body politic: "Take away the sewer and you fill the palace with pollution. Take away prostitution and you fill the world with sodomy." Derrick Bailey comments that "nothing could demonstrate more clearly the strange and often perplexing ambivalence and confusion of medieval sexual thought."[10]

[8.] Ernest C. Messenger, *The Mystery of Sex and Marriage in Catholic Theology*, Vol. II in *Two in One Flesh* (Westminster, MD, 1950, second ed.), 152.

[9.] Small, *op. cit.*, 75-76.

[10.] Bailey, *op. cit.*, 163.

The Reformation

The Reformation was a turning point in Western civilization that brought a theological perspective based principally on Scriptures (*sola scriptura*) that affected every area of life including sexual relations. Luther (1483-1564) denounced compulsory vows of chastity (as did Zwingli), asserting that God had ordained marriage and it was sinful for clerics to refuse matrimony if they knew they had been denied the gift of celibacy. Luther's view of sex in marriage was similar to Aquinas's and understood coitus as an unclean act but an effective remedy for the incontinence that troubles every man. "Had God consulted me about it," Luther said in one of his table talks, "I should have advised him to continue the generation of the species by fashioning human beings out of clay, as Adam was made."[11]

The giant theological mind of the Reformation, John Calvin (1509-1564), was known as a stern man — growing up, his fellow Latin students called him the "accusative case." Yet his views on intercourse in marriage were reformist. In his commentary of 1 Cor. 7:1, Calvin pays homage to the theological contributions of Jerome but repudiates his statement, "He who loves his own wife too ardently is an adulterer." Calvin affirmed that marriage was a high calling of God and coitus is "undefiled, honorable, and holy therein since it is a pure institution of God."[12] Sherwin Bailey has importantly noted that Calvin "allowed that the propagation of the species is a special and characteristic end of matrimony, he also taught that its primary purpose is rather social than generative."[13]

Andrew Eichhoff recapitulates the Reformation attitude writing, "The Reformation brought changes of great consequences to the teachings about sex in Christianity .... This reemphasis on marriage as the highest Christian ideal laid the foundation for a new estimate of coitus and sex in general. Although little was said about the nature of sex by the Reformers, the open and forceful denunciation of celibacy (particularly by Luther and John Tyndale who believed clerical marriage should be compulsory as the best preparation for the exercise of pastoral oversight, ed.) as the religious ideal, and the marriage and establishment of families by the professional clergy, raised the status of coitus and of marriage as much as any formal teaching could have done."[14]

[11.] Morton Hunt, *Intimate Life Styles* (New York, 1959), 222-224.
[12.] John Calvin, *Commentary on the Epistle of Paul the Apostle to the Corinthians* (Grand Rapids, 1959), 222-227.
[13.] Bailey, *op cit.*, 173.
[14.] Andrew R. Eichhoff, *A Christian View of Sex in Marriage* (New York, 1961), 28.

The Puritans

The recognition of intercourse in marriage for pleasure as well as procreation was further expressed by the Puritan movement. That this would be their position (which many today mistakenly fail to attribute to them) is not surprising in terms of their commitment to Scripture as their standard for doctrine and reality. Dwight Small writes, "we still tend to malign the Puritans, as though all present-day repression of sex is a carryover from their times and attitudes. Not so. They were a stern and severe brand of Calvinists, to be sure, but we must distinguish their concern for a Biblically sound sexual morality from their easy acceptance of sex as natural and necessary — yes, as a God-given blessing."[15]

If we are to glean anything from the works of the eminent divine Thomas Hooker (1586-1647), it is that Puritan marriage knew the warmth of conjugal love. They placed such love only second to their love for God himself. John Cotton (1584-1652) preached a sermon at a wedding in 1694 where he admonished the couple not to follow the example of a newly married couple "who without approaching the Nuptial Bed" decided to live a life of sexual abstinence, which Cotton referred to as "an effort of blind zeal, for they are the dictates of a blind mind they follow therein, and not that of the Holy Spirit, which saith 'It is not good that a man should be alone.'" Edmund Morgan states "that it is a mistake to charge the Puritans with asceticism ... they were a much earthier lot than their modern critics have imagined."[16]

The Victorian Era

The stereotype of a cold-hearted, prudish, non-romantic Puritanism that prevails in our day has been distorted by the neo-puritanism that emerged in the Victorian period in the nineteenth century. Morton Hunt's views are instructive: "Seventeenth-century Puritanism was tight-lipped, severe (in terms of their willingness to employ Biblical sanctions for sexual crimes) and pious, but it was simultaneously frank, strongly sexed, and somewhat romantic. The frigidity and neurosis associated with Puritanism belongs to a much later date."[17]

The precursor to the Victorian era was the anti-Christian Enlightenment which elevated the rational faculties of man and commensurately denigrated the spiritual, emotional, and sexual aspects of human nature. The emotional life of human beings, particularly the aristocracy, all but disappeared behind the repressive facade of reason and even perhaps more importantly, stylized manners. Of course, anything sexual was permissible if only emotions were

---

[15] Small, *op cit.*, 88.

[16] Edmund Morgan, *The Puritan Family* (New York, 1966), 62-63.

[17] Morton Hunt, *The Natural History of Love* (New York, 1959), 252.

concealed and rules of etiquette observed. Rationalist love was nonetheless lustful and lecherous, but the game was gallantly played by the rules. Pornography and prostitution flourished in Victorian England.

Sexual desire for some strange reason was limited to males. Lord Acton (who had a lot more to say than about power corrupting) commented that it was a "vile aspersion" to attribute sexual desires to females. Only prostitutes were thought to enjoy sexual intercourse while wives were to endure, without interest or pleasure, the necessary though admittedly distasteful coitus. As a result, many wives never experienced the pleasure of orgasm.

Women were denied access to any reading that might be sexually enlightening and even Shakespeare was considered by some as too coarse for female eyes. Prudery was the defining characteristic of the time, both in public discourse and in available reading matter. Pregnant women stayed inside their homes to avoid public display of what might be construed the sexual side of life. Rollo May summarizes:

> "In Victorian times, when the denial of sexual impulses, feelings, and drives was the mode and one would not talk about sex in polite company, an aura of sanctifying repulsiveness surrounded the whole topic. Males and females dealt with each other as though neither possessed sexual organs. William James (1842-1910) ... treated sex with the polite aversion characteristic of the turn of the century. In the whole two volumes of his *Principles of Psychology*, only one page is devoted to sex, at the end of which he adds, 'These details are a little unpleasant to discuss ....'"[18]

Finally, Schlesinger comments: "By barring the joy of sex from wedlock, the Victorian code at once degraded the sexual impulse and weakened the marital tie. By transferring romantic love to the fantasy world of the sentimental novel and emptying serious literature of adult sexual content, it misled the rational sensibility. The Victorians' unsatisfactory pursuit of happiness thus ended half on Main Street and half on Back Street, with marriage denied passion, and passion denied legitimacy."[19]

Pietism and its Faults

The response to the Victorian priggishness was not a reaffirmation of the Reformation-Puritan beliefs based on Scripture which honored and celebrated sexual relations within the marriage covenant, but rather a "pietistic movement" that was not much different from what the Victorians were saying. Count Zinzendorf (1700-1760), the noted Moravian Pietist, believed that there should be no more enjoyment of sex in marriage than the

---

[18.] Rollo May, *Love and Will* (New York, 1969), 39.

[19.] Arthur Schlesinger, Jr., "An Informal History of Love, U.S.A.," *Love, Marriage, Family: A Developmental Approach*, eds., Marcia E. Lasswell and Thomas E. Lasswell, (Glenview, IL, 1973), 19.

wine in communion — which of course is no big deal. Hiltner's comments on pietism are instructive: "The prudishness that made several generations of Protestant theologians discuss marriage with practically no direct reference to sex supports the notion that some aspects of later Protestantism distorted the Biblical and Reformation views of sex."[20]

Contemporary Life

Neither pietism nor Victorian ideals were able to survive the nineteenth century. The sexual ethos of Western civilization has been referred to as revolutionary, since former mores such as coitus performed only in matrimony has been discarded in the name of a self-gratifying ethic that permits nearly every kind of sexual expression as long as it is undergirded by personal consent. The principal factors contributing to this sexual ethos include: Freudian psychology which identified humans as sexual animals; humanistic liberalism, which defines ethics in terms of self interest; two world wars; the birth-control pill; and the popularity of sociological morality, which defines ethics fundamentally in terms of what people do rather than by a transcendent standard, *i.e.* Biblical law. As the century enters its final decade, the only viable restraint on the licentious mania which condones every form of sexual expression has been the pandemic spread of venereal disease, most notably, AIDS.

Biblical Teaching

Having considered this historical backdrop, let us consider the Biblical injunctions pertaining to the deadly sin of sexual lust. Since sexual immorality is one of the most prominent topics in Scripture, featured throughout the Pentateuch, historical books, wisdom literature, prophets, gospels and apostolic epistles, space restricts me from treating the subject exhaustively. However, we can summarize God's attitude and man's responsibility concerning the area.

The Significance of Sexual Intercourse

Since original intent is fundamental to understanding any rule, law, or subject matter, let us begin with God's words to the first man and woman. Adam was made first and was in an obviously inadequate situation which God deemed as "not good for a man to be alone" and subsequently created Eve. God instructed them shortly thereafter that the pattern for the human race was, "Therefore a man shall leave his father and mother and be joined [Literally, to cling or cleave] to his wife and they shall become one flesh" (Gen. 2:24). They were also mandated to "be fruitful and multiply; fill the

---

[20.] Seward Hiltner, *Sex and the Christian Life* (New York, 1957), 64.

earth and subdue it" (Gen. 1:28). God's plan for the race involves a man and woman choosing to leave their parents in order to be joined covenantally in marriage so that through sexual intercourse they become one flesh, a state which subsequently leads to the procreation of the race and the work of subduing the earth.

Sherman Bailey says that "sexual intercourse is an act which engages and expresses the whole personality in such a way as to constitute a unique mode of self-disclosure and self-committal. By engaging in it, a man and woman become 'one flesh' — mutually involved for good or ill in a relation of profound significance and consequence."[21] Understanding the full implications of this one-flesh union explains the necessity for monogamy. To engage in the one-flesh union apart from marriage is not only a violation of God's decrees against fornication and adultery, but also an identification with that illegitimate partner which in turn affects one's own body:

> "Do you not know that your bodies are members of Christ? Shall I then take the members of Christ and make them members of a harlot? Certainly not! Or do you not know that he who is joined to a harlot is one body with her? For 'The two,' he says, 'shall become one flesh.' But he who is joined to the Lord is one spirit with him. Flee sexual immorality. Every sin that a man does is outside the body, but he who commits sexual immorality sins against his own body" (1 Cor. 6:15-18).

The Scriptural meaning of sexual intercourse is far more encompassing than merely a physical or biological romp. The Hebrews describe coitus as "to know" the person, a knowledge that comprehends other aspects of the human personality. Dwight Small comments that

> "sex in the one-flesh union moves towards a progressive integration of the several dimensions of personal existence. Biologically, sex appeases passion and reduces tension. Psychologically, sex discloses otherwise unexpressed aspects of our selfhood. Socially, sex is a unitive factor in the paired relationship. Ethically, sex manifests the necessary interdependence between fulfillment and responsibility. Theologically, sex points to the mystery of a union divinely purposed and illustrative of that between Christ and the church."

Thus, monogamous marriage provides the only secure context in which sexual intercourse can prove its stability, lasting power, faithfulness to God's calling and the other partner's welfare. God's undeviating standard is for men and women to marry and to cleave faithfully only to one another. To violate this law is to invoke his judgment: "Marriage is honorable among all, and the bed undefiled; but fornicators and adulterers God will judge" (Heb. 13:4).

Sexual lust, the intense or unrestrained sexual desire for someone outside the marriage covenant, is an act that modern society, Hugh Hefner, Masters and Johnson, and Dr. Ruth may condone but one in which Scripture prohibits.

---

[21] Derrick Sherwin Bailey, *Sexual Ethics* (New York, 1962), 178.

The classic text on the topic is from the Sermon on the Mount wherein Jesus says, "You have heard that it was said to those of old, 'You shall not commit adultery.' But I say to you that whoever looks at a woman to lust for her has already committed adultery with her in his heart" (Mt. 5:27-28). Our Lord categorizes not merely illegitimate sexual intercourse with transgressing the seventh commandment but includes the mental activity of sexual lust as well. And the refrain from our sex-laden culture then is "who then can be saved?"

The power of sexual lust is both a spiritual and human problem and consequently is one with which God's people have long contended, including me. Like every other sin and temptation, God's grace is amply sufficient to overcome it, yet we discover in Scripture that this problem has subdued some of the greatest men of God in history. The strongest man who ever lived, Samson, could physically overthrow a nation but could not control the enticements of Delilah. David, the "man after God's own heart," possibly the most spiritually sensitive man ever to live as reflected by the psalms he composed, nevertheless permitted his baser instincts to reign in the presence of a Bathsheba. Solomon, we are told, was "the wisest man who ever lived"; yet his insight turned to dribble as his passions were directed to his hundreds of wives and concubines. If the strongest, the wisest, and most spiritually sensitive were vanquished by lust, what hope is there for us?

Hope for Victory

Our fallen nature manifests itself in many egocentric ways, yet when Paul delineates the "deeds" of the flesh, it is noteworthy that he first mentions immorality, impurity, and sensuality (Gal. 5:19f). These aberrations of our sexuality are rooted in man's ultimate sin: his desire to be like God. Man's fallen nature endeavors to assert itself above God, his law, and the rest of his created order. Every illicit sexual thought and action is an affirmation of man's desire to be his own god, determining for himself what is good and evil, and orbiting all others around self. Sexual lust is exploitative, possessive, and degrading to the inherent value of other humans who are created in the image of God. They become merely objects of our satisfaction, slaves to use in our minds as we so please.

My conversion to Christianity brought me a newfound sense of peace, yet at the same time it generated a new disturbance as well. Whereas before, my life had been dedicated to my own pleasure, now there were conflicting tugs and pulls engaging my decision-making process. In fact, becoming a Christian was a disorienting, schizophrenic experience for me. After reading Galatians for the first time, I realized that I had been launched into an internal battle between my flesh and my regenerated spirit in Christ. Nobody warned me that by accepting Christ, God had a wonderful *war-plan* for my life!

As a new Christian, I was disturbed and disgusted by my lapses into sexual lust. So I began to pray the only prayer I knew at that time: *"Help!"* My problem was magnified by my job as the manager of a restaurant in a university town where the summer attire of most women bore a distinct resemblance to the *Sports Illustrated* annual swimsuit issue. Several times I literally would run into the back room of the restaurant before my wayward mind would plunge into lust in the presence of these nubile and naturally endowed young ladies. I even thought about fleeing to the desert, as the fourth-century monks did, to seek refuge from my problem. (Keeping my eyes closed wasn't the solution either; I had to operate the cash register.)

Help eventually came through my studies of the finished work of Christ on the cross. This, I discovered, was the basis for his victory, and my victory over lust as well. Romans 6 became my battle cry: "For we know that our old self [the flesh] was crucified with him so that the body of sin might be done away with, that we should no longer be slaves to sin... [so] count yourselves dead to sin but alive to God in Christ Jesus" (Rom. 6:6, 11).

From verses like these I realized that the solution to my dilemma whenever I was tempted by lust was believing and experiencing the triumph that Christ had won for me at the cross. I discovered that it was impossible for my mind to dwell simultaneously on sexual lust and the cross of Christ. As I affirmed my victory at Calvary, similarly the power of lust was broken in my life.

Several other Biblical texts that have been particularly helpful to me personally as well as to others in my counseling work include:

Job 31:1: "I have made a covenant with my eyes; Why then should I look upon a young woman?" To commit consciously to turn away from the omnipresent sexual allurements that daily confront us through movies, magazines, and television is an essential step in curtailing the development of sexual lust.

Secondly, I Thes. 4:3-5: "For this is the will of God, your sanctification: that you should abstain from sexual immorality; that each of you should know how to possess his own vessel in sanctification and honor, not in passion of lust, like the Gentiles who do not know God...." These statements emphasize God's unequivocal concern and intention for our sexual lives. God's people should be distinct sexually from the practices and philosophy of the culture.

Finally, Pr. 6:23-29: "For the commandment is a lamp, And the law is light; Reproofs of instruction are the way of life, To keep you from the evil woman, From the flattering tongue of a seductress. Do not lust after her beauty in your heart, Nor let her allure you with her eyelids, For by means of a harlot a man is reduced to a crust of bread; And an adulteress will prey upon his precious life. Can a man take fire to his bosom, And his clothes not be burned? Can one walk on hot coals, And his feet not be seared? So is he who goes in to his neighbor's wife; Whoever touches her shall not be innocent."

These verses affirm that there are judgmental consequences for illegitimate sexual behavior. History is replete with individuals, cities, and even cultures that God has despoiled for bowing to the lustful whims of sexual humanism. The Bible does not affirm that man is merely a sexual animal who is bound by the forces of sexual determinism which thereby legitimizes lust as an inevitable and impregnable manifestation of human behavior. No, sexual lust is not the ultimate determinative force of human existence. Rather it is a twisted expression of our fallenness that God prohibits and condemns.

To successfully overcome sexual lust, our minds must be directed toward God's laws and promises. The battle is in the mind and the one who contemplates the power of the cross and the revelation of Scripture can and will achieve victory over this mortal enemy.

Joseph R. McAuliffe is a political leader, and senior pastor of a church in Tampa, Florida.

The Inseparability of Holiness and Dominion: The Relation of Psalm 1 and Psalm 2

Joe Morecraft, III

Christianity is the world's only true comprehensive faith. It can be applied to the whole of life and all of its details consistently and effectively. All other religions must either impose their alien principles on life squeezing it into their unnatural molds or else they must compartmentalize life, concerning themselves with only one aspect of it, tearing that one part loose from the whole fabric of the universe. Christianity explains the unity of life in this universe as well as the true meaning of all the individual aspects of life, without distorting one fact.

The comprehensive nature of this Faith is seen especially in the relationship of a Christian's inner, spiritual life (Ps. 1) to his responsibility in this world to exercise godly dominion over it (Ps. 2). These two responsibilities of the Christian man — holiness and dominion — are not at war with each other, but are two aspects of one common calling: to glorify and enjoy God in all we are and in all we do (1 Cor. 10:31). R. J. Rushdoony has made this point more clearly than most Christian scholars today:

> To be holy means to be a regenerate covenant man obeying the law of God. It means re-establishment in the covenant calling and Kingdom task of dominion. *Thus, without holiness, there is no dominion, and without dominion, there is no holiness.* Holiness means dominion over our lives, over our calling, and over our work. *The holy man is a dominion man.* To be separated to God means to manifest the righteousness or law of God, and to manifest the righteousness or law of God means to exercise dominion.

> Jesus Christ is alone our Savior. To be in fact his covenant people, we must manifest His righteousness, His law. We must be holy, because He is holy. Holiness means the law of God. It means that the earth must be separated and devoted to God, and God's law made the governing rule of land, life and thought. Holiness means dominion under God, over ourselves, our callings, and the earth. The holy man is a Dominion Man.[1]

Today the Christian reconstruction of society (dominion) and Christian spirituality in the individual (holiness) are frequently set over against each other, as if the choice had to be made for one or the other. Some, who opt for Christian spirituality, denigrate Christian Reconstruction as a worldly-minded deviation from the Christian's central work of Christ-likeness. Others, who opt for Christian Reconstruction, often ridicule Christian spirituality as an other-worldly disregard for the critical issues of this life.

---

[1] R. J. Rushdoony, *Law and Society, Vol. II of The Institutes of Biblical Law* (Vallecito, CA, 1982), 323-324.

Holiness Without Dominion

Some want holiness without dominion. The pietist, influenced unconsciously by neo-platonism, sees the spiritual, subjective and heavenly as the only legitimate concerns for the Christian. For him earthly, political, social, economic, and sexual concerns are degrading detours from his calling of striving to be like Jesus, producing the fruit of the Spirit and waiting to go to heaven at death. Neo-platonism is the pagan Greek philosophy which holds that material and physical things are base and evil while subjective, spiritual, contemplative and heavenly things are the only good concerns of man. However, pietism must not be confused with piety. Neo-platonic pietism is the distortion and truncation of Christianity. Piety is true, Christ-like holiness of life and Biblical godliness.

Many modern neo-puritans also want holiness without dominion, at least without cultural dominion. Neo-puritanism includes an emphasis on a revival of the church by the word and Spirit of God, and a return to our roots in the Protestant Reformation of the sixteenth century with its emphasis on the sovereign grace of God in Christ and the call to faith in Christ and obedience to God. But today's version of Reformed churches, in many instances, has narrowed the concerns of the Reformation to inner dominion by the power of the Holy Spirit, and to inner and personal conformity to God's will in prayer and worship, to the near exclusion of the duty of the Christian reconstruction of culture and society.[2] One representative of this narrowed vision has written that any attempt to conquer the world for Christ and to reconstruct cultures by his word is, in actuality, rebellion against Christ!

Dominion Without Holiness

On the other hand, however, there are those who want dominion (Christian reconstruction) without holiness (Christian spirituality). Of course, at the most basic level, that is the goal of humanism: the (anti-Christian) reconstruction of culture and society by the imposition of a humanistic worldview and its (im)moral order onto a culture by political force and intimidation, without any regard for submission to the transcendent God, who is categorically rejected. This view, greatly modified of course, has infiltrated

---

[2.] By Christian Reconstructionism I mean faithfulness to the Creation Mandate of Gen. 1:28 and to the Great Commission of Mt. 28:18-20. This mandate and commission comprise a unity. They must not be set over against each other. The Great Commission is Christ's restatement of the Creation Mandate taking into consideration fallen man's need of redemption in Christ. So then, Christian Reconstructionism is the work of rebuilding and renewing every idea, activity, relationship, motive and institution of human experience and society by the Word and Spirit of God, beginning with the human heart. Our motivation is Christ's Person. Our basis is Christ's work. Our power is Christ's Spirit. Our pattern is Christ's humanity. Our protection is Christ's Father. Our governing authority is Christ's Deity. Our strategy is Christ's word. Our hope is Christ's victory. Our mandate is Christ's law. Our food is Christ's sacraments. Our aim is Christ's glory. This is Christian Reconstructionism.

the ranks of those committed to Christian Reconstructionism. With its criticism of pietism, its reaction against legalism, antinomianism and today's synthetic version of Christianity and its emphasis on Christian liberty, some in this camp have exhibited unholiness, harshness, abrasiveness, arrogance and an absence of love in their responses to those with whom they differ, and in their approach to life in general. It would seem that they want dominion without holiness. One who appears guilty of this desire for global dominion without personal holiness, when confronted with his harsh manner in dealing with people, responded, "God did not call me to be nice, just to tell the truth!"

The point I am trying to make is simply this: *Dominion (Christian reconstruction) is impossible without holiness (Christian spirituality); and holiness is impossible without dominion.* Striving for holiness of life without total involvement in the Great Commission and Creation Mandate will not produce holiness of life. And total involvement in the carrying out of the Great Commission without the careful pursuit of holiness of life, *i.e.*, personal obedience to Biblical law for Jesus' sake, will be counter-productive and is not true Christian Reconstructionism. Both dominion-taking without holy living and holy living without dominion-taking are rebellion against Christ. *In other words, Psalm 1 and Psalm 2 must be seen as inseparable.*

The book of Hebrews makes this point in chapter twelve, verse fourteen: *Pursue peace with all men, and holiness, without which no one will see the Lord.* Peace is the restoration of God's order in the heart and in the earth as a result of Christ's victory over evil in his life, death, and resurrection (Lk. 2:14). It requires the transformation (or reconstruction) of life, both personally and corporately, privately and publicly. Holiness is personal and corporate obedience to Biblical law from the heart for Jesus' sake. In Heb. 12:14, we are not told simply to pursue peace or to pursue holiness, but to pursue both peace and holiness, without which pursuit no one will ever see the Lord. What God has joined together, let no man put asunder! Peace is impossible without holiness. Holiness is not holiness unless its aim is peace. And, of course, both peace and holiness are impossible without Jesus Christ and his Spirit.

Why Holiness and Dominion are Inseparable

Holiness (Christian spirituality) and dominion (Christian reconstruction) are inseparable for several important reasons.

First, man's being and calling are inseparable. The basis of the Cultural Mandate to fill the earth and exercise dominion over it (Gen. 1:28), is the fact that man and woman are created in the image of God (Gen. 1:27). He and she manifest God's image in their own life and character as they exercise dominion under God over the world. And they exercise dominion as God's image-bearers fully accountable to him to serve him exclusively and totally in terms of his word. This "image" and "mandate" define man's existence and calling in this world.

Second, sanctification is inseparable from mission. Sanctification, or maturation in the Christian life, is not for its own sake. Striving to be holy for the sake of striving to be holy produces ingrown, introspective, self-centered, self-righteous, unloving, and unholy individuals. Jesus made it clear in Jn. 17:17-19 that the reason he wants us to be sanctified by the truth of God is that we can be effective in the mission to which he has sent us into the world "Sanctify them in the truth; Thy word is truth. As Thou didst send Me into the world, I also have sent them into the world. And for their sakes I sanctify Myself, that they themselves also may be sanctified in truth." Involvement in the church's mission without sanctification by the truth will prove to be ineffective and ugly, just as sanctification without involvement in world mission will produce icy sterility. Activity in the King's business does not make up for neglect of the King; and adoration of the King does not excuse neglect of submission to his mandates.

Third, being in Christ is inseparable from living for Christ and serving Christ. Jesus called and set apart his disciples for a twin calling: to be with him and to witness for him, "And He appointed twelve, that they might be with him, and that He might send them out to preach...." (Mk. 3:14). On the one hand, Jesus told his disciples: "You are My friends, if you do what I command you" (Jn. 15:14). And on the other hand, it is only as we are working to make the nations of the world Christ's disciples, baptizing them and educating them in the whole word of God, in the authority of Christ, that we can claim the promise of Christ, "And lo, I am with you always, even to the end of the age" (Mt. 28:18-20).

Fourth, God's powerful blessing permeates the entirety of the holy person's life (Ps. 1), thereby making him productive in being used of God to establish and extend the triumphant kingdom of Jesus Christ over every aspect and institution of the world's nations (Ps. 2). As we live to obey God in Christ, we must keep in view the goals of the kingdom of victory, or we will stagnate. Moreover, as we strive for the goals of the kingdom, we must do so as God's separated and law-abiding people, or we will be domineering and unloving and unwise.

The Relation Between Psalms 1 and 2

All this means that we must constantly keep in mind *the relation between Psalm 1 and Psalm 2!*

Psalm 1 presents us with an exquisite picture of a person enjoying the fulness of divine blessing. It sets the stage for the rest of the psalter. It introduces themes that are developed throughout the 150 psalms. Its major emphasis is unmistakable: the only truly happy and blessed person is the holy person, the person who seeks to avoid evil and to conform the entirety of his life to Biblical law out of love for Jesus Christ and gratitude for the salvation we have in him. As John Calvin put it: "The meaning of the psalmist…is that it shall be always well with God's devout servants, whose constant endeavor it is to make progress in the study of his law …. God is favorable to none but to those who zealously devote themselves to the study of divine truth."[3]

This person's character is portrayed in verses one and two. In verse one we learn that in the totality of his conscious life (walking, standing, sitting), he is endeavoring to avoid any entanglement with evil. He does not adopt the principles of evil men as his rule of life. He *does not walk in the counsel of the wicked.* Nor does he persist in the practices of evil men. He does not *stand in the path of sinners.* Nor will he deliberately associate himself with those who mock Christianity, for he will not *sit in the seat of scoffers.* "… how impossible it is for anyone to apply his mind to meditation upon God's law, who has not first withdrawn and separated himself from the society of the ungodly. — The sum of the whole is, that the servants of God must endeavor utterly to abhor the life of ungodly men."[4]

In verse two we learn that the greatest delight of his life is the studying and applying of the revealed law of God: "But his delight is in the law of the LORD, and in his law he meditates day and night." God's law-word is his supernaturally revealed law, *i.e.*, the Bible, which gives direction (torah) to every facet of our thinking and living in this world. The true Christian (the holy person) studies Biblical law, cleaves to it, delights in it, meditates on it, and submits himself to it. He obeys it and applies it to his whole life, inside and out. In so doing, he protects himself against all the plots of the ungodly and fortifies himself against temptation (Ps. 17:4). This personal joy and delight in Biblical law presupposes the union of the human will and the divine will. And that is what happens in the new birth, when God renews our heart and writes his law on it, working in us the will and the ability to do his pleasure (Heb. 8:10; Phil. 2:13).

The Consequence of Obedience

The consequences of the blessing of the Lord on the person walking in the paths of holiness are three. First, his life is marked by stability, strength, productivity and prosperity: "And he will be like a tree firmly planted by streams of water, which yields its fruit in its season, and its leaf does not wither; and in whatever he does, he prospers" (Ps. 1:3). Calvin writes: "… the children of God constantly flourish, and are always watered with the secret influences of divine grace, so that whatever may befall them is conducive to

---

[3.] John Calvin, *Commentary Upon the Book of Pslams*, in *Calvin's Commentaries* (Grand Rapids, MI), 4:1,2.
[4.] *ibid.*, 4:2, 3.

their salvation; while, on the other hand, the ungodly are carried away by the sudden tempest, or consumed by the scorching heat."[5] Second, he will be sifted and separated from the worthless chaff, which God will destroy: "The wicked are not so, but they are like chaff which the wind drives away. Therefore the wicked will not stand in the judgment, nor sinners in the assembly of the righteous" (Ps. 3:4-5). Third, the holy person's way of life day by day is loved by God, and that love produces in him those things which please God. It brings him to his final destiny, eternal life and bliss with God: "For the LORD knows the way of the righteous, but the way of the wicked will perish" (Jn. 1:6). J. A. Alexander makes this concluding remark: "This completes the contrast, and sums up the description of the truly happy man, as one whose delight is in the law and his happiness in the favor of Jehovah, and whose strongest negative characteristic is his total lack of moral likeness here to those from whom he is to dwell apart hereafter."[6]

The blessed and happy life is the holy life, lived out in love for and obedience to God in Christ. There is no other kind of Christian life than this.

The Triumphant Kingdom

Psalm 2 presents us with the divine promise of the triumphant kingdom of Jesus Christ over the nations of earth. Psalm 1 introduced to us our duty before God. Psalm 2 introduces us to our Lord and Savior Jesus Christ. It is a psalm of victory, which note is sounded throughout the psalms (22:27f; 45:4; 47:1f; 66:4; 72:8; 86:9). It is a messianic psalm, referring to Jesus Christ, as is clear from such passages as Ac. 4:24f; 13:33f; Heb. 1:5,8; 5:5; Rev. 2:27 and 19:15. Its theme is also obvious: *the kingdom of Jesus Christ is God's answer to the rebellion of men.* It will triumph over all opposition in all areas (1 Cor. 15:24f). Therefore all men and all human institutions must submit to the supremacy of the Son of God or be destroyed by him. William Plumer put it succinctly: "We must love Christ or terribly perish."[7]

Verses 1-3 reveal that mankind (individuals through their political institutions) is in revolt against the authority of Almighty God over life. It is a conscious, universal, united, historical and continual attempt to build a world on a principle of revolt against Jehovah and his Christ. But it is all in vain: "Why are the nations in an uproar, and the peoples devising a vain thing? The kings of the earth take their stand, and the rulers take counsel together against the LORD and His Anointed: 'Let us tear their fetters apart, and cast away their cords from us!'" Calvin comments: "Let it be held as a settled point, that all who do not submit themselves to the authority of Christ

---

[5.] *ibid.*, 6.
[6.] J. A. Alexander, *The Psalms Translated and Explained* (Grand Rapids, 1975 reprint), 12.
[7.] William S. Plumer, *Psalms* (Edinburgh, Scotland, 1975 reprint), 47.

make war on God. Since it seems good to God to rule us by the hand of His own Son, those who refuse to obey Christ Himself deny the authority of God, and it is in vain for them to profess otherwise...."[8]

God's Response to Man's Rebellion

God's response to mankind's futile but vicious revolt is described in verses 4-6. It is a threefold response.

First, God laughs! "He who sits in the heavens laughs, the LORD scoffs at them." The sovereign and omnipotent God laughs in contempt at the feeble attempts of his enemies to overthrow his authority and overturn his government (Ps. 37:12f; 59:8). He does so because he is enthroned as sovereign Lord over all, actively ruling all men and nations according to his good pleasure, causing all things to work together for good for his people (Rom. 8:28; 1 Chr. 29:11-23; Is. 40:22f; Ac. 4:23f). All efforts to put down the kingdom of God are "as if a fly should attack an elephant, or a man endeavor to snatch the sun from the sky."[9] His revolt is like "the effort of an infant to stay the whirlwind or the unavailing yell of the maniac to calm the raging of the sea."[10] God's laughter guarantees the overthrow of all rebellion against him and his moral order.

Second, God speaks! It is God's revealed word that will overturn and confound all the conspiracies of his enemies against him. "Then He will speak to them in His anger and terrify them in His fury" (Ps. 2:5). 1 Cor. 1:18-29 reiterates this point when it quotes God as saying: "I will destroy the wisdom of the wise, and the cleverness of the clever I will set aside." Psalm 2 tells us that he will accomplish this by his word — the word of God preached, testified to, lived out, meditated on, and applied by God's people — which always accomplishes the conquering purposes for which God sends it forth (Is. 55:11). The word of God is *the sword of the Spirit* in the hands of the church resisting and defeating God's enemies on the battlefield of life (Eph. 6:17). By confirming the word of his servant, he will demolish all the "isms" of men raised up against him, and also firmly establish his church in the earth as a mighty force against whose endeavors of world conquest with the gospel the gates of hell will not prevail (Is. 44:24f). Rev. 12:11 says that the rebels of the earth are overcome by "the blood of the Lamb and because of the word of their testimony, and they did not love their life even to death."

Third, God establishes the kingdom of Christ in the earth! "But as for Me [God], I have installed my king [Jesus] upon Zion, My holy mountain." "I (Jesus) will surely tell of the decree of the LORD: He [God] said to Me [Christ], 'Thou [Christ] art My Son, today I have begotten Thee. Ask of Me

---

8. Calvin, *op.cit.*, 12.
9. Plumer, *op. cit.*, 41.
10. *ibid.*

[God], and I will surely give the nations as Thy [Christ's] inheritance, and the very ends of the earth as Thy possession. Thou [Christ] shalt break them with a rod of iron, Thou shalt shatter them like earthenware'" (Ps. 2:6-9). God completes the overthrow of his enemies by coming to the earth in the person of his Son, the Lord Jesus Christ (at his incarnation) and by establishing his victorious, invincible and universal kingdom on the earth. By advancing his kingdom he will squelch revolt in human hearts and societies; and he will restore and preserve his moral order. This messianic King will overcome his enemies by converting many of them (Ps. 22:27), and by destroying some of them (Rev. 19:11f). God promised Christ a great, global inheritance of the world's nations; then he instructed his Son to intercede in behalf of those nations that they will, in fact, be given to him. This intercession of Christ is the hope of the world (Jn. 17:20) and the guarantee of the success of evangelism, world missions and Christian Reconstructionism. Nothing can hinder the triumph of the gospel over all nations and peoples. Nothing can resist the progress of Christ's kingdom on earth. It is for this reason that the psalms continually emphasize the truth that "All the ends of the earth will remember and turn to the LORD, and all the families of the nations will worship before Thee. For the kingdom is the LORD's, and He rules over the nations" (Ps. 22:27).

"Kiss the Son"

Psalm 2 concludes in verses 10-12 with a solemn and universal call for submission to Jesus Christ from all individuals and all human institutions, particularly from judicial and political institutions: "Now therefore, O kings, show discernment; take warning, O judges of the earth. Serve the LORD with reverence, and rejoice with trembling. Kiss the Son, (*i.e.*, pay homage to him), lest He become angry, and you perish in the way, for His wrath may soon by kindled. How blessed are all who take refuge in Him."

This worshipful service and undivided allegiance demanded of kings and judges toward Christ is the only acceptable and proper response to such a kingly Savior described in this psalm. Anything else or anything less can only be considered continued rebellion against this king. Notice particularly that political institutions "of the earth" are called to bow in submission before the supremacy of God's Son and his rule. This calls for Christian reconstruction. Calvin wrote: "God is defrauded of His honor if He is not served in Christ. As Christ is not despised without indignity being done to the Father who has adorned Him with His own glory, so the Father Himself will not allow such an invasion of His sacred rights to pass unpunished."[11] John Newton continued this thought:

[11.] Calvin, *op. cit.*, 25.

"He is Lord over those who hate Him. He rules them with a rod of iron, and so disposes their designs as to make them (though against their wills) the means and instruments of promoting His own purposes and glory. They are His unwilling servants even when they rage most against Him. He has a bridle in their mouths to check and turn them at His pleasure. He can and often does control them, when they seem most secure of success, and always sets them bounds, which they cannot pass."[12]

Conclusion

From our brief study of these two psalms, it becomes clear that the divorce of holiness (Christian spirituality) from dominion (Christian reconstruction) is fatal. Such divorce is rebellion against Christ. God's mighty word conquers God's enemies as we preach and teach and live that word. As we delight in doing his word, God blesses us and we are productive for him in the work he has given us to bring every thought captive to Christ. Christ's triumphant kingdom is advanced through the members of that kingdom confessing relevently and in concrete ways that *Jesus is Lord*, and by living in obedience to their king. Rom. 16:17-20 tells us that as we separate from a sinful lifestyle and become consistent in obeying the Lord, "the God of peace will soon crush Satan under [our] feet. The grace of the Lord Jesus be with [us]."

We are to go to the nations, which are Christ's inheritance, and call individuals, kings, judges and nations with all their families and institutions, to repentance and submission to the government of Jesus Christ revealed in the Bible. We cannot compromise the message. The demands of the gospel of Christ must be made plain. Christ will conquer the nations of earth, in history, through our bold call to all men and nations to join us in unconditional surrender and submission to the King of kings and Lord of lords. Psalm 1 and Psalm 2 may not be separated without robbing one or the other of its power. *Holiness and dominion are inseparable. One is impossible without the other*: "Pursue peace and holiness, without which no one will see the Lord!"

Joe Morecraft of Roswell, Georgia, is a preacher and a noted lecturer on contemporary political and historical trends in the United States. He holds a B. A. degree in History from King College in Bristol, Tennessee, a Master of Divinity degree from Columbia Theological Seminary in Decatur, Georgia, and a Doctor of Theology degree from Whitefield Theological Seminary, Lakeland, Florida.

[12.] Plumer, *op. cit.*, 48.

Pierre Viret and the Sovereignty
of the Word of God
Over Every Aspect of Reality

Jean-Marc Berthoud

The Church inescapably invited war by its very existence as a Christian institution. It broke radically with the old unitary and immanent concept of society. It shattered the humanistic unity of society by declaring itself to be the representative of a transcendental King and order, Jesus Christ and the Kingdom of God. It held, moreover, that the State, and every aspect of society, is similarly duty bound to represent God's order, not man's. The Church therefore was more than new wine in an old wine skin; it was new wine demanding new wine skins, demanding that all things be mode new in terms of Christ.

R. J. Rushdoony, *Christianity and the State*

The distinctive vocation of Rousas J. Rushdoony and the particular place he holds in the history of the church are characterized by a whole lifetime of persevering labor in the task of calling back God's people to a renewed understanding of the significance, for every domain of life, of the written revelation, the Bible, and a summons addressed to the church to a renewed obedience to the whole counsel of God as at the same time law and gospel. This persistent call to repentance and faith, to spiritual understanding and thoroughgoing obedience, has resulted, as might have been expected, in much opposition and calumny both within the churches and beyond their walls. This has been specially true, unfortunately, in many circles which call themselves Reformed and openly adhere to the same doctrinal standards as Rushdoony. One aspect of this theological and ecclesiastical opposition to his teaching and influence has expressed itself in the accusation leveled against him of *originality,* of teaching things that the church has in the past not taught; of fomenting novelty by his insistence that man live by every word spoken by God in Scripture. Such an accusation must not be treated lightly. Within the church of God the concept of novelty is always closely linked to that of heresy, for it is our vocation to teach only those things which have always been taught from all time past in all faithful churches, and thus to maintain the unity and apostolicity of the church. Coming from various quarters we have heard: "Never has the church known such a fanatical determination to apply to every aspect of reality of every detail the revealed word of God." In this short paper, by examining the contribution to the on-going growth of the kingdom of God of a little known French Swiss reformer, Pierre Viret, I shall briefly endeavor to refute such unfounded accusations.

Background

Pierre Viret was born in 1511 in the ancient Roman and Burgundian town of Orbe at the base of the Jura mountains in what is today the canton of Vaud in French-speaking Switzerland. His father was by profession a draper and both his parents pious Roman Catholics. After following the parochial school of his home town, his parents sent him in 1527 at the age of sixteen to Paris to further his higher education with a view to his entering the priesthood. There he followed the strenuous academic discipline of Montaigu College, famous for such students as John Calvin and Ignatius of Loyola, founder of the Jesuit order. Not only did Viret in these Parisian years begin to acquire the encyclopaedic knowledge which marks all his writings, but he advanced greatly in that apprenticeship of the ancient tongues which later made of him not only a fluent Latin scholar but a pastor familiar with Hebrew and Greek. Far more important, however, it was in this context of arduous study, lighted by the bonfires in which the first French martyrs of the Reformation were burnt at the stake, that Viret came to see the deadly errors of that Roman religion in which he had been reared and his need for a personal Savior to deliver him from the curse a holy God laid on his sins. After a very painful and difficult struggle, he at last came to saving faith in the Lord Jesus Christ. For it was a time when all over the Kingdom of France, and more especially in Paris, the newly rediscovered gospel was being powerfully preached in a climate of dire persecution for any who dared question the established doctrines of a totalitarian religious and political order.[1]

This persecution led Viret, seeking refuge, back to his native Orbe. It was here that he met his vocation. In the spring of 1531, Guillaume Farel, that intrepid preacher of the gospel and political agent of the newly Reformed authorities of the Berne Republic, called Viret (as he was to do with Calvin a few years later) out of the tranquility of his studies into the battlefield of the Reformation of the church and the implantation in his country of God's mighty kingdom. At the age of twenty, Viret thus became the pastor of the small evangelical congregation of Orbe where he had the privilege of seeing his parents' conversion under his preaching of the word of God. The following years saw him engaged in a growing itinerant ministry all over French-speaking Switzerland. In the Abbey town of Payerne, some thirty miles north of Lausanne, an irate monk violently refuted his preaching by

---

[1.] No recent biography of Pierre Viret is available. See Jean Barnaud, *Pierre Viret, sa vie et son oeuvre* (Saint-Amans, 1911); Henri Vuilleumier, *Notre Pierre Viret* (Lausanne, 1912); Jean-Marc Berthoud, *Pierre Viret et le refus de l'Eglise de plier devant la puissance de l'Etat*, in *Des Actes de l'Eglise* (Lausanne, 1993), 45-58.

On Viret's theology the only substantial study available is by a Roman Catholic theologian, Georges Bavaud, *Le réformateur Pierre Viret* (Genève, 1986).

On the general history of the church of the canton of Vaud in the sixteenth century see Henry Vuilleumier, *Histoire de l'Eglise réformée du Pays de Vaud sous le régime bernois*, Tome Premier, *L'Age de la Réforme* (Lausanne, 1927).

running him through (in the back!) with a sword as he was crossing a field. In 1534 we find Viret at Farel's side breaking the ground for the free entrance of the gospel in the city of Geneva. There again, murder was on his path, this time in the shape of a poisoned soup which, if it did not kill him, nonetheless left him with permanently ruined health. In 1536 the canton of Vaud was overrun by the Bernese army, ostensibly at war to defend Geneva from the threats of the Counts of Savoy, but effectively working for the aggrandizement of Bernese power. These temporal ambitions, in God's merciful hand, opened up the whole region to the preaching of the gospel. After the famous Dispute de Lausanne in the same year,[2] a public disputation where Viret (with Farel) bore the brunt of the debate, the young pastor, now age 25, became the minister of the Cathedral Church. Apart from a brief period (1541-1542) where he very ably assisted Calvin on his return to Geneva after his exile in Strasbourg, the twenty-three years between 1536 and 1559 saw Viret as the principal minister of the Reformed church of the Vaud canton where he exercised the ministry of God's word under the heavy hand of the Bernese political and ecclesiastical power.

The Freedom of the Church

Very early Viret came to hold a high view of the authority and dignity of the church. As a result, he came to demand, with a mild but unshakable persistence, that the church be free to exercise its ecclesiastical discipline independently of the overweening Erastian ambitions of the Bernese authorities. The government of Berne saw themselves as the heirs of the undivided rule of the Roman republic and were on no account prepared to tolerate any kind of real spiritual independence in the church. In his polemical writings, Viret was often to declare that the Bernese Pope in short frock (the absolute state) was a far worse enemy for the Faith than the old Pope of Rome in his long gown. The conflict was inevitable, long-drawn and brutally climaxed in February, 1559, when those Messieurs de Berne, as they styled themselves, demanded of the recalcitrant pastors of Vaud either total submission to their undivided authority or immediate resignation and exile. More than thirty opted for faithfulness and exile and this at the very moment when God, in his Providence, had opened the doors for a great expansion of his kingdom in neighboring France. Between 1559 and 1561 Viret exercised a much appreciated ministry in Geneva at the side of his great friend Calvin, but his failing health forced him to seek a milder climate in the south of France. His health partly restored, he was instrumental in bringing about a remarkable revival, first in Montpellier and Nîmes, then in the second city of the realm, Lyon. There he exercised a highly blessed ministry during the early

---

[2.] On the Dispute de Lausanne, see Arthur Piaget, *Les Actes de la Dispute de Lausanne, 1536* (Neuchâtel, 1928) and the study by Georges Bavaud, *La Dispute de Lausanne* (Fribourg, 1956).

years of the civil wars, ending a very fruitful and eventful life as Chief Pastor and Academic Superintendent of the Reformed Church of the Kingdom of Navarre where he died in 1571.

Viret's Significance

Now Pierre Viret, Calvin's most intimate friend,[3] known under the name of the Angel of the Reformation, was by no means the minor or insignificant figure which most Reformed histories of the Reformation lead us to imagine. He had, in 1537, founded in Lausanne the first Reformed Academy. He gave much of his time to the teaching of theology to students who flocked from every corner of Europe. This Lausanne Academy (and not the Genevan, as is too often thought) became the model of all future Reformed Academies. By the time of the expulsion of Viret in 1559, the Academy had nearly a thousand students enrolled. For many years, the Principal was none other than the celebrated Greek scholar and poet, Théodore de Bèze. Amongst the students we find men of the stature of the authors of the Heidelberg Catechism, Ursinus and Olevianus, ample proof of the quality of the teaching dispensed in Lausanne. In 1559 the whole staff of the Academy resigned and constituted the teaching base of the newly founded Genevan Academy.[4]

But this mild and gentle Christian, a man of the highest spiritual mettle, was also one of the great preachers of the Reformation. Of Calvin Bèze wrote, *"None have taught with greater authority"*; of Farel, *"None thundered more mightily"*; but of Viret he said, *"None has a more winsome charm when he speaks."*[5]

> His speech was so sweet that he would continually hold the attention and the interest of those who heard him. His style, which married strength to harmony, was so caressing to the ear and to the intelligence that even those of his hearers least interested in religious matters, those most impatient of other preachers, would hear him out without difficulty and even with pleasure.[6]

Melchior Adam remarked of his preaching:

> In Lyon, preaching out in the open, he brought thousands to saving faith in Jesus Christ. By the power of his divine eloquence he would even cause those passing by to stop, listen and hear him out.[7]

[3] Henri Meylan, "Une amtié au XVIe siècle: Farel, Viret, Calvin," in *Silhouettes du XVI siècle* (Lausanne, 1943) 27-50.

[4] *idem., La Haute Ecole de Lausanne, 1537-1937* (Lausanne, 1937).

[5] Henry Vuilleumier, *Notre Pierre Viret*, (Lausanne, 1912), 142.

[6] Jean Barnaud, *Pierre Viret, sa vie et son oeuvre* (Saint-Amans, 1911), 539-540.

[7] *ibid.*, 540.

Writings

But in addition to exercising such great gifts, Viret was in his own right a prolific writer, author of some forty books, some almost a thousand pages long.[8] A number of these were translated into English during the sixteenth century,[9] others into Dutch, German and Italian. If very few of Viret's works have been reprinted, they nonetheless had a marked influence on Reformed thinking up to the time of that last great dogmatician of the Genevan school, Benedict Pictet, in the early years of the eighteenth century. Viret wrote a small number of treatises in Latin, but the immense majority of his books were written in French, in a familiar style and in the popular form of dialogues between clearly differentiated and attractive personages designed to reach a public privileged with little formal instruction. But if the style is pleasant, the matter is profound, the knowledge of the Bible impeccable, and the scholarship immense. The pattern of his dialogues: affirmations — objections — refutations — and finally the clear, authoritative and balanced doctrinal synthesis, harks clearly back, in a popular form but without the philosophical jargon, to the scholastic method of formal discussion learnt at the feet of the Scottish master of Philosophy and Theology at the Collège Montaigu, John Major.

Pierre Viret was undoubtedly (with Martin Luther) one of the finest popularizers of the Christian Faith in the sixteenth century. But his deep concern for the spiritual needs of the common people never led him (as is all too common today) to debase the content of his theological teaching. It is impossible, in the brief space assigned to this paper, to do proper justice to the astonishing achievements of this extraordinary Christian. If his good friend, John Calvin, was the consummate dogmatician and the prince of exegetes, Pierre Viret must be considered as the finest ethicist and the most acute apologist of the sixteenth century. His monumental *Instruction chrétienne en la doctrine de la Loy et de l'Evangile et en la vraie philosophie et théologie, tant naturelle que supernaturelle des chrétiens* [10] ("Christian instruction in the doctrine of the law and the gospel and in true Christian philosophy and theology, both natural and supernatural") is without doubt his major theological work and can well bear comparison, in its own domain, with Calvin's *Institutes*. The first 248 pages of Vol. I (large folio pages, small

---

[8.] Very little of Viret's voluminous writings has been reedited in the twentieth century. Charles Schnetzler, Henri Vuilleumier et Alfred Schroeder, *Pierre Viret par lui-même* (Lausanne, 1911); idem., *Quatre sernnons français sur Esaïe 65* (Lausanne, 1961); idem., *Deux dialogues* (Lausanne, 1971); idem., *L'interim fait par dialogues*, (Berne, 1985); idem., *La cosmographie infernale* (Paris, 1991).

[9.] *A very familiar and fruitful exposition of the XII articles of the Christian faith*, 1548; *A Christian instruction containing the Law and the Gospel*, 1573; *Christian disputations*, 1579; *A faithful and familiar exposition upon the prayer of our Lord Jesus Christ*, 1582; *The school of beasts*, 1585.

[10.] Volume I; Volume II (Genève, 1564). The third volume was published apart with the title *De la providence divine* (Lyon, 1565).

print) comprises a treatise on the subject of God's general revelation as manifested in creation. The refreshingly simple and direct character of Viret's teaching on general revelation makes it clear that this work was written in a period prior to the philosophical insanity of Cartesian rationalism and of Kantian idealism. Pages 249 through 674 constitute a complete treatise on the detailed application of the Ten Commandments to every aspect of reality. It is the finest exposition of the law of God that it has been my privilege to read. The only work I know which in any way bears comparison to this masterpiece is Rushdoony's *The Institutes of Biblical Law.*[11] Not only do we find there a detailed application of God's word to the practical problems of Christian living in every aspect of personal and social life, but this is done with an admirable sense of theological balance and of the delicate relation of dogmatics to ethics, together with the constant, implicit purpose of favoring the preaching of the gospel, of extending God's kingdom, and of bringing all honor and praise to the Lord Jesus Christ. In the *Preface* Viret sets forth his central purpose with the utmost clarity:

> My aim in this volume has been to produce an exposition of the Law of God, Law which must be regarded as the rule for every other law through which men are to be directed and governed.[12]

and adds,

> Every science, human prudence and all wisdom of men must be put into relation to God as a gift which proceeds from him.[13]

Then Viret goes on to define his purpose more precisely:

> Thus God has included in this Law every aspect of that moral doctrine by which men may live well. For in these Laws he has done infinitely better than the Philosophers and all their books, whether they deal with Ethics, Economics or Politics. This Law stands far above all human legislation, whether past, present or future and is above all laws and statutes edicted by men. It follows that whatever good men may put forward has previously been included in this law, and whatever is contrary to it is of necessity evil .... This law, if it is rightly understood, will furnish us with true Ethics, Economics and Politics. It is incomparably superior to what we find in the teachings of Aristotle, Plato, Xenophon, Cicero and like thinkers who have taken such pains to fashion the customs of men.[14]

And Viret concludes his *Preface* with these words:

> For as it can only be God Himself who is able to give us such a perfect Law by which we are truly enabled to govern ourselves, likewise it is

---

[11.] R. J. Rushdoony, *The Institutes of Biblical Law* (Nutley, NJ, 1973).

[12.] Pierre Viret, *Instruction chrestienne en la doctrine de la Loy et de l'Evangile* (Genève, 1564).

[13.] *ibid.*, 274.

[14.] *ibid.*, 255.

only He who can provide us with Princes and Magistrates, Pastors and Ministers gifted with the capacity of applying this Law. Further, He is fully able to shape such men into adequate instruments for his service and to grant them the authority necessary for the accomplishment of the duties of their office. Thus armed they are enabled by God to maintain those over whom they rule (and of whose welfare they are accountable to God) in a spirit of due subjection. For, just as He has granted us this Law in order that we might clearly know what we lack, so he likewise grants us, through Jesus Christ his Son, the Holy Ghost by whom our hearts are renewed and through whom we receive those gifts and graces so necessary for the accomplishment of our vocation.[15]

Such a view of the overarching authority and of the supreme wisdom of God's law led Pierre Viret to an examination of the particular duties of men within the bounds of their specific vocations. To this task he more particularly addressed himself in a masterly treatise entitled *Métamorphose chrétienne, faite par dialogue.*[16] The chapter titles of the sections of the first part entitled *Man* go as follows: 1/ The natural man. 2/ Man deformed. 3/ The transformation of souls. 4/ The true man, or man transformed. The second part concerns *The school of beasts* and is composed of the following sections: 1/ Economics, or good management. 2/ Politics, or the Republic. 3/ Military art. 4/ The Arts. 5/ Ethics, or moral behavior. 6/ Religion. 7/ Language and, finally, 8/ Prophesy or Theology. One can imagine the interest such a work provoked at the time it was written.

Finally, among his numerous writings in the field of apologetics (a good number of which were devoted to a running polemic with the errors of the Roman Church) we cannot pass without comment his satirical examination of the politics of his time and development of what we must call *the theology of history,* a book entitled, *Le monde à l'empire et le monde démoniacle.*[17] This title, with its pun on the word *empire* (meaning both *empire* and *to worsen),* could be tentatively translated *The corruption of the world's empires and the world demonized.* This work bears ample witness to the extraordinary prophetic insight granted to those who, like Viret, make it their business to see and understand every aspect of reality in the light of God's law-word.

Viret's Political Thinking

Here of great value is Robert T. Linder's path-breaking study on Viret's political thinking.[18] After having described what for Viret was the normative rule of the word of God for both ecclesiastical and theological matters, Linder defines his thinking in these terms:

[15.] *ibid.*, 255-256.

[16.] *idem., La métamorphose chrétienne* (Genève, 1561).

[17.] *idem., Le monde à l'empire et le monde démoniacle fait par dialogues,* (Genève, 1561).

[18.] Robert T. Linder, *The Political Ideas of Pierre Viret* (Geneva, 1964).

The Scriptures also contained statements concerning the state and, insofar as they applied to secular government, they represented God's will for that institution. Thus the secular state was seen by Viret as a de facto creation derived directly from God himself but governed in harmony with the rules and precepts contained in the Holy Scriptures.[19]

Linder adds:

God's plan for men included a peaceful and orderly existence and the state was the means whereby this kind of life was assured. The rulers of the secular state were to legislate in accordance with the Bible and fulfill the office outlined for them in the Scriptures. Viret had to make the civil authorities see that all justice and law emanated from the sovereign will of God and that they were the dispensers of God's justice and law. If they did not do this, these secular authorities were considered "wicked tyrants" and in danger of the judgment of Almighty God. [20]

For, in Viret's eyes,

The secular state was a direct creation of God and because of this was delegated a certain amount of authority directly from God himself. However, according to Viret, the Holy Scriptures not only described and confirmed temporal authority but also defined and limited it.[21]

Viret felt that all laws affecting public morals and related to spiritual values should be drawn directly from the moral law of God. However, he believed that these absolute and eternal laws of God had to be geared to the times in which people lived and the national temperament of the country to which the laws were to be applied.[22]

Further,

Viret made it plain that civil laws could be both good and bad. He believed that men had a certain amount of freedom in choosing the legal codes under which they lived. Nevertheless, he felt that "good laws" in a truly Christian state always would be based on the Ten Commandments of God found in the Holy Scriptures. According to Viret, unless human laws were built upon God's moral law, men could not expect for them to be just and equitable. In this sense, all "good laws," come from God himself for they are derived from God's Word which is the written record of his will for mankind ....

Viret's great emphasis was upon government under civil law, and particularly under civil law derived, as fully as possible within a given political context, from the moral law of God.[23]

Linder states, moreover:

---

[19] *ibid.*, 55.
[20] *ibid.*, 56.
[21] *ibid.*, 57.
[22] *ibid.*, 58, note 29.
[23] *ibid.*, 58-59.

Viret's notion that the prince was below the law is extremely interesting and very different from the absolutist theory placing the king above the law that Jean Bodin was to advocate in his *De Republica* in the latter part of the sixteenth century. The idea that the secular ruler was always subject to the law was one of several recurrent strains in Medieval political thought in Western Europe and was not a new concept.[24]

Viret put it this way:

For prince and magistrate must be subject to the laws of the land and conform their rule to them. For they are not rulers of the law but servants thereof, as they are servants of God from whom all good laws proceed.[25]

And Linder comments:

Viret stressed that in every instance the true Christian should subjugate the Justinian Code and all Roman Law to the Word of God.[26]

Linder concludes:

Viret's pattern of thought led him to advocate what would be called today the legislation of morals. For example, he favored the adoption of civil statutes against adultery, blasphemy and idolatry, and was a proponent of regulating certain economic activities on Sunday. In addition, he linked true Christianity with the support of such laws as those controlling public corruption and the purchase of public offices, against usury, against the exploitation of the poor by the rich, and legislation fixing ceiling prices and land purchases.[27]

From all this it is clear that Viret's great friendship for John Calvin (his elder by only two years) in no way prevented him from, on occasion, expressing divergent theological views whilst, of course, sharing on all fundamental points of doctrine the same Reformed convictions. The Reformation thus gives us a striking example of the way basic doctrinal unity is in no way exclusive of a certain theological diversity. It is the mechanical conformism of a narrow-gutted age which cannot stomach disagreements on secondary matters in the church. Thus, on the question of extent of the application of the detail of the Mosaic law to our present situation, Viret held a significantly different position from that of Calvin. This is how Linder defines this difference:

Viret, unlike Calvin, was ready to extend openly the authority of the Bible over the State.[28]

---

24. *ibid.*, 59-60.
25. *idem.*, *Le monde à l'empire el le monde démoniacle fait par dialogues*, 91-92.
26. Linder, *op. cit.*, 61.
27. *ibid.*
28. *ibid.*, 63.

One must here in passing draw the reader's attention to the influence, on this particular point, of the teaching of Thomas Aquinas[29] on the political and legal theology of John Calvin. On this point Viret's position, though not explicitly theonomic, was far more consistently and thoroughly Biblical than that of his Genevan colleague who, in his application of God's law to the body politic, ambivalently ranged between the affirmation of the existence of a *natural law,* a *law of nations* (nonetheless inspired, be it said by, Biblical *principles)* on the one hand in his *Institutes,* and, on the other, a more careful and precise coordination of the legal and political implications of Biblical law in his commentaries and in his sermons.[30] It is enlightening to compare Viret's and Calvin's exegesis of specific texts. In his sermons on Deuteronomy, for example, we often find that Calvin, while not ignoring the detailed practical implications of the Mosaic law, nonetheless pays but scant attention to their application to the political and social problems of his time. He often rapidly passes from these practical ethical and social considerations to, in his eyes, more essential matters and goes on to draw out the doctrinal and spiritual implications of the text. Viret, on the other hand, while never minimizing the doctrinal aspect of his text, paid far more attention to the immediate literal meaning of the specific law under consideration and to its application for his own time. This may explain the fascination his preaching exercised even on those who were foreign to the Faith. But in spite of these different and complementary orientations we do not find the slightest indication of personal and theological tension in the friendship that united these two great Christians leaders in their common vocation to further the kingdom of God. In this they have much to teach us latter-day Calvinists who are all too often inclined to give way to that sectarian spirit which so banefully characterized the Corinthian church.

Viret's Discernment

I would like to conclude this all too brief appreciation of one of the great figures in the history of the church (often unknown to those who consider themselves heirs of the Reformation) by showing the extraordinary lucidity and discernment by which his great respect for God's law endowed Pierre

---

[29.] Thomas d'Aquin, *Somme Théolgique* (Paris, 1984, Vol. II, *La loi ancienne,* Questions 98-105), 627-715. The corresponding passage is to be found in John Calvin, *L'Institution Chrétienne* (Genève, 1958, Book IV, Chapter XX, 447-481, *Du gouvernement civil).* It is clear that the classic Reformed distinction between the moral law, the judicial law and the ceremonial law has, for better or for worse, a scholastic origin. Such a distinction (and opposition) between the moral and the judicial law is, as far as I can tell, not to be found in the Bible, neither in Augustine, nor in the teachings of the Church Fathers. On these questions see, Jean-Marc Berthoud, *Une religion sans Dieu. Les droits de l'homme contre l'Evangile* (Lausanne, 1993) and my forthcoming book, *Une apologie pour la Loi de Dieu.*

[30.] Here it is necessary to put aside the *Institutes* and examine Calvin's exegetical teachings, in particular his *Sermons on Deuteronomy* and his *Harmony of the Pentateuch.*

Viret. In a book on the nature of the study of history in the latter part of the sixteenth century, the Marxist historian, Claude Gilbert Dubois, pays considerable attention to Viret's Biblical vision of history and in so doing brings to light the remarkable economic discernment of our Swiss reformer.[31] Dubois' analysis is concentrated on the study of Viret's masterpiece in apologetics, *Le monde a l'empire et le monde de'moniacle.*[32] This book, says Dubois, could well be considered a treatise in economics written some two hundred years in advance of its time. Though in total disagreement with Viret's theocentric conservatism, Dubois is nonetheless outspoken in his admiration of our author's perception of contemporary economic currents. For Viret saw in the anarchical monopolistic capitalism developing before his indignant gaze a growing practical opposition to God's law and the rise of a thoroughly anti-Christian society. Viret saw in the progressive attachment of many of his contemporaries to material wealth (a fascination severed from all sense of stewardship and of accountability to God for the use of one's riches), a particularly vile form of idolatry where the rapidity of growth in opulence was in direct proportion to the loss of religion and morality. This is how Dubois expresses Viret's preoccupations:

> Behind the official public laws which are supposed to govern society one can discern the existence of those hidden perverse principles of our fallen nature that have now come to be officially accepted by society which imposes as the norm of a new morality the perverted rules of a chaotic nature.[33]

Viret directed a continual polemic against the heresies of the Church of Rome and the social abuses they engendered. But here his polemic is not only directed at the unproductive accumulation of wealth by the Church of Rome but against those incoherent *evangelicals* of his time who saw in the process of the *Reformation* a liberation from the historical constraints of a partly Christianized society and thus refused all submission to the social and economic disciplines implied by the law of God. It was this godless antinomianism, often to be seen in what he called *deformed* (rather than *Reformed)* Christians, that Viret attacked with biting irony. He saw an expression of this anti-social behavior in the *nouveaux riches* who had been quick to forget their modest origins and glory in their recent prosperity, often acquired at the expense of the poorer classes who had been impoverished by the new economic order founded on monopolistic speculation. Dubois writes:

> Viret's indignation has a theological base — these Christians have betrayed that spirit of poverty which characterized the apostles; but it

---

[31.] Claude-Gilbert Dubols, *La conception de l'histoire en France au XVIe siècle (1560-1610),* (Paris, 1977).

[32.] idem., *Le monde à l'empire et le monde démoniacle fait par dialogues* (Genève 1561).

[33.] Claude-Gilbert Dubois, *op. cit.,* 442.

also bears a social character — this sterile and unproductive wealth provokes the economic enslavement of the poor to the newly enriched ruling class. What this 16th century economist reproaches the Roman Church for is that its accumulation of riches had the effect of freezing its wealth in unproductive activities rather than letting it circulate freely in the money market where eventually it would also come to benefit the poorer classes.

And he asks,

What is the true character of the social degradation Viret perceives in the history of his time? Its origin is theological in nature, linked as it is to human sin. It manifests itself immorally by the perversion of the created order. But it takes on the modern form of a specifically economic scandal: a perverted economic order, a unethical distribution of riches, provoked by the circulation of wealth in one direction only, its accumulation in the hands of a few. Such are the signs of the corruption that reigns in the world today.[34]

Viret writes:

The greatest evil that can be imagined is when the public purse is impoverished and individual men wealthy. This is an evident sign that the commonwealth is in an unhealthy condition, that public policy is in weak and incapable hands and that the state is under the domination of thieves and bandits who make of it their prey.[35]

For Viret such a cultivation of sterile wealth represents nothing less than an iniquitous pact with the Prince of this fallen world. It is nothing less than idolatry, the cult of the creature and the forgetting of the Creator. Such an egotistical cumulative concentration of wealth runs completely counter to the Biblical doctrines of stewardship, of charity, and of personal sacrifice. In itself it is a clear indication of the decadence of a society and calls forth future purifying social disasters and divine judgments. For the economic mechanisms which lead to such an unfruitful concentration of wealth in the hands of a financial oligarchy prepares the way for those social and political catastrophes which will inevitably destroy such an amoral and irresponsible ruling class. For this infernal cycle of economic injustice must of necessity breed revolution. Economic oppression has as direct origin an inordinate desire for the accumulation of wealth but, in the long run, it must produce popular impatience. And such a feeling of social frustration, when it becomes conscious, ends in revolt. For Viret very lucidly perceived, and here the Marxist Dubois parts ways with him, that sedition cannot be constructive. Viret saw very clearly that this new oligarchy made abundant use of its monopolistic domination of the apparatus of the state to appropriate the riches of the whole nation by disrupting the natural circulation of wealth in the usual channels of production and exchange. For Viret, this stifling of the economic

---

[34.] *ibid.*, 453.
[35.] *Le monde à l'empire et le monde démoniacle fait par dialogues*, 156.

blood flow of industrial production and commercial exchange by a parasitical oligarchy must be broken if an equitable distribution of wealth is to be reestablished and the economic health of the society restored. In spite of his explicit opposition, both to Viret's social and political conservatism and to his Christian pessimism as to the benefits to be drawn from revolutionary action, Dubois at the close of his analysis of Pierre Viret's diagnosis of the economic evils of his time (and ours!) exclaims:

> Is it not indeed extraordinary that Viret, taking as his point of departure a number of vague theological propositions, ... should manifest such a sure sense of historical judgment, such precision in his economic analysis of the trends of his time and so marvelous a perspicuity in his analysis of the new economic mechanisms which were transforming society before his very eyes?[36]

But Viret's *vague theological propositions* are not as sterile as Dubois imagines. We here see the wonderful practical and intellectual wisdom that comes from a long-standing meditation of God's law, particularly, in this instance, with regard to the law's economic implications. And if Viret sees all too well, in the outworking of the principles of evil the judgments of God towards a rebellious and ungrateful world, he on the other hand, shows us all the more clearly the blessings which flow from faithful obedience to God's commandments. Speaking of the blessings and judgments being so clearly worked out before his attentive gaze, he writes:

> If we but consider what the grace of God has in our time manifested through the renewed revelation of his Holy Gospel and the restoration of letters and of every excellent discipline that has followed, we can without hesitation call our age, the age of gold and affirm that, since the time of the Apostles, none have been so blessed as we are today. But if, on the contrary, we oppose our malice and ungratefulness to God's abundant goodness and to the grace he so generously offers us, then we can certainly call this age, an age of iron and consider ourselves the most miserable of men who have ever lived under heaven's implacable dome.[37]

This brief evocation of the astonishing life and labors of Pierre Viret, that faithful servant of Almighty God who all his life labored to bring every thought of his contemporaries captive to the obedience of Jesus Christ and of his word, makes it absolutely plain that R. J. Rushdoony stands squarely in that Biblical tradition which manifests to the world what is without a doubt the most vigorous and the most fruitful heritage of the church of the living God.

[36.] Claude-Gilbert Dubois, *op. cit.*, 459.

[37.] *idem.*, *Le monde à l'empire et le monde démoniacle fait par dialogues*, 271.

Jean-Marc Berthoud, who lives in Lausanne, Switzerland, holds a Bachelor of Arts with Honors degree from the University of the Witwatersrand (Johannesburg) in the Republic of South Africa. He is the editor of the review Résister et Construire, *President of the* Associaton vaudoise de Parents chrétiens *in Switzerland, and of the* Association Création, Bible et Science *and is the author of numerous articles and a number of books.*

The Influence of German Biblical Criticism on Muslim Apologetics in the Nineteenth Century

Christine Schirrmacher

This present article has been written in remembrance of the suffering of R.J. Rushdoony's Armenian family from Islamic persecution:

> Let me add that a powerful factor in my childhood were the stories by escapees of Turkish atrocities against Christians.[1]

The aim of this paper is to trace the development of a new Muslim view of Christianity in the nineteenth century, which still has an enormous impact on today's Muslim apologetical works. The composition of anti-Christian books has changed in character due to the achievement of a different view of Christian dogmas and Christianity itself in the nineteenth century.[2]

Background

The development of Muslim-Christian polemics dates back to an event in the middle of the nineteenth century. On the tenth and eleventh of April in 1854, we find ourselves in the schoolroom of the British missionary agency, Church Missionary Society (CMS) in Agra, India, among several hundred Muslims and Europeans, mostly Christian missionaries, but also a few government officials of the British colonial power. They had all gathered to listen to a public debate initiated by the Muslim community of Agra. The debate was carried out between the German missionary, Karl Gottlieb Pfander (1803-1865), coming out of the pietistic movement in Württemberg, Swabia, and an Indian Muslim Shî'î theologian, Rahmatullâh Ibn Khalîl al-'Uthmânî al-Kairânawî (1818-1891).[3] Despite the fact that this debate took place nearly 150 years ago, both of the opponents are still well remembered in the Muslim world today pertaining to matters of the dialogue. The subject of discussion at this public debate, which lasted for two days, was mainly the deviation of the Christian Scriptures (tahrîf).[4]

[1.] From a letter by R. J. Rushdoony printed in John Graham Child, *Biblical Law in the Theology of R. J. Rushdoony: A Systematic Theological Analysis and Appreciation*, Master of Theology (University of South Africa, 1985), 323.

[2.] The following text is based on material of my dissertation, C. Schirrmacher, *Mit den Waffen des Gegners, Christlich-Muslimische Kontroversen im 19. und 20. Jahrhundert, dargestellt am Beispiel der Auseinandersetzung um Karl Gottlieb Pfander's 'mîzân al-haqq' und Rahmatullâh ibn Khalîl al-'Uthmânî al-Kairânawîs 'zhâr al-haqq' und der Diskussion über das Barnabasevangelium* (Berlin, 1992).

[3.] For a more detailed description of the debate see *e.g.* A. A. Powell, *Contact and Controversy between Islam and Christianity in Northern India 1833-1857: The Relations between Muslims and Protestant Missionaries in the North-Western Provinces and Oudh* (unpublished Ph. D. thesis) (London, 1983), 273 f.

[4.] Arabic theological terms in parentheses.

The challenger of the debate in 1854 was the Muslim theologian al-Kairânawî, who intended to publicly demonstrate the inferiority of Christianity and make it clear once and for all that Muslims should not be shaken in their faith because of the proclamation of the Christian creed by Protestant missionaries in India in the past decades.

India had been opened to Protestant Christian missionary activities by a decree of the British Parliament in 1813, and the first Anglican Bishop was secretly consecrated on May 8, 1814 in Lambeth Palace, Calcutta.[5] In 1832-1833, non-British missionary agencies were allowed to follow and began to establish their net of Christian missions all over India, more or less officially supported by the Britains. It is interesting enough that the Shî'î al-Kairânawî represented himself in 1854 as the defender of the Muslim religion and obviously was accepted as such by the whole Muslim community.

Although it was planned to extend the discussion to subjects of the Trinity (tathlîth), the Qur'ân being the Word of God and the sending of the prophet Muhammad, the debate did not proceed further than the deviation of the Christian Scriptures. The discussion centered on this point of controversy: al-Kairânawî insisted that the Christian scriptures had been abrogated, and tried to prove this with examples taken out of the Bible itself, while the Christian missionaries persistently affirmed the integrity of the Old and New Testament. After two days the opponents separated and "both sides claimed the victory."[6] Also, a few conversions to Christianity took place following the debate. Besides the well-known Safdar 'Alî,[7] who was baptized in 1864, perhaps the most famous Muslim convert to Christianity in India had been 'Imâd ud-Dîn (ca. 1830-1900), who was baptized in 1866, and ordained as an Anglican priest in 1872.[8] He had been involved in mosque-preaching against Christian missionary work before, and afterwards wrote several apologetical works against Islam such as the famous book *Guidance for Muslims* (hidâyat al-muslimîn) or *Inquiry into the Faith* (tahqîq al-imân).

But why is this 1854 debate of such significance? Have there not been many more debates before and up until the present which have concentrated again and again on the main points of encounter between Islam and Christianity, like the deviation of the Christian Scriptures (tahrîf)?

[5] H. H. Dodwell, ed., *The Cambridge History of India* (New Delhi, 1932), 6:124.

[6] E. Stock, "The C.M.S. Missions to Mohammedans," *The Muslim World*, 2(1912), 128; W. H. T. Gairdner, *The Reproach of Islam* (London, 1909), 248.

[7] The story of Safdar 'Ali's conversion to Christianity appeared in *Church Missionary Intelligencer*, 2 NS (July 1866), 215-221. Parts of his own report of his conversion are published in D. R. Paul, *Lights in the World*, Life Sketches of Maulvi Safdar Ali and the Rev. Janni Alli [sic] (Lucknow, 1969), 20-23, 28-30.

[8] The German magazine of the Basle Mission Society EMM (*Evangelisches Missions-Magazin*) published the story of his conversion under the title "A Mohammedan brought to Christ, being the Autobiography of a Native Clergyman in India" 14(1871), 397-412, being probably a summary of his own tract, in Urdu, dealing with his conversion which was republished in 1957 in Lahore and 1978 in Vanyambadi.

The 1854 Agra-debate is a historical milestone. Experts of the religious situation of India in the nineteenth century have asserted: "... there was in these days no debate on the scale of the high drama of the Rahmatullâh-Pfander debates of the 1850s."[9] I will attempt to analyze the significance of this Muslim-Christian debate in India and its effects on future Muslim apologetical works.

Significance of Place and Time

Concerning the nineteenth century onwards, Jacques Waardenburg has written:

> [W]e see another period of confrontation, now mostly political, between Muslim states and the expanding West, heir to Christian tradition. In this time we witness a growing polemics of Islam, at first linked with the national movements, against religions like Christianity, Hinduism and Judaism ....[10]

This is perfectly true for India: in the nineteenth century, Agra, the former symbol of the Mughal power, developed into one of the centers of Muslim learning and culture in India. The British government transformed it into their administration center of the North-West-Provinces. In addition, the British government allowed foreign mission agencies to enter the country. Especially in Agra, mostly British missionaries were stationed and they opened a huge orphanage after a disastrous famine in 1837. Several children were baptized as Christians, so that the growing influence of the Christian mission was universally recognized. In Agra itself, several polemical Christian books against the Muslim creed had been published.[11] All of these facts made the Muslim population extremely aware of the presence of Westerners and missionaries as an instrument of British colonialism.

So we find ourselves in the heat of Christian-Muslim tensions in Agra in the middle of the nineteenth century: the Muslim "ulamâ" felt threatened by the presence of European Christian missionaries, and during the 1840s and 1850s underwent a severe crisis due to the decline of values of their own religion and culture. Different parties gathered in the middle of the nineteenth century in Agra and various lines intersected at this historical turning point: 1) The representatives of India's colonial power, being Great Britain, the protector of the European missionaries; 2) The German pietist and Protestant missionary Pfander himself, his co-workers and perhaps a few of his

---

[9.] N. Gupta, *Delhi Between Two Empires 1803-1931, Society, Government and Urban Growth* (Delhi, 1981), 79.

[10.] J. Waardenburg, "World Religions as Seen in the Light of Islam," in ed., A. T. Welch, P. Cachia, *Islam: Past Influence and Present Challenge* (Edinburgh, 1979), 248.

[11.] See A. A. Powell, "Maulânâ Rahmat Allâh Kairânawî and Muslim-Christian Controversy in India in the Mid-19th Century," *Journal of the Royal Asiatic Society*, 20(1976), 42-63.

converts; 3) Representatives of the Anglican church, who were neither against the debate nor wholeheartedly for it. Thomas Valpy French (1825-1891) should be named, who later became the first Anglican bishop of Lahore. He himself was not overly convinced of the benefit or the necessity of open encounter and proselytizing, but having been challenged by the Muslim theologians, was determined to defend the integrity of the Bible;[12] 4) Roman Catholic missionaries in Agra, who obviously disliked the work of their Protestant colleagues and materially supported Muslims who helped them to refute the Protestant missionaries; and 5) The Muslim audience, including Shî'îs and Sunnis, while the Shî'î theologian al-Kairânawî prepared himself to defend the Muslim creed against Christian mission with the help of Dr. Muhammad Wazîr Khân, having worked since 1851 in a British medical hospital. He had received parts of his medical training in Great Britain where he collected material in order to prove Christianity false.

Significance of Individuals Involved in the Controversy

Karl Gottlieb Pfander (1803-1865)

The German missionary Karl Gottlieb Pfander, who was involved in the controversy, was a few decades after his death still considered as "the greatest of all missionaries to Mohammedans"[13] or "one of the most interesting figures among the Missionaries to Muhammedans of the nineteenth century."[14]

In the West, he remained nevertheless quite unknown until the very present, but especially his controversial book *Balance of Truth* (mîzân al-haqq) is still a current topic of debate in the Muslim world today. This apologetical work, written in 1829, originally in German[15] in refutation of Islam, intends to convince its readers of the supreme values of Christianity, mostly by defending the integrity of the Old and New Testaments and refuting the Muslim charge of the deviation of the Christian Scriptures (tahrîf). After its first publication in 1831 in Armenian, it was quickly translated into at least half a dozen Muslim languages, including, *e.g.*, Urdu (1840), Persian (1835), Turkish (1862), and Arabic (1865)[16] and has had an enormous influence. This

---

[12.] S. Neill, *A History of Christianity in India, 1707-1858* (Cambridge, 1985), 344.

[13.] Church Missionary Society, ed., *One Hundred Years, Being the Short History of the Church Missionary Society* (London, 1898), 78.

[14.] Translated from: J. Richter, *Mission und Evangelisation im Orient* (Gütersloh [1908], 1930), 71.

[15.] The original handwritten text is still to be found in the archives of the Basle Mission Society headquarter (Basler Mission), Switzerland.

[16.] In Turkey, where Pfander was missionary from 1858-1865, "the circulation of the Mîzân seems to have brought matters to a crisis..." (*Pfander's letter of 16th Sept. 1862 to the CMS*, Doc. No. 63a; archives of Heslop Room/University of Birmingham). The Ottoman government resolved to expel all missionary agencies in consequence of the baptism of several converts to Christianity by Pfander and his co-workers in 1864.

book *Balance of Truth* (mîzân al-haqq) still is both quoted and refuted by Muslim apologists today. It has remained a subject of controversy in the Muslim world. Twelve years after Pfander's death, a participant of the Agra-debate of 1854 wrote: "He has passed away, but the stir and movement he excited has not passed ..."[17]

Balance of Truth (mîzân al-haqq), the "standard work of encounter between Christianity and Islam"[18] was used by generations of Christian missionaries as an apologetical tool to refute Islam, and for this reason was reprinted many times up to the present. Despite the fact that we also hear severe critiques concerning the work, especially in the twentieth century,[19] we can date the last Arabic and English reprints back to the year 1986,[20] and these reprints are still used today for missionary activities among Muslims.

The author of the book, Karl Gottlieb Pfander, having been stationed as missionary of the British mission agency CMS in India from 1837-1857, was requested on the tenth of April, 1854, by Muslim theologians of Agra to publicly defend the Christian dogma of the integrity of the Bible. In fact, it was he himself who had opened the discussion by public preaching on the bazars, and by writing and distributing books for several years. It should also be noted that Pfander tried to prove the high value which the Qur'ân attributes to the Bible with the help of Qur'ânic statements. He also quoted Muslim commentators in order to hint at the difference of their judgement about Christianity: "... the Christians were trying to show that in the Qur'ân itself Muhammad shows respect for Christianity and veneration for its beliefs and teachings."[21]

Rahmatullâh Ibn Khalîl al-'Uthmânî al-Kairânawî (1818-1891)

Nevertheless, Pfander's opponent is much more interesting for the theme of Muslim-Christian historical encounter.

The Shî'î theologian Rahmatullâh Ibn Khalîl al-'Uthmânî was engaged in the battle against the presence of Christian missionaries in India from the beginning of the 1850s, and in 1855 had already written three polemical works against Christianity in order to defend Islam, probably with the help of

---

[17] H. Birks, *The Life and Correspondence of Thomas Valpy French, First Bishop of Lahore* (London, 1895), 1: 70.

[18] Translated from H. R. Flachsmeier, *Geschichte der evangelischen Weltmission* (Giessen, 1963), 446.

[19] See *e.g.*, L. L. Vander Werff, *Christian Mission to Muslims: The Record, Anglican and Reform Approaches in India and the Near East 1800-1938* (Pasadena, 1977), 42; E. Kellerhals, *Der Islam. Seine Geschichte, seine Lehre, sein Wesen* (Basel, 1956, 2nd ed.), 334 f.

[20] The publishers of the 1986 English edition wrote in their introduction to the book: "Perhaps the way of discussion seems questionable to some theologians in our century, but until today the book touches the central points in sincere dialogue between Muslims and Christians." "The Publishers," *Introduction*, in C. G. Pfander, D. D., *The Mîzân-ul-Haqq, Balance of Truth* (Villach, 1986).

[21] H. G. Dorman, *Toward Understanding Islam* (Edinburgh, 1948), 31.

the Bengali physician Muhammad Wazîr Khân. al-Kairânawî and Wazîr Khân belong to the most outstanding figures of Indian Muslim defense against Christian mission in the nineteenth century. They came into contact at the beginning of the 1850s in connection with their apologetical work. In 1854 both of them took part in the public Agra debate, al-Kairânawî being the challenger and the leader of the discussion, Muhammad Wazîr Khân acting as interpreter between the Urdu- and English-speaking participants.

The Influence of al-Kairânawî on Nineteenth Century Muslim Views of Christianity

al-Kairânawî's influence is not restricted to this single event in Agra. This was only a prelude to his future impact, which is due to his written works. When it comes to Muslim apologetics, al-Kairânawî certainly comes to mind: The reason for this is his famous book *Demonstration of the Truth* (izhâr al-haqq), which he composed as a response to Pfander's *Balance of Truth* (mîzân al-haqq). Written in Arabic in 1867 by request of the Ottoman sultan Abdülaziz I (1861-1876),[22] the book has seen several translations into Turkish (1876/1877), French (1880), English (ca. 1900), Urdu (1968), *i.e.*, into almost the same languages as Pfander's *Balance of Truth* (mîzân al-haqq) has been translated. Like *Balance of Truth*, the book *Demonstration of the Truth* (izhâr al-haqq) has been reprinted until the present. In 1964 a new edition came out, supervised by the Department for Islamic Affairs of the Kingdom of Morocco, and a foreword was added by the adab-professor 'Umar ad-Dasûqî. The last Arabic editions date from the year 1978; one of the two was authorized by the late Shaikh 'Abd al-Halîm Mahmûd of al-Azhar-University, Cairo. In 1989 a short version in English appeared, published by Ta-Ha Publishers in London.

Only a few polemical Muslim works have become as famous as al-Kairânawî's *Demonstration of the Truth* (izhâr al-haqq). It has been stated, "The first great classic of modern Muslim polemic has never been superseded."[23]

Ignaz Goldziher reported that during his visit in 1877 in Damascus, everybody was talking of al-Kairânawî's *Demonstration of the Truth*.[24]

[22.] Ahmad Hijâzî as-Saqqâ, ed., Rahmat Allâh al-Hindî, *izhâr al-haqq* (Cairo, 1978), 29-30. al-Kairânawî had to go into exile because the British government suspected him of having participated in the anti-British revolt of 1857. al-Kairânawî fled to Mecca, and when the Ottoman sultan made his pilgrimage (hajj) to Mecca at the beginning of the 1860s, he was informed about the events in India of 1854. al-Kairânawî had to stay in Mecca until his death in 1891.

[23.] H. G. Dorman, *op. cit.*, p. 44.

[24.] Goldziher wrote: "Während meines Aufenthaltes in der umajjadischen Chalifenstadt übte eine enorme Zugkraft auf das Lesepublikum aus das arabisch geschriebene polemische Werk izhâr al-haqq von dem indischen Muhammedaner Sheikh Rahmat Allâh gegen die mîzân al-haqq betitelte Missions- und Controversschrift eines englischen Predigers des Evangeliums, welcher mit den Geschützen christlicher Theologie die Bollwerke des Islam erschüttern wollte." I. Goldziher, "Ueber muhammedanische Polemik gegen Ahl al-kitâb," *Zeitschrift der Deutschen Morgenländischen Gesellschaft*, 32 (1878), 343-344.

Undoubtedly, the book played a key role for Muslim polemics in the past but it is still currently on the "top ten" of Muslim apologetical works. Concerning the significance of the book, Georges C. Anawati wrote in 1969: "C'est le grand ouvrage de base qui a servi et continue à servir d'arsenal pour les apologistes musulmans de la fin du siècle jusqu'à nos jours,"[25] and again in 1981: "... et aujourd'hui encore, il reste le livre par excellence où les musulmans traditionalistes et peu ouverts au christianisme, puisent leurs arguments."[26]

Concerning *Demonstration of the Truth* (izhâr al-haqq) it was stated in 1968: "The editor of the Urdu version has expressed the strong opinion that nothing written in the intervening hundred years on the theme of Islam and Christianity has replaced the books which were generated in the mind of Maulânâ Rahmat Allâh Kairanawî by the situation of extreme tension which faced the 'ulamâ' of northern India in the first half of the nineteenth century."[27]

The popularity of this apologetical work is also due to the fact that only a very cautious Shî'î coloring can be found in the book. As far as it can be seen in the different editions form 1867 onwards, the reason for this is not any revision, but rather the original tone of al-Kairânawî himself, who only once hinted at his own Shî'î background when dealing with hadîth. Therefore it could become the standard work of Muslim apologetics as well as in "orthodox" circles like al-Azhar.

In order to realize the influence of *The Demonstration of the Truth* (izhâr al-haqq), it can be noted that the Sunni nineteenth century "reform-wing" theologian Rashîd Ridâ made extensive use of al-Kairânawî's book when dealing with Christianity. Coming to the question of Muhammad's mission, he quoted in the famous 'Abduh/Ridâ Qur'ân commentary "Exegesis of the wise Qur'ân" (tafsîr al-qur'ân al-hakîm) about 60 pages from al-Kairânawî's *Demonstration of the Truth* (izhâr al-haqq).[28] Another name of a Muslim polemicist, making use of it, which should be mentioned is Muhammad Muhammad Abû Zahra.[29] In his famous *Lectures on Christianity* (muhâdarât fî n-nasrânîya) he made use of al-Kairânawîs commentaries on the Christian creed.[30]

[25.] G. C. Anawati, "Polémique, Apologie et Dialogue Islamo-Chrétiens," Positions Classiques Médiévales et Positions Contemporaines, *Euntes Docete*, 22 (1969), 420.

[26.] G. C. Anawati, *Les grands courants de la pensée religieuse musulmane dans l'Égypte comtemporaine*, in: G. C. Anawati, M. Borrmans, *Tendences et courants dans l'Islam arabe contemporain*, vol. 1: Égypte et Afrique du Nord, Entwicklung und Frieden, Wissenschaftliche Reihe, (München, 1982), 26: 58.

[27.] A. A. Powell, *Maulânâ Rahmat Allâh Kairânawî and Muslim-Christian Controversy in India in the Mid-19th Century*, loc. cit., 63.

[28.] Muhammad Rashîd Ridâ, ed., *tafsîr al-qur'ân al-hakim* (Cairo [1347], 1928, first ed.), 9: 231-293.

[29.] This is mentioned by the editor of one of the newest editions of izhâr al-haqq: Ahmad Hijâzî as-Saqqâ (ed.), Rahmat Allâh al-Hindî, *izhâr al-haqq, op. cit.*, 33

[30.] Quotations of al-Kairânawî by Muhammad Muhammad Abû Zahra in his *muhâdarât fî-n-nasrânîya* (Cairo, 1966, 3rd ed.), 32

Reasons for the Influence of izhâr al-haqq

The very reason for the immense influence of al-Kairânawî's book *Demonstration of the Truth* (izhâr al-haqq) can be found in his developing of a new method to prove Islam to be the only true religion: it is quite obvious that al-Kairânawî does not restrict the defense of Islam to a mere devaluation of the Christian creed or to a praise of Islam. al-Kairânawî took advantage of the new orientation of European theology which had taken place especially during the nineteenth century. From a former conservative standpoint in regard to the integrity of the Christian Scriptures, European theology had undergone a rapid change to a more and more critical standpoint regarding the reliability of historical and textual questions especially since the nineteenth century. Critical and liberal standpoints found their way into universities and churches. In this evolution, Germany was the forerunner for the whole Christian Occident. Numerous theologically liberal works appeared and found their way into the Muslim world rather quickly.

al-Kairânawî was ostensibly the very first apologist in the Muslim world who referred to these books and Bible commentaries in order to fight Christianity with its own weapons. For the first time, he used different works of famous European theologians who were influenced by liberalism and historical criticism of European theology of the nineteenth century. During the Agra debate, al-Kairânawî quoted these representatives of liberalism in order to show the conservative missionaries that Christian theology had already produced evidence that the Bible is unreliable.

European Theology and Philosophy Influences Muslim Apologetics

This is not the only example where the Muslim world borrowed fruits of European theology or philosophy which affirmed Islam. Before the nineteenth century, there had been a movement in European theology which was called rationalism. Representatives of German rationalism, *e.g.*, Karl Friedrich Bahrdt (1741-1792) or the famous Heinrich Eberhard Gottlob Paulus (1761-1851) maintained that Jesus Christ has been crucified, but they denied that he had really died on the cross, a standpoint which is again an "outside" position today. Bahrdt writes at the end of the nineteenth century:

> This is my opinion on this last part of the history of Jesus. Jesus has been put to death: he underwent all the sufferings of an evil-doer, he endured the suffering of death, but he overcame death — he came from death to life — he came out of the mausoleum... on the third day after having been put to death ... and he has shown himself to his disciples as somebody being revived from the dead.[31]

[31.] Translated from: K. F. Bahrdt, *Ausführungen des Plans und Zweks [sic] Jesu* (Berlin, 1784-1793), 10: 187.

It is possible, even if not probable, that the Ahmadîya standpoint (the Ahmadîya being a Muslim sect of Indian-Pakistani origin) of Jesus having died a natural death in India after he survived his crucifixion, did not originate in Islam itself, but was fostered by developments in Europe like rationalism; Muslim apologists claimed: "European theologians and scientists have proven that Jesus Christ survived the crucifixion."

Some Christian university theologians even went so far as the climax of theological liberalism, which is, historically considered, connected with the Enlightenment, that they neglected Jesus as a historical figure or at least his deity or his being part of the Trinity. Muslim apologists have used these theories as proofs for their old affirmation that according to Sura 4,157-158 Jesus never died on the cross, even if he was perhaps crucified, which they consider doubtful.

The Gospel of Barnabas Confirms Muslim Apologists

Doubts of European theologians and philosophers concerning the death and resurrection of Jesus Christ or concerning the reliability of the four canonical gospels also played a key role when the "Gospel of Barnabas" was defended in numerous books and pamphlets by Muslim apologists as the only true Gospel of Jesus Christ, mostly in the twentieth century. Muslims had mostly taken over positive statements about the value of the "Gospel of Barnabas" by European critics of conservative theology of the eighteenth and nineteenth century, while at the same time Christian missionaries tried to prove that it is impossible to date this gospel back to the first centuries A. D. The "Gospel of Barnabas" proves that Jesus Christ did not die on the cross; Judas was transformed into the likeness of Jesus and crucified, while everybody thought he was Jesus himself; so the Qur'ân is again affirmed in its refutation of the crucifixion of Jesus.

The Qur'ân is confirmed by "objective," "scientific" results: Muslim apologists name European theologians or philosophers like the well-known English deist John Toland (1670-1722), who positively mentioned the announcement of Muhammad in the "Gospel of Barnabas." Muslim apologists concentrate on European authors who, on the one hand trace the "Gospel of Barnabas" back to the first centuries and herewith accept its value and who, at the same time, doubt and critique the integrity of the Bible and the inspiration of the Old and New Testaments.[32]

[32.] *e.g.*, J. Toland, *Christianity Not Mysterious* (London, 1696) had a rationalistic understanding of the wonders narrated in the Bible. In his work *Nazarenus* he attributes at the same time a great probability to the "Gospel of Barnabas" going back to the very first centuries A. D.: J. Toland, *Nazarenus or Jewish, Gentile and Mahometan Christianity* (London, 1718). He defended the "Gospel of Barnabas" against the common charge from the Christian side as being a willful forgery of a renegade of the Middle Ages: "How great … is the ignorance of those, who make this an original invention of the Mahometans." J. Toland, *Nazarenus, op. cit.*, 17, or: "After this mature examination I coul'd safely say, that this Gospel might in the main be the antient 'Gospel of Barnabas'…." J. Toland, *Tetradymus* (London, 1720), 148.

It is possible that al-Kairânawî himself "brought" the "Gospel of Barnabas" to the Moslem world by mentioning it for the first time in 1854 in his Urdu work i'jâz-i 'Isâwî[33] and afterwards in *Demonstration of the Truth* (izhâr al-haqq) from 1867 onwards as an old Christian gospel which foretells the coming of the prophet Muhammad. In the middle of the nineteenth century, the "Gospel of Barnabas" was not even published as a whole. Only a few fragments were known to the Western world when al-Kairânawî used it as a weapon against the Christian rejection of Muhammad, who had been foretold from the beginning of revelation. It is quite probable that Muhammad Rashîd Ridâ, who defended the gospel as the only surviving reliable gospel of the time of Jesus, and who published the first Arabic edition of the "Gospel of Barnabas" in 1908 under the title *True Gospel* (al-injîl as-sahîh), was led to this gospel through the work of al-Kairânawî. Several translations have appeared since 1908 to promote this "only true Gospel of Jesus Christ" (Urdu 1916, English 1916, Persian 1927, Indonesian 1969, Dutch 1990, German 1994).

Changes of Muslim Apologetics are Due to Developments in European Theology

In the nineteenth century a new wave of criticism emerged in Europe and quickly found its way into the Muslim world. In European universities all miracles reported in the Old and New Testaments were called into question, historical events were doubted, the formulation of Christology, Trinity, and the deity of Jesus Christ, his crucifixion and resurrection were disputed from their very foundation. All these doubts and critical remarks of European theology entered the Muslim world and were enthusiastically taken as proofs of the traditional Muslim view of a corrupted Christian Bible. This way of arguing against the reliability of the Old and New Testaments has marked the form of controversy especially since al-Kairânawî.

During the Agra debate, this method of controversy was used for the first time. al-Kairânawî confronted the theologically conservative missionary Pfander and his friends in 1854 with the newest results of European critical research. Pfander, who had already left Europe in 1825 as a missionary, had not witnessed the important developments which had taken place in European theology in the nineteenth century. Moreover, the leaders of the conservative Basel Mission Society (Basler Missionsgesellschaft), where Pfander was educated from 1821-1825, had allowed their pupils to visit the theological

---

[33.] Rahmatullâh Ibn Khalîl al-'Uthmânî al-Kairânawî, *i'jâz-i 'Isâwî* (Agra, 1853/Delhi, 1876).

seminary at Basel, but had restricted its influence on the candidates.[34] David Friedrich Strauss' world-famous book *Das Leben Jesu* (*The Life of Jesus*) was not published until 1835, when Pfander had already been ten years abroad. As the Agra debate took place in 1854, Pfander had already suspected that his Muslim opponents were busily studying European theological works, but he either underestimated the far-reaching effects of these studies or he did not have enough knowledge himself of these new developments. Pfander wrote concerning his Muslim opponents: "... several of their friends in Delhi, have been for the last two or three years hard at work in studying the Bible, reading the controversial books we have published, and searching out our commentaries and critical writers ..., only to obtain material for refuting it."[35]

al-Kairânawî and Muhammad Wazîr Khân presented during the Agra debate the newest critical remarks on textual variations and on contradictions between different Biblical texts of the latest theories in Europe. al-Kairânawî seemingly inherited most of his material from Muhammad Wazîr Khân, who received part of his medical training in Great Britain where he came into contact with European theologically critical works. In addition, al-Kairânawî received the latest European works from the Roman Catholic missionaries in India, who strongly disliked the work of their Protestant colleagues.[36]

In several polemical works against Christianity in Agra and later on, the Muslim theologian al-Kairânawî presented, for the first time, the latest scientific research from Europe. Against this new sort of attack Pfander was helpless since his books responded to the traditional Muslim charges against Christianity and not to the European results of higher or lower criticism presented from the Muslim side.

Europe did not have the slightest idea about the effects of its theological evolution on the Near East. Protestant missions were comparatively new to the Muslim countries, only dating from the nineteenth century[37] in which a new branch of Christian mission was extended to the Muslim countries, apart from single attempts in former centuries as for example undertaken by Henry

---

[34.] Teachers of the Basel Mission Seminary thought about the lectures at Basel university, given from one of the most famous theologians of the nineteenth century and representative of Biblical criticism, Wilhelm Martin Lebrecht de Wette (1780-1849): "Doch trug man Bedenken, sie bei De-Wette hospitieren zu lassen und sie so in die historische Kritik einzuführen. Überhaupt fürchtete man, die Zöglinge möchten aus diesen Vorlesungen nicht denjenigen Gewinn davontragen, der dem Zeitaufwand entspräche," P. Eppler, *Geschichte der Basler Mission 1815-1899* (Basel, 1900), 16-17.

[35.] Undated letter, perhaps to Thomas Valpy French, participant of the Agra-debate 1854: H. Birks, *The Life and Correspondence of Thomas Valpy French, op. cit.*, 1: 71.

[36.] E. Stock, *The History of the Church Missionary Society: its Environment, its Men and its Work* (London, 1899-1916), 2: 171

[37.] The nineteenth century is called the "Missionsjahrhundert" (century of mission) in Europe because of the founding of numerous Protestant missionary agencies and seminaries for the education and sending of missionaries to foreign countries.

Martyn or Bartholomäus Ziegenbalg. It can be added here that after the debate, Pfander sought in Basel, European authors who were refuting these theories, but only in order to demonstrate to the Muslim polemicists that the standpoint of these theologians is only one part of the prism of European theology.[38]

Apart from the Agra debate, we are able to witness that al-Kairânawî developed this method of proving the corruption of the Bible with European voices. In his book *Demonstration of the Truth* (izhâr al-haqq), al-Kairânawî draws all the evidence from European sources he can procure: he quotes Luther's critical attitude concerning the pope and King Henry VIII of England, European critical remarks on the apostle Paul's devastating influence on early Christianity; he refers to doubts among theologians as to whether the epistles of Jacob or Judas belong to the original Biblical canon or not, he criticizes the forming of dogmas by the first Christian councils like Nicea about three hundred years after the death of Jesus Christ. Furthermore, he refers to doubts about the authorship of the books of Moses, Joshua, and Judges. When he comes to the genealogies of Christ, he detects "errors and contradictions," "absurdities" in the narrative of Elijah being fed by ravens, and he quotes commentaries on the Bible from Eichhorn, Horne, or Henry and Scott. I could continue with hundreds of contradictions al-Kairânawî "detects" between single Biblical texts.[39] In six thick volumes, *The Demonstration of the Truth* (izhâr al-haqq) served as a summary of all possible charges against Christianity and was therefore used after al-Kairânawî's death as a sort of encyclopedia, since al-Kairânawî extended the material of former polemicists like 'Ali Tabarî, Ibn Hazm or Ibn Taymiyya to a great extent.

European Theology Changes Muslim Views of Christianity

Here it is obvious that al-Kairânawî has changed the former Muslim view of the deviation of the Christian Scriptures (tahrîf) and the Muslim view of Christianity as a whole: The dogma of the deviation of the Christian Scriptures (tahrîf) should, according to al-Kairânawî, no longer be understood as mere single alterations in the texts of the Old and New

---

[38.] He asked for the books in a letter to his former school in Basel "... um den Mo-hammedanern, die sich mit denselben gar sehr brüsten, zu zeigen, daß diese Neologen und Pantheisten weit über den Koran hinausgehen und also gefährliche und schlechte Hilfsgenossen seien, teils um nachzuweisen, daß Strauß und Konsorten längst ihre Widerlegung gefunden haben ..." C. F. Eppler, *D. Karl Gottlieb Pfander, Ein Zeuge der Wahrheit unter den Bekennern des Islam* (Basel, 1888), 152.

[39.] It is true what H. G. Dorman states for the real apologetical literature until the present time: "Through most of this material there moves a strain of suspicion and re-sentment. In only a few of the books is there an open friendliness in the approach. For the most part the polemists are fighting hard to win a declared battle and to overthrow the enemy. There is surprisingly little difference from the classical polemical methods of the earlier centuries," H. G. Dorman, *op. cit.*, 113.

Testaments, which had crept into the texts throughout the process of copying them during the centuries. Apologists in former times only criticized certain Biblical dogmas such as the Trinity or the dogma of the deity of Jesus Christ as the Qur'ân itself does. al-Kairânawî expanded the Qur'ânic criticism of the corruption of the Bible to a much larger extent. Leading Muslim apologists now follow the example of al-Kairânawî's *Demonstration of the Truth* (izhâr al-haqq) and take over the "results" of the textual studies of European theologians. al-Kairânawî came to the conclusion that the Biblical texts are totally distorted, corrupted and unreliable in all their historical, dogmatical and narrative passages. This is for al-Kairânawî no matter of dispute, since the Christian "ulamâ" of Europe themselves admit the complete distortion of all Biblical texts. So al-Kairânawî and his followers feel confirmed in the traditional Muslim view that the Bible is corrupted just as the Qur'ân states: Muslim apologists had known this for centuries already, but now European theologians have confirmed it themselves through scientific studies in history, geology or archeology.

The effect of this use of European theology can be summarized: in today's Muslim apologetical works against Christianity, we find numerous results of the severe studies in textual exegesis and different sciences undertaken in the West. With this transformation of the dogma of the deviation of the Christian Scriptures (tahrîf) in Christianity and the acknowledgment of European theology serving as a proof for the Muslim statements, the whole Muslim view of Christianity has changed. In former times, only certain dogmas of Christianity had to be refuted, but Christianity as a whole contained the same message as Islam. Now Christianity seems to have been proven to be corrupted as a whole: if Christian scientists and theologians in the West determine that it is untenable to believe in this collection of fanciful stories and legends originating in heathenism or Greek platonic philosophy, it is no longer tenable to praise this revelation. Muslim apologists only take seriously what the religious authorities of Christianity have discovered about their own creed. In contrast to this great error, Islam is the religion of understanding and intelligence. The Islamic dogmas are clear, understandable and reasonable.

Furthermore, we witness that Muslim polemical works following the al-Kairânawî-Pfander battle always pursue this fundamental attitude: Christian theologians themselves admit, that the Old and New Testaments are not inspired by God as we have it today, but both parts of the Bible are full of errors, misconceptions, contradictions, absurdities, if not willful distortions. Thus Muslim theologians are confirmed in their interpretation of the Christian Scriptures.

We can witness this form of controversy today when it comes to Muslim apologetical works: Muhammad Rashîd Ridâ used the results of European theological studies in his Qur'ân commentary "tafsîr." For him the apostle, Paul, is especially guilty for having introduced heathenism into Christianity.

It was not until the council of Nicea in the year 325 A. D. that the dogma of Trinity and redemption through the crucifixion of Jesus were established. With this development, the dogma of the unity of God (tauhîd) was replaced by polytheism (shirk).[40] We witness the same tendency in Abû Zahras *Lectures on Christianity* (muhâdarât fî-n-nasrânîya): Jesus Christ himself preached monotheism, but this dogma was distorted by the influence of syncretism, new-platonic and Greek philosophy and Roman heathenism.[41] Ahmad Shalaby considers Christianity as a mixture of heathenism and of the convictions of the apostle, Paul,[42] and Jesus' miracles narrated in the four gospels as unreliable.[43]

Elwood M. Wherry remarks according to his personal view concerning the beginning of the twentieth century: "The Muslims were obliged to abandon their own works and endeavour to save the day by a counter-assault, in which they scrupled not to use the stock arguments of European infidelity in their effort to overthrow the authority of the Christian Scriptures. This characteristic has marked the Muslim method of controversy ever since."[44]

Summary

1. In the nineteenth century a Muslim-Christian debate took place far away from the traditional centers of Muslim learning. In Agra in 1854, probably for the first time, Muslim theologians used European critical works as proofs against Christian missionaries.

2. The nineteenth century marks a turning point when it comes to Muslim apologetics: the Muslims developed a completely new method to prove Christianity to be the "false religion" with the help of European sources being mainly Christian theological works (*e.g.*, Bible commentaries).

3. After the publication of al-Kairânawî's *Demonstration of the Truth* (izhâr al-haqq) this method of controversy became common among Muslim apologists such as Muhammad Rashîd Ridâ or Muhammad Muhammad Abû Zahra to prove the traditional charge of the deviation of the Christian Scriptures (tahrîf).

4. The deviation of the Christian Scriptures (tahrîf) is the center of Christian-Muslim apologetics of the nineteenth century (Christology or redemption is the center of apologetics in the twentieth century).

---

[40] Muhammad Rashîd Ridâ, *al-manâr* 10 (1325-1326), 386.
[41] Muhammad Muhammad Abû Zahra in his *muhâdarât fî-n-nasrânîya, op. cit.*, 11.
[42] Ahmad Shalaby, *muqâranat al-adyân*, Vol. 2: al-masîhîya, (Cairo, 1965, 2nd ed.), 64.
[43] *viz.* 62.
[44] E. M. Wherry, *The Mohammedan Controversy* (London, 1905), 2.

5. This leads to a new Muslim view of Christianity during the nineteenth century. The dogmas of Christianity are no longer distorted in fragments but rather as a whole.

Christine Schirrmacher, M. A. and Dr. Phil., both in Islamic Studies, Ph.D. at State University Bonn, Germany, is a visiting professor of Islamic studies in Philadelphia (USA) as well as lecturer at Independent Theological Seminary (STH) Basel (Switzerland) and author of a standard introduction to Islam.

The Solution to Our Social Dilemma:
Theoretical or Theocentric?

Man's problem is not his environment but sin, man's desire to be his own god, his own law and principle of ultimacy. Man cannot save himself, either by politics, works of law or morality, or by any other means. Jesus Christ is man's only savior. Man must live under God's law order in order to live freely and happily, but the law order cannot save man, nor will that law order long survive, if there be not a sizable body of believers whose life is the law of God.

R. J. Rushdoony, *The Foundations of Social Order*

Background

Man was created as a social creature. Shortly after he created man, God said, "It is not good that man should be alone; I will make him a helper comparable to him" (Gen. 2:18). God created Eve. Seeing her, Adam began to communicate with her saying, "This is now bone of my bones and flesh of my flesh; she shall be called *Woman* because she was taken out of man" (Gen. 2:23). Adam and Eve could now communicate with one another and, more importantly, with their Creator — God.

Sin brought great changes to the social order of man (Gen. 3). Man became totally depraved:

> What total depravity means is that the infection of depravity is total in man's being; i.e. every aspect of man's nature is corrupted and governed by his fall. The principle of the fall governs man's mind and will, his heart and his tongue, and his every thought and act is governed by this false religious principle which governs his being.[1]

Fallen Adam and Eve sought to blame others for their sin (Gen. 3:12,13), rather than accepting responsibility for their actions. Social relationships and society as a whole immediately became disordered. This climaxed within one generation in the murder of Abel by his brother Cain (Gen. 4:8). Man was not only at war with God but also with mankind. Lamech, a bigamist, killed a man and then sang about his action. Rushdoony comments, "It made no difference to Lamech whom he dealt with, a stranger or a son. If he were hurt or bruised, his vengeance would require death."[2] More importantly, Lamech evidences no guilt for his actions. Within a few generations "the Lord saw that the wickedness of man was great in the earth, and that every intent of the thoughts of his heart was only evil continually" (Gen. 6:5). Although man was not as

---

[1.] R. J. Rushdoony, *Revolt Against Maturity* (Fairfax, VA, 1977), 70.
[2.] *ibid.*, 99.

bad as he could be, his sinful nature was in every fiber of his being, including his thought life.

Scripture does not end on this note. God's eternal Son came to earth and became the elect's substitute in his active and passive obedience. Through the work of the Holy Spirit, God's people become a new creation in Christ Jesus by means of God-given repentance and faith. Social relationships can be restored. Problems, even great social problems, can be worked out.

The Contribution of Rushdoony

Providentially, God has allowed R. J. Rushdoony to live in a time of social disorder. On all sides we see the collapse of a society that was once rooted in the terms of God's word. In his writings, Rushdoony has addressed many evidences of the collapse of humanistic culture. Twenty-five years ago he wrote of some of the social indicators of this collapse:

> Material progress there has been, but man finds himself increasingly engaged in deadlier wars with the world and himself, facing deadly problems of air, earth, food and water pollution, and progressively suicidal in his own impulses.

> Much is said about the "communication gap," about the failure of young and old to communicate, and of the inability of any man to find common ground with other men. Again this loss of communications is a sign of the end of an age; the essential faith of an age, which binds man to man, has then lost its cohesive power, and, as a result, communication is lost.[3]

In the ensuing twenty-five or more years this societal breakdown has been exemplified time and again. The limits of this essay allow for only a few examples.

Social Erosion

First, a generation has been born and grown never knowing a time when abortion in the U. S. and in many other countries was illegal. Beginning with the 1973 *Roe v. Wade* decision, U. S. citizens could legally rid themselves of their unborn children. The Supreme Court, denying the clear teaching of Scripture (Ps. 51:5, 139:13ff; Lk. 2:41-44, etc.), declared its ignorance in determining the beginning of new human life. By its ruling the Court declared that life did not begin prior to birth. As a result, man was not at war only with those outside the nation or the family but now could legally be at war with members of his own family — unborn children. Women were on the frontlines of this war as they entered the abortion clinics and allowed their unborn child to be legally aborted. No doubt some went at the insistence of

---

[3] *idem.*, *The One and the Many* (Nutley, NJ, 1971), 368.

the father or perhaps at the insistence of their own father. Others went without the knowledge of the male God had established as their head.

More recently, euthanasia is becoming acceptable. Such acceptance is consistent with the legality of abortion. In our social upheaval the family is making war on itself. It is killing off its future — unborn children — and allowing its past — the elderly members — to legally be put to death. The present is all that matters in today's existentialist mindset.

A reaction to legal abortion has been the desire of some pro-life advocates to resort to murdering those who are actively involved in abortion. By implementing capital punishment, they have taken on themselves a responsibility that God has given civil government (Rom. 13:1-4). Early in Scripture, God makes it clear that individuals do not have the responsibility to carry out the death penalty. God's law is eternal. Thus, prior to the law being written down, Cain realized he deserved death: "... and it will happen that anyone who finds me will kill me" (Gen. 4:14b) for his murderous action. God would not allow this (v. 15). The only human inhabitants on earth at that time were Cain's parents, brothers, sisters, and perhaps nieces and nephews. No civil government existed at that time. God had not given family government the duty of capital punishment. Regarding this, Rushdoony's remarks are clear:

> The power of the family does not extend to the death penalty. As the cradle, nursery, and school of life, its function is restricted to the discipline of life. The death penalty is the function of the state. Because the family has such great powers, to give it also the power of death is to make it totalitarian. Since mankind in Cain's day was one family, father, mother, sons, and daughters, God at the very beginning restricted the power of the family in this area. It was more important to preserve the boundaries of the family's power than to bring judgement in time to a murderer.[4]

Individuals cannot assume to themselves the power of capital punishment.

Secondly, just as individuals are not to assume responsibility of civil government, neither is the civil government to usurp powers that God has given to other institutions, such as individuals, families and churches. This has brought immeasurable social disorder to society. Fathers have no need to care for their families when "Daddy" government can provide in their absence. There is little motivation to get a job when the paycheck may provide less money than a welfare check or housing subsidy. Accountability and responsibility are unnecessary words in the vocabulary of socialism, for the paychecks will arrive regularly without work or moral faithfulness.

The point is well made elsewhere in this book that charity is a family responsibility. If that fails, then the church is to step in. This is God's means

---

[4.] *idem.*, *Revolt Against Maturity*, 99.

of maintaining social order. The failure of families and church to exercise their God-given responsibility is evidenced in growing entitlement programs, decreased family capitalization due to increased taxation, and successive generations being on welfare rolls. As the young widows in Paul's day, many today have learned to be idle (1Tim. 5:13). This is in direct violation of God's command that man earn his living by the sweat of his brow (Gen. 3:19); that the head of the home is to provide for that household (1 Tim. 5:8); that we are to help others in need (Dt. 24:14,15,19, etc.); and that the church is to minister to the needy (Ac. 6:1ff).

Because it is antithetical to Biblical teaching, Rushdoony pointed out the ingredients for socialism and its certain failure:

> In order to have socialism, there must be a population of spoiled children who want a great father who can provide them with more than their parents can, take their parents off their hands, and protect them from the necessity of growing up. Whenever and wherever the family breaks down, socialism results as the substitute for the family. But socialism destroys itself, because it cannot truly replace the family, and, unless the family re-establishes its godly order, the result is chaos. There are not short-cuts to liberty. The godly family is basic to a free country.[5]

Thirdly, one cannot overlook the contribution the false doctrine of pluralism has made to social disorder. Pluralism teaches that all religions are to be accepted as equal within society. No religion can claim to be a basis for the law of a society or exert undue influence on a law structure. Of course, such thinking is impossible. A good example is the teaching regarding man's origin. Creation is not allowed instructional time because it is religiously (Christian) based. Instead, total instructional time is given to teaching that man evolved. However, that too is based on religion — the religion of humanism. Proof for evolution is non-existent; yet fallen man, desiring to be god (Gen. 3:5), has declared it to be valid.

Sadly, many within the church oppose the implementation of God's law in the civil realm. Their basis? Pluralism. Those within the church who support pluralism fail to realize that they are proclaiming anti-Christian teaching and are promoting a law structure that is anathema to godly social order. Supporters open the door for humanism to become the basis for law. Consequently, homosexuality is legal. Can incest and bestiality be far behind? If not, why not? A moral code based on religion is illegal according to pluralists. But without such, criminal behavior becomes rampant. With a breakdown of godly law, many become victims. Those fearful of crime must remain inside at night, only to be victimized again as their tax dollars are used for the upkeep of criminals in prison.

---

[5] *idem.*, *Law and Liberty* (Nutley, NJ, 1971), 107.

And yet, it is often the Christian who must guard his speech because a Biblical reference to homosexuality and abortion as grievous sins are profane statements in the eyes of many. In many jobs, employees are forced to attend sensitivity training sessions to "learn" how to respond to people with "alternative life-styles." Humanism, man becoming god and declaring right and wrong, has replaced godly teaching on morality.

Although written in the late 1960s, Rushdoony's following words have increasing relevance in our day as the consequences of pluralism are more evident.

> The foundation of law is morality, but what is the foundation of morality? Every morality rests on a religion, on a faith concerning the ultimate power in or over the universe. Buddhism has one kind of morality. Mohammedism another. Every religion has a different moral code because their religious foundations differ.
>
> The foundation of our American law is Christianity, Biblical faith. Our American system of laws will not last long without the foundation of Christian morality and faith.[6]

Years later, his thinking remains unchanged. He continues to faithfully point out the insidious lie of pluralism. There remains but two bases for law in society. Either God's law or man's. They are antithetical to one another. To accept one is to reject the other. The realm of each is all-encompassing to the exclusion of the other:

> The issue is the word of God or the word of man. Whose word shall prevail? If we limit the word of God to the realm of faith, we have denied it. The word of God is His infallible word and law for the whole of creation, for every man. His word is the binding word for every realm, and His law governs all things. Any man who attempts to build a theology on any other foundation than the sovereign and triune God whose word governs all of creation "is like a man that without a foundation built a house upon the earth; against which the stream did beat vehemently, and immediately it fell; and the ruin of that house was great" (Lk. 6:49).[7]

Much more could be said regarding social ills. But, pointing out problems in society is not Rushdoony's main focus, nor should it be ours. Rushdoony takes God's word seriously. He clearly understands that the earth is God's (Ps. 24:1). God will have the evident victory in every social realm. The last enemy to be defeated is death itself (1 Cor. 15:26). Christ "must reign till He has put all enemies under His feet" (v. 25, see also Ps. 2:7ff).

[6.] *idem.*, *Bread Upon the Waters* (Nutley, NJ, 1969), 15.
[7.] *idem.*, *Systematic Theology* (Vallecito, CA, 1994), I: 56,57.

Rushdoony's Solution

In dealing with societal ills, his writings do not reflect social theory. He understands and his writings clearly illustrate that God is lord over all of life. His written works speak to every "nook and cranny" of life and, of course, of society as a whole. His books fully endorse the inspired Paul's words on the sufficiency and extent of Scripture (2 Tim. 3:16,17). His writings are not given over to despair over our social ills; rather, his work reflects consistent teaching on how society can be reconstructed through applying God's word to every aspect of life. As an antidote to the social ills of our culture he has never offered a theory or a theoretical approach. Instead he has continually pointed out that the only valid answer is God's solution — a theocentric answer.

While the Christian sees the collapse of institutions throughout society, he can remain steadfast and hopeful because his hope is in God, not in man. God is working out all things "for good to those who love God, to those who are the called according to His purpose" (Rom. 8:28). This working out is in time and history. Rushdoony's writings evidence one who is aware of Christ's kingship. Life is to be lived and reconstructed under that kingship. The demise of humanism, void of answers, thus provides the Christian with manifold opportunities to faithfully live out and provide godly answers to life and culture. Our age is not a time of helplessness. As we act in terms of God's word, it is a time of great hope and helpfulness:

> Facing thus the end of an age, particularly one which deserves to die, the Christian must again re-assert Christianity as a total way of life. This means that the Christian and the churches are derelict in their duty if they do not re-think every field of life, thought, and action in terms of scripture. Christian schools are an excellent beginning, but no area of thought can be permitted to remain outside the dominion of Christ. To the extent to which the churches and Christians pursue a crumb-picking operation rather than an exercise of dominion, to that extent the world will founder in its own decay and ruin before renewal comes.[8]

Rushdoony's works point to a need for Christians to return to a proper understanding of the Trinity if our social ills are to begin to be corrected in our day. In his *Systematic Theology* he rightly states:

> Without the doctrine of the Trinity, there is no Christianity. Apart from the Trinity, there is no God. Without this doctrine man's thinking faces an endless blind alley, and an inability to account for the facts of unity and plurality. The reality of unity in creation and the reality of particularity or individuality rests on the fact of the Trinity. The Triune God is the Eternal One-and-Many, and the basis for the possibility of a created or temporal one-and-many. Neither particularity nor unity are

---

[8] *idem.*, *The One and the Many*, 374.

illusions, as they have been in non-Christian religions and philosophies because in God Himself we have both unity and particularity.[9]

The philosophical problem of the one and the many is of such importance that he authored a book addressing the subject.[10] In *The One and the Many*, Rushdoony insightfully shows that man has no answers to problems outside a belief in the Triune God. The issue is of great importance sociologically. The Triune God is important. Each person in the Godhead is also important. The Father planned salvation and all things (Eph. 1:4,11). The eternal Son died for the elect on the cross of Calvary (Mt. 1:21). The Holy Spirit opens the hearts of sinners and applies the word therein (Jn. 16:7ff, 1 Cor. 2:10ff).

Within creation we see the importance of the one and the many. The father is head of the home and very important. Yet he cannot take his earnings and selfishly spend the money on himself. The family (the many) is important. The father is worse than a non-Christian is he does not meet the need of his family members (1 Tim. 5:8).

Societal institutions exemplify the importance of understanding the concept of the one and the many. The defense of the nation as a whole and the institutions within are so important that men may have to leave their families for a time to defend their country. Yet the institution of the family (the one) is of such vital importance that the newly married husband was not to engage in battle or be regularly away from home for a period of one year after his marriage (Dt. 24:5). The family is the central institution of society. Thus it was of utmost importance that each new family obtained a good start. Without strong families there would be no unified nation to defend.

The Example of the War Between the States

One and many is also seen today in the increased interest in the War Between the States. The issue involved — the relationship of a strong central government (the one) versus the rights of the individual states (the many) — certainly reflects the impact of this concept.

By their passing the Tenth Amendment the states kept for themselves the rights and powers not elsewhere given to the central government. Prior to the War Between the States the right of secession had been understood to belong to the individual states. As early as 1811, secession was mentioned by Massachusetts Congressman Josiah Quincey. In fact, the War of 1812 was so unpopular that the New England states held a secession convention. Later, John Quincy Adams (1839) and Abraham Lincoln (1847) argued for the states' right to secede.[11] When the South voted in each individual state to

---

[9] *idem.*, *Systematic Theology*, I: 175.

[10] *idem.*, *The One and the Many*.

[11] James R. Kennedy and Walter D. Kennedy, *The South Was Right* (Baton Rouge, LA, 1991), 143ff.

secede, the one central government wrongfully exercised its power against the Constitutional rights of the many — the individual states. The South considered itself, and rightly so, a separate nation, and sought to defend itself from the Northern invaders. The Confederate loss has resulted in a continual growth, as seen in Reconstruction onward, in the power of the central government and the decreased power of local and state governments. Thus it should not be surprising to see renewed interest in the historical incident that spawned prolific government growth that in many ways enslaves its citizens today. Many have come to realize that when the South lost the war the nation as a whole also lost.

One can only surmise how many in the South understood the importance of the one and the many concept. Clearly the South was different in religion and culture when compared with the North and the West. The South was greatly influenced by the important revivals in colonial history — the First Great Awakening, the Second Great Awakening and then the revival that began immediately prior to the secession action and continued in the Confederate army until 1863. The North was greatly influenced by Unitarianism. Influenced greatly by the theology of Charles Finney, the West and the North were also marked by the acceptance of Arminianism, a man-centered theology.[12]

Although Deism and Unitarianism were evident in the South and Arminianism made inroads, Calvinistic thought was important and influential. Rushdoony has pointed out:

> Moreover, while Calvinism had receded in New England by 1787, it was coming into new power in the central states and in the South. And, when Princeton Seminary was a lonely bastion of Calvinism in the North, that faith held sway in the South. Indeed an important aspect of the Civil War was the Unitarian statist drive for an assault on its Calvinistic enemy, the South.[13]

Calvinistic thought stresses the importance of the Trinity and the one and many concept in the realm of salvation as well as in all of life.

Certainly the South was imperfect in some of its social views. Regarding mid-19th century southern theological leaders, Douglas Kelly has pointed out that "they did not take into serious consideration the fact that the blacks had been stolen from their homeland and that for Christians to buy stolen property is wrong."[14] However, it must also be noted that approximately six percent of the Southern population were slaveholders. Records show that 300,000 out of

---

[12.] See Iain H. Murray's *Revival and Revivalism: The Making and Marring of American Evangelicalism, 1750-1858* (Edinburgh, Scotland, 1994).

[13.] R. J. Rushdoony, *The Nature of the American System* (Nutley, NJ, 1965), 49.

[14.] Douglas Kelly, *Preachers with Power: Four Stalwarts of the South* (Edinburgh, Scotland, 1992), xxiii.

a population of 5.3 million whites in the South owned slaves.[15] It must be stressed that the central issue in the war was the states' right to make laws and decisions when those states would not be usurping the Constitutional authority of the central government. The Confederate defeat allowed the constitutional balance between the one and the many to be disregarded in favor of the one (central government) becoming far more powerful than the many (the states).

Personal versus Political

Rushdoony has also stressed the need for personal change preceding effective political change. Sadly, many conservative Christians today put too much hope on a new political party in power as greatly effecting social change. While Christian involvement in politics cannot be neglected, we must remember that individual hearts must be regenerated and converted before the heart of a nation can be changed. God brings true societal change from the grassroots up, not from the top down.

In Scripture this is clearly seen in the reign of Jotham. Jotham "did what was right in the sight of the Lord, according to all that his father Uzziah had done (although he did not enter the temple of the Lord). But still the people acted corruptly" (2 Chr. 27:2). The contrast is clear. The ruler pleased the Lord in many ways; those ruled did not.

In 1964, Rushdoony wrote:

> The Constitution still stands, basically the same document despite certain amendments, and its character has changed little in the past fifty years. The interpretation thereof has changed, reflecting a now deeply rooted revolution in American faith and life. The outcome of the struggle between the older faith and the newer approach will certainly be reflected at the polls and in the Courts, but it will be settled first of all in the religious decisions of men. Inescapably, history is the outworking of religious commitments.[16]

Religious commitment must be grounded in Jesus Christ as Savior and Lord. Discussions of the application of Biblical law to society too often forego the need for a change in the heart of many citizens. Only then can God's law be implemented nationally. Rushdoony did not overlook this foundational need. "At the heart of Christian faith is the fact that sinful man, incapable of making atonement to God, is redeemed by the atoning work of Jesus Christ."[17]

In another work, he wrote:

[15.] J. Steven Wilkins, *America: The First 350 Years* (Monroe, LA, 1988), 153.

[16.] R. J. Rushdoony, *This Independent Republic* (Nutley, NJ, 1964), 159.

[17.] *idem.*, "The Atonement Analyzed and Applied," *The Journal of Christian Reconstruction*, VIII:2 (Vallecito, CA, 1982), 9.

In the New Testament, faith is saying Amen to Christ and His salvation; it means accepting the verdict of death on ourselves which the law pronounces to law-breakers, and accepting the atoning work of Christ as our vicarious substitute. It means also the response of gratitude in the forms of works of law, the obedience of faith as the means of setting forth God's kingdom.[18]

Reconstruction is important; however, it must begin in the individual's heart. Once redemption has been applied, man willingly living under Christ's lordship can begin to live out his life in terms of God's law and work toward the Biblical reconstruction of every realm of life.

Christ summarized the moral law with two commandments (Mt. 12:29-31): loving God with our total being and loving our neighbor as ourself. It is often easier to apply God's law to others than to ourselves. Being saved, we are confronted with the greatness of God's love toward us, especially in light of our great sinfulness. Realizing this, we are compelled to live in terms of God's law-word. One cannot truly love others without first, by God's grace, loving God with his heart, mind, and soul. A remembrance of our own salvation reminds us that God's word must be applied to our lives, then to others, then to society at large.

Conservatism is evidencing new life today, as seen in the popularity of some conservative talk shows and publications. This will have little long-term effect without our political stands being defined by God's word. There is nothing wrong with being a conservative as long as that word is defined in Christian terms. We want to conserve what God says is worth keeping: "The Christian will thus conserve that which is godly and conforms to the law of God, working always to reform it in terms of that word. He will uproot whatever is not of God, not by revolution but by reconstruction."[19]

The regeneration of man and his living out his life and relationships in terms of God's law cannot help but have a positive impact on society. Once a man loves God, it follows he will love his fellowman. Biblically, this love is defined as keeping God's law (1 Jn. 5:2,3). Our social relationships will be governed by God's law-word.

As I mentioned earlier, Calvinism that had been so important as a religious basis in the colonial period began to wane in the early nineteenth century, especially in the northern and western states. Calvinism and its influence was mainly concentrated in the South. Of course, the War Between the States and the years following brought great change in Southern society. Until recent years the South was noted as being a "Bible belt" region because of the impact of Christianity on society. Thus a native Southerner recently wrote, "The South is still known for hospitality, personal courtesy, generally quiet

---

[18.] *idem.*, *Salvation and Godly Rule* (Vallecito, CA, 1983), 414.

[19.] *ibid.*, 148.

and calm manners in public, and the saying of 'Sir' and 'Ma'am' by children to adults."[20]

We do not, however, set our sights on the return to the social order of a certain region. Instead we must desire a change that pleases God in the totality of life and society. It is a change that will come in God's timing. Our duty is to be faithful to love God and then to love our neighbor, in Scriptural terms.

Biblical social change takes work and prayer. In his lectures, counsel, correspondence and testimony given in support of the right of Christians to educate their children, Rushdoony has often been confronted with criticism from those within the church. On the subject of standing for the Faith, Kelly writes:

> It also means the animosity of the compromising churchmen whose conscience disturbs them and who therefore lash out against the courageous men who make a stand. I know that, when I support any who resist, I am usually given "friendly" warnings by these compromisers that it would be inadvisable for a man of my stature to associate with such men, and I have no doubt that these resisting Christians are warned against associating with the likes of R. J. Rushdoony![21]

Providing the theocentric solution for social life has been a hallmark of Rushdoony's writings. He has performed the task admirably. Through these writings, many in our day have seen that godly social change is possible and is even commanded by God himself. This change will take place in time and history. Our duty? We are to take God's word and prayerfully work, by God's grace, to apply it to our lives first, then to social relationships throughout the nation, and even the world at large. We leave the results to God. We can be assured he will never disappoint us.

Byron Snapp is an Associate Pastor at Calvary Reformed Presbyterian Church in Hampton, Virginia. A native of Virginia, he graduated from King College in Bristol, Tennessee (B. A. History) and from Reformed Theological Seminary in Jackson, Mississippi (M. Div.). He has held pastorates in Mississippi, South Carolina, as well as Virginia.

[20.] Douglas Kelly, *op. cit.,*(Edinburgh, 1992), xix,xx.
[21.] Kent Kelly, *The Separation of Church and Freedom* (Southern Pines, NC, 1980), 99.

Education and Christian Reconstruction

Samuel L. Blumenfeld

When a world disintegrates, nothing more quickly becomes contemptible than its dead values, nothing more dead than its fallen gods, and nothing more offensively fetid than its old necessities .... If the new order is capable of breaking with statism, it will in due course turn on every citadel of statism, the school no less than any other.

R. J. Rushdoony, *Intellectual Schizophrenia*

There is no doubt that Rousas J. Rushdoony has done more to advance the restoration of educational freedom in America than any other Christian theologian. Not since the death of J. Gresham Machen in 1937 have we had as consistent, uncompromising, and intellectually profound a voice maintaining the importance of Christian education as we have in the prolific writings of Rushdoony. His classic study, *The Messianic Character of American Education*, first published in 1963 and recently reissued, is a monument to Christian scholarship and historical investigation. In that book he clearly delineates the philosophical conflict between humanism and orthodox Christianity raging in America's public square where these two opposing visions of the nation's future depend on the education of American children for their fulfillment.

Humanism and the State

That humanism not only threatens Christian education *per se* but educational freedom in general is well demonstrated by the link Rushdoony shows existing between religious liberty and educational freedom, for education is basically a religious function even if its statist version is atheistic, and Christian education is hardly viable without religious liberty. As Rushdoony writes in *The Roots of Reconstruction*:

> Among Nietzsche's manuscripts, after his death, was found a slip of paper on which he had written these words: "Since the old God has been abolished, I am prepared to rule the world." This is the meaning of humanism's inescapable totalitarianism. Total government is a necessity, and everything in man requires it. If there is no God to provide it, then man must supply it ....
>
> In the United States, the efforts of federal and state governments to control churches and Christian Schools are the logical results of their humanism. There must be sovereignty and law, and it must be man's, not God's, is their faith. Clearly, we are in the basic religious war, and there can be no compromise nor negotiation in this war. Humanism seeks to abolish the God of Scripture and rule the world.[1]

[1.] R. J. Rushdoony, *The Roots of Reconstruction* (Vallecito, CA, 1991), 11.

In America, the aims of humanism can be achieved only through the control of children and their education. The ultimate issue, therefore, is the ownership of children. Rushdoony writes:

> The first and basic premise of paganism, socialism, and Molech worship is its claim that the state owns the child. The basic premise of the public schools is this claim of ownership, a fact some parents are encountering in the courts. It is the essence of paganism to claim first the lives of the children, then the properties of the people.[2]

Thus, religious and educational freedom essentially rest on the foundation of God's ownership, and the issue of Christian liberty can only be resolved in a philosophical confrontation between Christians and the state. Rushdoony observes:

> The church and the Christian School are not the property of the state, nor are they the property of the congregation: they are the Lord's, and can be surrendered to no man.[3]

This principle of God's ownership was implicitly understood by the Founding Fathers who wrote the U.S. Constitution and upheld God's sovereignty over man. As long as the civil government remained subsidiary to God's sovereignty, it was legitimate and thereby supportable by Christians. But the introduction of secular, government-owned-and-controlled schools and colleges began to erode that basic understanding in the minds of the American people. Hegelian statism, with its pagan-inspired pantheism, slowly absorbed the loyalty of the academic elite so that the state, in Hegel's words, became "god walking on earth." Slowly but surely, the concept of religious freedom gave way to that of religious toleration. Religious freedom had meant that the state had no jurisdiction over the church, its schools, or its affairs. But the new doctrine of religious toleration meant that the state granted certain privileges to churches and religious schools at its own pleasure, privileges, such as tax exemption, which could be withdrawn at any time for some "compelling state interest." Rushdoony writes quite bluntly:

> The fact is that religious liberty is dead and buried; it needs to be resurrected. We *cannot* begin to cope with our present crisis until we recognize that religious liberty has been replaced with religious toleration .... [4]

> We may be able to live under religious toleration, but it will beget all the ancient evils of compromise, hypocrisy, and a purely or largely public religion. It will replace conscience with a state license, and freedom with a state-endowed cell of narrow limits. This is the *best* that toleration may afford us in the days ahead. [5]

---

2. *ibid.*, 10.
3. *ibid.*, 22.
4. *ibid.*, 150.
5. *ibid.*, 151.

The simple fact is that we already have a public, government-sanctioned religion. It is called humanism, and its most popular festival is Halloween, of pagan, Druidic origin. Today, it is lavishly celebrated in all of the public schools of America and is one of the many means now being used by government educators to paganize or de-Christianize American children.

The Role of the Family

However, Rushdoony's most noteworthy contribution to the heated debate over educational jurisdiction is his profound analysis of the central role of the family in Christian society as based on Biblical principles. He writes:

> In Scripture, the family is the basic institution of society, to whom all the most basic powers are given, save one: the death penalty. (Hence, the death penalty could not be executed on Cain.) The family is man's basic government, his best school, and his best church ....
>
> To review briefly the basic powers which Scripture gives to the family, the *first* is the control of children. The control of children is the control of the future. This power belongs neither to church nor state, nor to the school, but only to the family ....
>
> *Second*, power over property is given in Scripture to the family .... God gives control of property into the hands of the family, not the state, nor the individual ....
>
> *Third*, inheritance in Scripture is exclusively a family power, governed by God's law ....
>
> *Fourth*, welfare is the responsibility of the family, beginning with the care of its own ....
>
> *Fifth*, education, a basic power, is given by God to the family as its power and responsibility. The modern state claims the right to control and provide education, and it challenges the powers of the family in this area also ....
>
> Humanistic statism sees control of the child and the family as basic to its drive towards totalitarianism.[6]

Even though this was written in 1979, we see the accuracy of the analysis in the federal government's recent enactment of Goals 2000 and, in various states, of Outcome Based Education, which calls for greater and greater state intrusion into family life. The extensive data-gathering projects of the National Center for Education Statistics will give bureaucrats the private information needed to impose government control over children and families. Since the aim of humanistic education is not to educate in the traditional sense, but to change the beliefs, values, and behavior of the students, behavioral scientists have emerged as the true developers of the American

---

[6.] *ibid.*, 35-36.

curriculum. Their aim has been to transform the American public school into a humanist parochial school, and they have devoted years to developing the means to bring this about. One of the basic tenets of behaviorism is that the younger the child, the easier it is to change his values. Professor Benjamin Bloom, the godfather of Outcome Based Education, wrote in 1956 in his famous *Taxonomy of Educational Objectives*:

> The evidence points out convincingly to the fact that age is a factor operating against attempts to effect a complete or thorough-going reorganization of attitudes and values ....

> The evidence collected thus far suggests that a single hour of classroom activity under certain conditions may bring about a major reorganization in cognitive as well as affective behaviors. We are of the opinion that this will prove to be a most fruitful area of research in connection with the affective domain.[7]

Forty years later, the research has been completed and the programs are now in the schools! Note the presumption of the psycho-educators that they have the right to reorganize the attitudes and values of the students without the parents' knowledge or consent. But according to Scripture, as Rushdoony makes quite clear, the family, not the agents of the state, has the responsibility for the education of its children.

Thus, Rushdoony stresses the importance of parental responsibility in education if Christian children are to be spared mental reorganization — better known as brainwashing — at the hands of government psycho-educators. Only parents can ensure the continuity of Christian life in America. But it will take years of Christian reconstruction to reverse the humanist trends and restore acknowledgment of God's sovereignty over our institutions.

It is obvious that the return to Christian education is central to the future of Christian Reconstructionism. The decision by Christian parents to remove their children from the public schools and place them in reliable Christian schools or home schools is the necessary first step that must be taken not only to restore the family as a God-centered institution, but to withdraw financial and moral support from the secular humanist institutions that seek to destroy Christian culture. While many Christian leaders continue to support the public schools, and others provide a kind of lukewarm Christian education in a variety of church schools, Rushdoony has stressed the fact that we are at war with humanism and that any compromise with that enemy cannot in the long run be beneficial to Christianity. He writes in *The Philosophy of the Christian Curriculum*:

---

[7] Benjamin Bloom *et al.*, *Taxonomy of Educational Objectives* (New York, 1956), 85, 88.

A humanistic philosophy of education alternates between anarchism and totalitarianism .... [T]he purely existentialist purpose is really no purpose at all but rather whim. *Purpose* implies transcendence, a goal to be attained, an inadequacy in the present situation or condition of man, and therefore a determination to reach a superior place ....

A Christian liberal arts curriculum is therefore a purposive curriculum in terms of the doctrine of the resurrection and the calling of man to exercise dominion and to subdue the earth .... [T]he student must be enabled to grow in his dominion over himself as a necessary first step towards exercising dominion over the earth ....[8]

The purpose of the Christian school should be to prepare generation after generation to dominate every area of life and thought ....

The student must be schooled to see every legitimate area as an area of necessary dominion. He must be taught that the people of God must assert the crown rights of King Jesus over every area of life. There can be no compromise nor any diminution of this goal.[9]

The lukewarm Christian school which simply adds occasional Bible reading to a basic state-approved secular curriculum can hardly carry out the mandate set forth by Scripture. And therefore some of these schools do more harm than good by giving their students an erroneous idea of what a truly Christian education consists of.

Home Schooling

As a champion of the Bible-centered Christian family, Rushdoony has been a pioneer in the advocacy of home schooling because he recognizes that there can be no true Christian reconstruction without the responsible Christian family at its core. He has testified in various courts throughout America at more hearings and trials involving home schoolers than any other Christian leader, and his testimony has helped clarify the legal and philosophical issues involved. The Christian home schooling family is of particular significance because it has made a sharp and clean break with the humanist institutions of the state. This is surely a revolutionary act because it rejects the power of the state to impose its will on the Christian family. The cause of Christ cannot be advanced by so-called Christians who sacrifice their children on the altar of public education, thereby glorifying the sovereignty of the pagan state.

There is no doubt that the decline of Christianity in America is due to the capture of its educational institutions by the enemies of the Triune God. The process started as early as 1805 when the Unitarians took over Harvard University and began their long-range campaign to eradicate Calvinism as the chief spiritual and cultural force in America. Rushdoony documents all of this

---

[8.] R. J. Rushdoony, *The Philosophy of the Christian Curriculum* (Vallecito, CA [1981], 1985), 28.
[9.] *ibid.*, 29.

in *The Messianic Character of American Education* through the simple but most effective means of providing biographical studies of the major individuals — :rom Horace Mann to John Dewey — who transformed American education from its God-centered origins to its present atheist-humanist philosophy. All of these "educators" had one thing in common: they rejected Christ as the true Messiah and created a new messianic vision based on science, evolution and psychology, the chief apostles of which were Darwin, Marx, and Freud. A reading of this one book alone will convince any Christian that America's secular educational institutions are the primary cause of the nation's moral and spiritual decline. That is why an exodus by Christians from these institutions and the creation of new God-centered institutions is imperative if America is to regain its moral and spiritual health. And that is basically the message of Christian Reconstructionism.

Conclusion

It is obvious that Rushdoony's profound analysis of America's educational and cultural crisis has provided the Christian Reconstruction movement with a solid foundation of scholarship. As Rushdoony writes in *Intellectual Schizophrenia*:

> Scholarship is a prophetic, priestly, and kingly function, a central part of man's creative mandate. The godly scholar is the true man, and the school an essential part of the Kingdom of God.[10]

But it is also obvious that the days and, no doubt, years ahead will be ones of great struggle and philosophical turmoil as the entire liberal messianic cultural fabric unravels. But Rushdoony not only sees light at the end of the tunnel, but blazing daylight on the horizon. He captured the climate of the times quite dramatically with these words written over 30 years ago:

> The end of an age is always a time of turmoil, war, economic catastrophe, cynicism, lawlessness, and distress. But it is also an era of heightened challenge and creativity, and of intense vitality. And because of the intensification of issues, and their world-wide scope, never has an era faced a more demanding and exciting crisis. This then above all else is the great and glorious era to live in, a time of opportunity, one requiring fresh and vigorous thinking, indeed, a glorious time to be alive.[11]

To that we can all say "Amen"!

[10.] *idem.*, *Intellectual Schizophrenia* (Phillipsburg, NJ: 1961), 20.
[11.] *ibid.*, 113.

Samuel Blumenfeld graduated from the City College of New York in 1950, studied in France for two years, then worked for ten years as an editor in the New York book publishing industry. In 1970 he began writing full time. His book, Is Public Education Necessary?, *has been described by one critic as one of the most important books about education ever written.*

Mr. Blumenfeld also edits The Blumenfeld Education Letter, *a monthly newsletter that monitors the ongoing struggle between humanism and Judeo-Christian values in education.*

Law and Beauty

David Estrada-Herrero

Man creates planned chaos in every realm in the expectation of fertility. Not order but chaos rules in art. Art that moves on terms of law is regarded as dull, sterile, and academic

R. J. Rushdoony, *Law and Liberty*

Law and the Created Order

In God's created order, law is everywhere the indispensable condition of life. Law is an all-embracing reality in all realms of the universe. God's sovereignty is inseparable from his law. In all his works and eternal purposes, God moves in terms of his law. Our God is a God of order; chaos and order are incompatible. The principle of order is the law. To speak of God's order of creation is to refer to a *nomistic* principle of life and fulfillment. Through the law, God affirms the principle of life and reveals the purposes of his justice towards his creation. The law permeates all of God's attributes. To confess that God is love is to confess that he is just. In no way does salvation imply the suspension of law and justice. The purpose of grace is not to set aside the law but to fulfill the law and to enable man to keep the law. If the law was so serious in the sight of God that it required the death of Jesus Christ, the only-begotten Son of God, to make atonement for man's sin, we are not to think that it has now been abolished. The law has not been superseded in the soteriological sphere, nor in any other realm of God's creation. This concept of God's law as an all-encompassing reality in all of his handiwork is pivotal in Rushdoony's teaching. In all his writings the global significance of the law is stressed and the implications of the nomic principle is stressed.

God reveals himself as a God of order — and order is compliance with law. This is equally the case in the sphere of art. The God-given instructions for the construction of the tabernacle and the building of the temple show that art is not outside the lordship of the Creator. Art must follow the *pattern* principles of God's law (Ex. 25:40). The religious purposes of both the tabernacle and the temple, and everything in them, did not exclude another goal: the creation of beauty. And thus we read that Solomon "garnished the house with precious stones for *beauty*" (2 Chr. 3:6). In some form or another, the law is omnipresent in every aspect of man's life and culture. As a religious, social and cultural being, man was placed in a nomistic context. Any attempt to efface nomism — in whatever realm it unveils itself — has proved to be destructive and negative for man. On the other hand, in those spheres and endeavors in which man has followed the dim light still left in his lapsarian condition, the productions of his creativity demonstrate the positive results of observing the nomic principles. And this precisely is what we shall endeavor to show in this essay as we consider the relationship between *law and beauty*.

The Meaning of Beauty

As we reflect on the word *beauty,* we find that its meaning has been framed in the context of nomism. It is indeed remarkable that for more than two thousand years the concept of *beauty* has been developed in close relationship with the nomistic notions of *order, proportion, and harmony.*

In the art and accomplishments of the non-regenerate, we have to see the Divine image and inspiration of God's Spirit. As Calvin points out, "the image of God was not utterly effaced and destroyed in man." To charge "the intellect with perpetual blindness so as to leave it no intelligence of any description whatever, is repugnant not only to the Word of God, but to common experience." According to the reformer, the laws of society, the capacity for "manual and liberal arts," and the "knowledge and development of the sciences," openly attest to a universal reason and intelligence naturally implanted; this universality is of a kind which should lead every individual for himself to recognize it as a special gift of God. These gifts, since

> "they are bestowed indiscriminately on the good and on the bad, are justly classed among natural endowments. Therefore, in reading profane authors, the admirable light of truth displayed in them should remind us that the human mind, however much fallen and perverted from its original integrity, is still adorned and invested with admirable gifts from its Creator. If we reflect that the Spirit of God is the only fountain of truth, we will be careful, as we would avoid offering insult to him, not to reject or condemn truth wherever it appears. In despising the gifts, we insult the Giver."[1]

The study of the history of art eloquently corroborates Calvin's standpoint: the great works of art are a testimony of "how many gifts the Lord has left in possession of human nature, notwithstanding of its having been despoiled of the true good."[2]

Art in Antiquity

The great works of art of all ages exhibit an unmistakable note of *beauty.* And the remarkable thing in this connection is that already from the early days of Greek culture the concept of *beauty is* inseparably joined with that of *law.* Beauty is defined in a nomistic context, to the point that where there is no law — in the sense of an artistic norm, there is no beauty. Beauty

---

[1] John Calvin, *Institutes of the Christian Religion* (Grand Rapids, 1957), Vol. 1, Bk. 1, Ch. 15, 164, 234-237.
[2] *ibid.*, 236.

presupposes order and harmony, and this is not possible unless the principle of law regulates the structure of the artistic form. Where the principle of law is not found, ugliness finds its way. According to Homer, the ugliness and monstrosity of Poliphemus and all the Cyclops is explained on the grounds that they have neither laws, nor arts, nor *agorai* (*Oddyssy,* IX). In its Greek origin, the term *classical* points to a type of culture in which the principle of law establishes a note of moderation, restraint, harmony and balance in all its productions. Classical Greek art was based on the conviction that beauty depended on the law of number and measure. This is what is implied in the concept of *canon.* The term *canon* was the equivalent in the plastic arts of the term *nomos* in music. Apart from an abiding law or norm, art cannot be beautiful.

The old Pythagorean definition of beauty embodies a recurrent asthetical conception of excellency in art: "order and proportion are beautiful and useful, while disorder and lack of proportion are ugly and useless." The norm of "law and proportion" (*taxis kai simmetría*) has been the backbone of the main definitions of beauty in Western aesthetics. For the Pythagorean, the norm which issues in beauty or harmony, is a property of the cosmos; it is an expression of the *number* which is an objective property of things. The Greeks took it for granted that nature, and the human body in particular, display mathematically defined proportions and inferred from this that the representations of nature must show similar proportions. The finest temples, like the Parthenon, and the most celebrated statues as the Apollo Belvedere and the Venus of Milo, were constructed according to the proportion of the so-called *golden section.*[3] The Greek concept of beauty is inseparably joined with the concept of nomistic harmony.

The Pythagorean doctrine of measure and proportion appeared also in Plato's aesthetics and became its permanent feature. In order to fulfill its function, art must follow the laws governing the world. Every deviation from the laws governing the world is a fault against that which is *right* (*orthotes*). Aristotle equated order and proportion with the norm of *moderation.* The Stoics followed the Pythagoreans in saying that order, proportion, and harmony rule the world; and on these principles lies the beauty of the universe (*pankalia*).

The Christian View of Beauty

The norm principle is not absent in the Christian concept of beauty. Far from it. At the light of revelation, the law character of the principles of beauty is seen as grounded in and derived from God — supreme law-giver and legislator of the created reality. The Greek and Latin Fathers of the early

---

[3.] This is the name given to the division of a line in which the smaller part is to the greater as the greater is to the whole.

church embraced the norm character of ancient beauty and developed the concept within the framework of a theocentric cosmology. However, the task of purifying aesthetic notions of heathen elements encountered some difficulties. The main problem originated in the Greek translation of the Old Testament, the so-called *Septuagint.* This version was made in the third century by Jewish scholars living in Alexandria and strongly influenced by Hellenistic thought and culture.[4] Some Hebrew words, containing specific Biblical aesthetical meaning, lost their original meaning in the Greek rendering. This is the case, for instance, with Gen. 1:31, where the Septuagint reads: "And God saw everything that he had made, and behold, it was very *beautiful.*" The Hebrew word *tob* is translated by *kalos,* beautiful. The Hebrew word is an adjective of wider meaning, denoting the inner and external excellencies of God's creation; the emphasis centers around the idea of success and accomplishment in accordance with God's purposes. We cannot discard the *kalos* element in the meaning of *tob,* but the full purport of the Hebrew term is far broader and richer. The Biblical concept of beauty places the nomistic meaning under a wider and deeper significance than it had in ancient Greece. The law of the beautiful is a reflection of God's own law, manifested in his handywork and in the unfolding of his purposes for the universe. The world is beautiful — because God created it. The world has measure and number — because these have been conferred on it by a God of order and law.

St. Basil (329-379) sums up the concept of beauty of the Greek Church Fathers. When we read in the Genesis account that God praised the beauty of the world, this was not because the world was pleasing "to His senses," but because it had fulfilled the purpose for which it was created. That is, the universe is beautiful because of its purposefulness. Every individual thing is beautiful to the extent that it fulfills its purpose; it is beautiful according to the function it serves, according to the nomistic perfection with which it performs its appointed task. Nothing in creation is superfluous, nor made without reason. And since the world is beautiful because it is purposefully constructed, it is similar to a work of art: all has been made according to law and order. "We walk the earth, says Basil, as though visiting a workshop in which the divine sculptor exhibits his wondrous works. The Lord, the creator of these wonders and an artist, calls upon us to contemplate them" *(Hom. in Hex.,* IV, 33).

Since the world is governed first and foremost by the law of God *(lex Dei),* this should also be reflected in the beautiful works of art. "God is the cause of all that is beautiful," wrote Clement of Alexandria. The criterion of beauty

---

[4.] The Hellenistic influence must also be traced to the *Book of Wisdom* and *Ecclesiasticus,* received as canonical by the Ancient and Medieval Church. Both books contained basic substantial Greek aesthetical ideas. In the *Book of Wisdom* beauty is defined as "measure, number and weight."

— more and above conformity with nature — expressed conformity with the idea of a perfect, suprasensual and spiritual beauty. Athanasius writes: the beautiful creation, "like the words of a book, points, by its *order* and *harmony,* to its master and creator and speaks loudly of him" (*Contra gentes,* 34). In this quotation Athanasius uses the words *order* (*taxis*) and *harmony* (*armonia*), that is: the Pythagorean terms for nomistic beauty.

St. Augustine (354-430) can be regarded as the great representative of Western aesthetics. For over a thousand years his ideas exercised a decisive influence on the views on Christian art. Not even after his conversion did he lose his early love for aesthetics. In the study of beauty and related subjects, Augustine practiced what we would call a "sanctified eclecticism" from Greek and Latin sources, and set the great ideas of the past under the converting effects of God's revelation. Once more, for Augustine beauty has an objective and nomistic identity. Measure and number ensure order and unity and, therefore, beauty. The nomic concept of beauty is to be seen in the idea of *rhythm* — a basic notion of his whole aesthetics. He regarded it as the source of all beauty, extending its meaning to include visual rhythm, bodily rhythm, the rhythm of the soul, and the rhythm of the universe. Art was not supposed to depict the real world for its own sake, but to demonstrate the wisdom and power of the Creator.

In the Middle Ages, it was believed that art was subject to universal laws. Art was regarded as a form of knowledge — especially on account of its nomistic mathematical structure. The basis of beauty is clearly seen in the concept of music. Music was treated as a branch of cosmology. It was assumed that harmony is a property of the universe (*musica mundana*), and not an invention of man; man does not create it, he merely discovers it. The law of harmony governs not only the physical world, but also the spiritual world (*musica spiritualis*). Every object in nature has its *module,* or unit of measure, and is built on the principle of multiplying the module; its proportions can be expressed in terms of numbers. Like nature, the artist should accomplish his work on the principle of the module. Music, therefore, established the model for nomistic beauty in all the arts.

Medieval art was essentially religious. Art was not supposed to represent the real world for its own sake, but to show the wisdom and power of the Creator. But within the religious framework there was room for a striving after beauty. Artists of the Middle Ages believed that art was subject to universal laws: in the service of the Christian Faith, it had to keep the truth, and adapt itself to the laws of creation. Romanesque architecture was based on rules and relied mainly on *proportion*. It was the only European architecture which derived its main beauty from its *weight*. Romanesque architects were able to bring out the beauty of heavy walls and massive pillars. Relying mainly on proportions, they enlivened the rough surfaces with closed arcades, friezes, galleries, and sculpture. Romanesque sculpture was not only a display of harmonious forms, but also an epitome of knowledge — especially theological. Romanesque artists depicted reality in a joyful and lively manner, to the point that the sculptor was called "master of living stone" (*magister lapidis vivi*).

Gothic art was a continuation of Romanesque art, but the use of new techniques introduced important changes in the appearance and structure of the building. The technique of *cross-ribbed vaulting* allowed the buildings to be higher, more slender, with thin walls and wide apertures. The ogive — the distinctive mark of Gothic — was the result of the new vaulting. Natural beauty was sought in conjunction with spiritual beauty. Bodies were to be made beautiful by bringing into prominence the beauty of the soul. Gothic figures were more ascetic, narrower and slimmer than those of antiquity. Beauty was dependent on rules of proportion. The churches had a fixed relationship between the height and width of the nave, and fixed proportions in projection, elevation and all three dimensions. The towers had the same proportions as the nave. Altars and fonts, pinnacles and the tiniest details of the exterior and interior decoration followed the same rule of proportions.

The light and brightness of the Gothic churches was not only a source of joy and fruition to the eye, but also an object of mystical reverence, and embodiment of beauty. As in the Solomonic temple, in the applied arts, the things which were most highly valued were richness and costliness of material, gold, precious stones and trinkets; and in buildings, "the resplendent marble columns." But as Ruskin reminds us: the offering of precious things has to be understood in a deep religious context: "It may be infallibly concluded that in whatever offerings we may now see reason to present unto God, a condition of their acceptableness will be now, as it was then, that they should be the best of their kind. Costliness was *generally* a condition of the acceptableness of the sacrifice" (*The Seven Lamps of Architecture*, 20). Ruskin quotes here the words of David: "I will not offer unto the Lord my God of that which doth cost me nothing" (2 Sam. 24:24). The sight of a beautiful church, on account of its religious connotations, was said to free man from sadness and fill him with joy.

The Secularization of the Renaissance

In the Renaissance the idea of beauty lost the theological foundations of the Middle Ages, but retained the basic ancient normative structure. The main ideas were borrowed from the *Ten Books on Architecture* of Vitruvius and centered on the idea that beauty consists in a harmony of parts and in a harmony with reason, and has in nature an eloquent model for art. In Baroque aesthetics the norms of beauty became more subjective, as is seen in the fact that they were "intuitively discovered." G. L. Bernini acknowledged the importance of "measurements and proportions" in the beautiful art, but also stated that he worked "without blindly serving rules, but equally without violating them." In the seventeenth century classical revival, the correlation between beauty and law is again stressed. Art must be based on *principles,* and adhere to general *rules.*

Although the philosophers of the seventeenth century had little to say about beauty and art, their views paved the way for the loss of objectivity and rationality in aesthetics, and, through Romanticism, led to the contemporary idea of an art "free from rules and external impositions." For Descartes, Spinoza, and even Hobbes, the "beautiful" falls within the purely subjective, and there are no rules for it. According to Leibniz, beauty cannot be rationally grasped; it falls within the realm of the *nescio quid* — the "I do not know what." For Kant the aesthetic judgment is "without concept." He cannot accept, however, an art without norms, and therefore in his theory of *genius* he acknowledges the existence of some *rules* in artistic productions. These rules are not previously known, but are the spontaneous manifestation of the artist's own nature. This would lead to the romantic idea of the genius as legislator in the realm of art. Beauty has not an objective foundation in God's created order and nomistic reality, but is the product of man's autonomous decision.

The Views of John Ruskin

The early writings of John Ruskin reflect the Christian aesthetics of past ages. He defends an objective basis for beauty in accordance with the laws of God's creation. Over and over he appealed to the artist to escape from the prison of his own subjectivity and to look at the world objectively in order to trace the "laws of aesthetic government." In the *Seven Lamps of Architecture* (1849) he states that the "artist cannot advance in the invention of beauty without imitating natural form": "Orderly balance and arrangement are essential to the perfect of the more earnest and solemn qualities of the beautiful, as being heavenly in their nature, and contrary to the violence and disorganization of sin" (*Works,* XV, 118). His aim in writing *Modern Painters* was "to bring to light, as far as may be in my power, that faultless, ceaseless, inconceivable, inexhaustible loveliness which God has stamped upon all things. The beauty of nature is in God's image. He has made all things beautiful. In all perfectly beautiful objects there is symmetry ... and symmetry is a type of Divine justice" (*Works*, IV, 125). The visual forms are symbols of the Divine, and the artist is to discover in creation the excellencies of God's providential government. Biblical theology holds the key to the secrets of artistic beauty. Thus, no supreme power of art can be attained by impious men. Above and beneath perceived beauty there is "felt beauty": an acknowledgment that all beauty has in God its source. The discovery and fruition of beauty leads to a "sacrifice of praise and adoration. It is not the church we want, but the sacrifice; not the emotion of admiration, but the act of adoration: not the gift, but the giving" (*The Stones of Venice*, 26).

For a time the writings of Ruskin represented a stronghold of evangelical aesthetics. It seemed that he was going to become the greatest Christian aesthetician of all times; nevertheless, by the time he completed the last volume of *Modern Painters* in 1860, he was a changed man. Along with many other Victorians, Ruskin had succumbed to evolutionary thought. In a tragic tone, as early as 1851, he foresaw the shipwreck of his evangelical faith: "My faith is being beaten into mere gold leaf, and flutters in weak rags from the letter of its own forms .... If only the geologists would let me alone, I could do very well, but those dreadful *hammers*! I hear the clink of them at the end of every cadence of the Bible verses" (*Works*, XXXVI, 115). Like the artists whom he had warned against the new trends of art, he also fell in the dark prison of subjectivity and agnosticism.

The Modern Age

The Victorian Age bequeathed its legacy of agnosticism to the twentieth century. Never has an age of history produced such profuse literature of lost faith. The nineteenth century marked the end of Western nomistic cosmology. With the Nietzschean "death of God," the sovereign Creator was dethroned and the brave new age of humanistic chaos introduced. The abyss of irrationality and chaos superseded the law and order of the triune God of heaven and earth. With the "death" of God the universe has ceased to possess any meaning. Once the existence of God is overthrown, no absolute moral order is possible. In the sphere of art, Western breakdown of law has meant the *death of beauty*. The norms and rules of beauty have been substituted by the tyrannic laws of irreducible creative *freedom*. And as Shakespeare already warned, with "beauty dead, black chaos comes again" (*Venus and Adonis*).

Contemporary art is a mirror in which the nihilism of today's life and culture is graphically depicted. Francis Bacon, the famous English painter, repudiated traditional art as a mere fiction to hide from human eyes the emptiness of a senseless universe and the futility of a nauseating existence. In some of his works the "human" figure is attached to the sewer drain as an integral part of the body. Today's art is an exponent of a culture that has been shaped by relativism and nihilism in the absence of a God of order and law. Early in our century, Dadaism championed the cause of anti-nomism with its radical rejection of norms and rules for the arts. The rebellion was directed against the art of the past and it was fought under the banner of total and absolute freedom for the artist. The Dadaists aimed to destroy classical art and to replace it with productions in which the "laws" of nonsense, absurdity and irrationality were to be the guiding principles. A few years later, Dadaism led to Surrealism and to other varied forms of anti-nomistic -*isms*. Anti-nomism in art has meant the death of beauty. Ugliness — and not beauty — is the distinct mark of today's art.

Modern thought contains a note of deep contempt for anything which stands for law and order. Man was created "to enjoy God forever." But today, in his rebellious and defiant attitude, man takes Satanic pleasure in the denial of God's existence and in the effacing of his imprints in the order of his creation. Nietzsche speaks of art as eliciting "an ecstatic nihilism." In many of his works Picasso shows a special delight in deforming the forms of nature and in introducing chaos in the assembling of the figures and shapes of reality:

> The creative person is seen, not as the disciplined man, but as the undisciplined, chaotic person, a lawless creature whose every act is the ritual invocation of chaos. Bohemianism in art rests on this faith. The artist is an alchemist who can only invoke the basic fertility of the universe by means of chaos. By returning to chaos, he supposedly leaps ahead in time; he becomes the man of tomorrow, with more vigor and power because he is more lawless. In religion, we are told that conformity to God's infallible word is sterile and deadening. Man's religious freedom supposedly involves rebellion against God's ordered, final, and infallible truth. Man must turn from God's ordered world to the chaos and abyss of existentialism, and then, somehow, out of this will come forth true religion. The dark night of the soul as the chaos of unbeing is invoked as the way to the future.[5]

In the alchemy of modern art, and in the impetuosity of his rebellion, man has turned law into chaos and beauty into ugliness. Frankenstein, the new Prometheus of Mary Shelley, put all his knowledge, his science, and "good intentions," into creating a better being than God's original Adam. But he failed. Unable to endure the aspect of the being he had created, he rushed out of the room in anguish and fear, and confessed that "a mummy endued with animation could not have been so hideous as that wretch... it became a monster such as even Dante could not have conceived." Modern man, proud and lawless, has created an ugly culture, an art void of beauty.

David Estrada-Herrero is professor of aesthetics at the University of Barcelona, Spain, and the author of numerous journal articles.

---

5. R. J. Rushdoony, *Law and Liberty* (Vallecito, CA, 1984), 48.

"But It Does Move!" and Other Legends About The Galileo Affair

Thomas Schirrmacher

The bland scholar and the bland university, is similarly a myth, as is the apparent United Nations ideal of the bland man. No person or institution possesses the ability to be neutral and objective, to transcend itself and its historical context. This is no less true of science. Some would claim for the instruments of science, if not for scientists, this capacity for neutrality. But do scientific instruments make for objectivity? They are the refinement of a perspective, namely, that the truth or utility of a thing rests in measurement, a highly debatable proposition. Scientific instruments are helpful, towards accuracy for a perspective, but they do not thereby give it truth, objectivity or neutrality.

R. J. Rushdoony, *The Nature of the American System*

Galileo and Creationism

The process against Galileo Galilei in the seventeenth century is frequently used as an argument against creationist scientists and theologians, who make their belief in the trustworthiness of the Bible the starting point of their scientific research. Absolute faith in the Bible, critics say, blinds creationists for scientific progress and hinders science. Thus, Hansjörg and Wolfgang Hemminger wrote in their book against creationism:

> Today's Creationism, in rejecting the radical experimental orientation of Scriptural research, turns against the great Christian naturalists of the 15th and 16th century, against Copernicus, Galileo, Kepler and Newton. It repeats the proceeding against Galileo and argues in principle with the Inquisitors, for the issue at the trial was, among other things, whether the natural scientist had the freedom to set experimentation and observation above Scripture, which was understood to be natural history and was interpreted according to Aristotalian principles. Today's Creationists in principle have the same standpoint as the Inquisitors because they follow their empirical-biblicistic method.[1]

This, of course, is nonsense. One could view the situation just the other way around in favor of the creationists, even though this probably would be just as one-sided: Galileo was a scientist believing in the trustworthiness of the Bible and trying to show that the Copernican system was compatible with it. He was fighting against the contemporary principles of Bible interpretation, which, blinded by Aristotelian philosophy, did not do justice to the Biblical text. Galileo was not blamed for criticizing the Bible but for disobeying Papal

---

[1] H. Hemminger, W. Hemminger, *Jenseits der Weltbilder: Naturwissenschaft, Evolution, Schöpfung* (Stuttgart, 1991), 201-202.

orders. Even today, most creationists are natural scientists who allow themselves to read the Bible differently from the contemporary school of Biblical interpretation, higher criticism, and therefore are criticized by the theological establishment, especially by the huge liberal churches and by other established natural scientists. (Hansjörg Hemminger, quoted above, is, for example, paid by the German liberal state churches to fight sects and fundamentalist endeavors.)

But here we will discuss a different topic. The picture of the Vatican process against Galileo Galilei, used by the Hemmingers and others, is not drawn from historical research but from heroic hagiography. The picture of a life-and-death battle between a completely narrow-minded Christian church and the genius and always objective natural science in the Galileo affair depends on too many legends.

Examples of hagiographies on Galileo full of legends are the biographies of the Anthroposophical author, Johannes Hemleben,[2] the official Galileo biography of the former German Democratic Republic by Ernst Schmutzer and Wilhelm Schütz,[3] and the chapter on Galileo in Fischer-Fabian's book *The Power of Conscience.*[4]

There are many examples of a virtually religious "adoration"[5] of Galileo, in juvenile[6] as well as in scientific literature.[7]

I know of only one printed answer by a creationist to the misuse of Galileo's trial by evolutionists, in the Doorway Papers by Arthur C.

[2.] J. Hemleben, *Galileo Galilei, mit Selbstzeugnissen und Bilddokumenten dargestellt*, rowohlts monographien 156 (Reinbek,1969). Hemleben in the end regards the line from Galileo through Newton up to modern times a detour and offers the line to Novalis and Goethe up to the occultist and founder of Anthroposophy, Rudolf Steiner. Hemleben has written several volumes in the famous biographical series "Rororo-Bildmonographien." Especially his volumes on Biblical persons are heavily influenced by Anthroposophy. Probably the publisher is very close to Anthroposophy himself, which is true for many other German publishers and book stores, as one can see looking into their bookshelves.

[3.] E. Schmutzer, W. Schütz, *Galileo Galilei*, Biographien hervorragender Naturwissenschaftler, Techniker und Mediziner 19 (Leipzig, 1983).

[4.] S. Fischer-Fabian, *Die Macht des Gewissens* (München, 1987), 149-200 (chapter 4: Galilei oder "Eppur si muove"). Fischer-Fabian starts his chapter on Galileo with examples of legends on Galileo, which have long been disproved (149). Nevertheless he wants to use them as anecdotes, which are not historical but contain a grain of truth (150). Even though he frequently speaks about Galileo legends (*e.g.* on 193 he shows that Galileo never was tortured), his chapter on Galileo is a pure hagiography full of heroism.

[5.] H. C. Freiesleben, *Galilei als Forscher* (Darmstadt, 1968), 8.

[6.] *e.g.* the hero-worship with many legends on Galileo in the book for the youth by the French professor of physics J. P. Maury, *Galileo Galilei: Und sie bewegt sich doch!*, Abenteuer - Geschichte 8 (Ravensburg, 1990) (cf. my review in *Querschnitte* Jan/Mar 1991) 1 [*Jan-Mrz*], (23), *e.g.* Galileo is said to have discovered through his telescope "irrefutable proofs for the Copernican worldview" (*viz.* backcover).

[7.] *e.g.*, H. Mohr, "Naturwissenschaft und Ideologie," *Aus Politik und Zeitgeschichte* (Beilage zur Wochenzeitung Das Parlament) April, 3, 1992, 10-18, especially 11-12.

Custance.[8] An even more extended comment by creationists on the Galileo affair is necessary. This article will give a first evaluation and list important literature, but only can help to start discussion, because Koestler is right when he states:

> Few episodes in history have given rise to a literature as voluminous as the trial of Galileo.[9]

In view of more than 8000 titles on the Galileo affair and the 20 volumes of the complete works of Galileo himself, one article cannot discuss all aspects of the whole issue.

Galileo legends

> The most popular Galileo legend, which put the courage saying "But it does move!" into the mouth of the Florentine scholar, after his denial under oath of the teaching of the moving earth in 1633, dates back to the time of Enlightenment. Apart from this glorifying picture every epoch created the Galileo, it needed: Galileo, the pioneer of truth or the renegade, the martyr of science or the cunning and tactical zealot, in short, the positive or negative ... hero.[10]

With these words, Anna Mudry starts her introduction into the German collection of works and letters by Galileo Galilei.[11] She goes on:

> In reality the biography of the cofounder of modern science contains many shifts, inconsequences, and withdrawals, which had already been realized by Galileo's contemporaries. On the one hand they praised the "Columbus of new heavens"; on the other hand they reacted openly against his inner conflict. "A clever man he will be wanting and feeling, what the Holy Church wants and feels. But he ignites himself on his own opinions, has irritable passions in himself and little power and wisdom to overcome them ...." This reports the Tuscan ambassador of the prince, Piero Guicciardini, on the 4th of March 1616 to Florence with little benevolence, but with an intelligent awareness of Galileo's inner conflict.[12]

[8.] A. C. Custance, "The Medieval Synthesis and the Modern Fragmentation of Thought," in A. C. Custance, *Science and Faith*, The Doorway Papers VIII (Grand Rapids, 1978), 99-216, here chapter 3: "History Repeats Itself," 152-167.

[9.] A. Koestler, *The Sleepwalkers: A History of Man's Changing Vision of the Universe* (London, 1959), 425.

[10.] A. Mudry, "Annäherung an Galileo Galilei," editor's introduction, in G. Galilei, *Schriften, Briefe, Dokumente*, (Berlin and Munic, 1987), 1:7-41, quoted 8.

[11.] G. Galilei, *loc. cit.*

[12.] A. Mudry, *op. cit.*, 8; see a further quotation of the ambassador in the explanation to Thesis 4.

Similarly, Arthur Koestler starts the section on Galileo in his famous and much discussed history of astronomy, *The Sleepwalkers*:[13]

> The personality of Galileo, as it emerges from works of popular science, has ever less relation to historic fact than Canon Koppernigk's. In his particular case, however, this is not caused by benevolent indifference towards the individual as distinct from his achievement, but by more partisan motives. In works with a theological bias, he appears as the nigger in the woodpile; in rationalist mythography, as the Maid of Orleans of Science, the St. George who slew the dragon of the Inquisition. It is, therefore, hardly surprising that the fame of this outstanding genius rests mostly on discoveries he never made, and on feats he never performed. Contrary to statements in even recent outlines of science, Galileo did not invent the telescope; nor the microscope; nor the thermometer; nor the pendulum clock. He did not discover the law of inertia; nor the parallelogram of forces or motions; nor the sun spots. He made no contribution to theoretical astronomy; he did not throw down weights from the leaning tower of Pisa, and did not prove the truth of the Copernican system. He was not tortured by the Inquisition, did not languish in its dungeons, did not say *"eppur si muove"*;[14] and he was not a martyr of science. What he did was to found the modern science of dynamics, which makes him rank among the men who shaped human destiny.[15]

Gerhard Prause, author of several books and articles on famous legends in historical research,[16] writes about the view that the Galileo affair was the greatest scandal of Christianity and proof for the backwardness of the church:

> The truth is that this is a primitive stereotype, a falsifying story book tale, a legend which seems to be immortal, even though it has long since been corrected by historians. These corrections have been made widely known by bestselling authors — most impressively by Arthur Koestler.[17]

[13.] A. Koestler, *loc. cit.* Koestler discusses Copernicus, Kepler and Galileo and made many new heavily discussed theses; cf. the literature in favor or against Koestler in J. Hemleben, *op. cit.*, 159 and A. C. Custance, *op. cit.*, 152f, especially footnote 106. Custance often appeals to Koestler and views his book as an excellent discussion of the original records. He does not agree with Koestler's philosophical starting point that Galileo was the first one to really grasp and promote the incompatibility of faith and reason.

[14.] "But it does move!"

[15.] A. Koestler, *op. cit.*, 353. But K. Fischer, *Galileo Galilei, op. cit.*, 34 shows that even if all of Galileo's doubtful inventions and discoveries really would be Galileo's, this would not cover the real Galileo and his importance.

[16.] Especially Gerhard Prause, *Niemand hat Kolumbus ausgelacht: Fälschungen und Legenden der Geschichte richtiggestellt* (Düsseldorf, n.d.).

[17.] Gerhard Prause, "Galileo Galilei war kein Märtyrer," *Die Zeit* Nov, 7, 1980, 78; cf. the whole article and the full version in Gerhard Prause. *op. cit.*, chapter 7: "Galilei war kein Märtyrer," 173-192.

The Leaning Tower of Pisa

The best example of a Galileo legend aside from the never-uttered legendary sentence "But it does move!" is Galileo's supposed experiment from the leaning tower of Pisa. Alexander Koyré has written an article "The Experiment of Pisa: Case-History of a Legend,"[18] in which he shows that Galileo never carried out this experiment, yea, he even could not have done so! He writes: "The average reader of today connects Galileo's name firmly with the picture of the leaning tower."[19] "The history of the 'experiments' of Pisa meanwhile is part of our heritage. It can be found in handbooks and guides."[20] Even scientific literature is no exception,[21] although E. Wohlwill already in 1909 proved the legendary character of the experiments beyond doubt.[22]

The battleground pro and con on this legend is a text of the early biography of Galileo by Vincenzo Viviani,[23] which was written 60 years after Galileo's death. Alexander Koyré writes:

Neither Galileo's friends nor his enemies mention it [the experiments]. Nothing is more improbable than such a silence. We would have to suggest that Galileo, who describes experiments he had only thought about as experiments which he carried out, at the same time purposely concealed a glorious actual experiment.[24]

Koyré has shown that Galileo could not have even imagined such experiments, as he held to a physical theory different than the one those experiments would have proved (and later did prove).

Sixteen Theses on the Galileo Affair

The following sixteen theses will show why the Galileo affair cannot serve as argument for any position on the relation of religion and science. Thereby I mainly follow Galileo's own writings,[25] K. Fischer's biography,[26] A.

[18.] Chapter heading in A. Koyré, *Galilei: Anfänge der neuzeitlichen Wissenschaft*, Kleine kulturwissenschaftliche Bibliothek (Berlin, 1988), 59 (cf. 59-69); cf. also W. A. Wallace, "Galileo's Concept of Science: Recent Manuscript Evidence," in ed. G. V. Coyne, M. Heller, J. Zycinski, *The Galileo Affair: A Meeting of Faith and Science: Proceedings of the Cracow Conference 24 to 27 May 1984* (Vatican City, 1985), 15-40.

[19.] A. Koyré, *op. cit.*, 59.

[20.] *ibid.*, 68, footnote 1.

[21.] Beispiele in *ibid.*, 59-62.

[22.] Emil Wohlwill. "Die Pisaner Fallversuche," *Mitteilungen zur Geschichte der Medizin und Naturwissenschaft* vol. 4 (1905); E. Wohlwill, *Galilei und sein Kampf für die copernicanische Lehre*, vol. 1: *Bis zur Verurteilung der copernicanischen Lehre durch die römischen Kongregationen* (Hamburg, 1909), 115; vol. 2: *Nach der Verurteilung der copernicanischen Lehre durch das Decret von 1616* (Hamburg, 1926), 260.

[23.] A translation of the original text can be found in Alexander Koyré, Galilei, *op. cit.*, 63.

[24.] *ibid.*, 64.

[25.] *Galileo Galilei, op. cit.*

[26.] K. Fischer, *op. cit.* Fischer discusses very well how far Galileo produced real scientific progress in his time.

Koestler's research on the original documents of the Galileo process,[27] the creationist essay by A. C. Custance[28] and the scientific research of the Czech author Zdenko Solle.[29]

The intent of the theses can be summarized with Koestler's judgment:

> In other words. I believe the idea that Galileo's trial was a kind of Greek tragedy, a showdown between "blind faith" and "enlightened reason," to be naively erroneous.[30]

It goes without saying that the sixteen theses neither intend to defend the Inquisition nor aim at denying any scientific value of Galileo's thinking or research. But Solle is correct, when he writes:

> The picture full of contrast, showing a heroic scientist in front of the dark background of Inquisition will develop many different nuances.[31]

1. The Ptolemaic system had been denied by many high officials and Jesuit astronomers even before Galileo was born. Many of them followed the Copernican system.

An open defense of the Copernican system in principle was without danger, as the example of the Imperial Court astronomer, Johannes Kepler, proves:[32]

> The Jesuits themselves were more Copernican than Galileo was; it is now well recognized that the reason why Chinese astronomy advanced more rapidly than European astronomy was simply because Jesuit missionaries communicated to them their Copernican views.[33]

> While Martin Luther called the author of "De revolutionibus orbium coelestium" [*i.e.* Nicolaus Copernicus] a "fool," which will turn "the whole art of Astronomiae upside down," the book had not been fought by the Vatican. It was seen as "mathematical hypothesis," but had already been used as an aid in astronomical calculations for a long time. Only some time after leading Jesuit scientists like Pater Clavius had

---

[27.] A. Koestler, *op. cit.*, 352-495; cf. footnote 10.

[28.] A. C. Custance, *loc. cit.*

[29.] Z. Solle, *Neue Gesichtspunkte zum Galilei-Prozeß, (mit neuen Akten aus böhmischen Archiven),* ed. Günther Hamann, Österreichische Akademie der Wissenschaften, Philosophisch-historische Klasse, Sitzungsberichte 361, Veröffentlichungen der Kommission für Geschichte der Mathematik, Naturwissenschaften und Medizin 24 (Vienna, 1980). A very good introduction (without footnotes) into an alternative view of the Galileo affair can be found in the mentioned texts of Gerhard Prause. Roman Catholic historians have produced several refutations and justifications on the Galileo affair which have not been used in our article, although they argue similarly, see *e.g.* several articles in G. V. Coyne, M. Heller, J. Zycinski, *op. cit.* and W. Brandmüller, *Galilei und die Kirche: Ein 'Fall' und seine Lösung* (Aachen, 1994).

[30.] A. Koestler, *op. cit.*, 426.

[31.] Z. Solle, *op. cit.*, 6.

[32.] cf. A. Koestler, *op. cit.*, 355-358.

[33.] A. C. Custance, *op. cit.*, 154 with further literature; cf. the addendum in A. Koestler, *op. cit.*, 495.

agreed to the trustworthiness of Galileo's observations, Copernicus and his followers became "suspicious."[34]

The book by Copernicus was not placed on the Vatican index until 1616 to 1620 and was readmitted to the public after some minor changes.[35] Only Galileo's *Dialogue* remained on the Index from 1633 till 1837.[36]

2. Until the trial against him, Galileo stood in high esteem among the Holy See, the Jesuits and especially the Popes of his lifetime. His teachings were celebrated.

"The visit" in Rome in 1611 after he had published his *Messenger from the Stars* "was a triumph."[37] "Pope Paul V welcomed him in friendly audience, and the Jesuit Roman College honored him with various ceremonies which lasted a whole day."[38] Jean-Pierre Maury writes about this visit:

> Now Galileo's discoveries have been acknowledged by the greatest astronomical and religious authorities of his time. Pope Paul V received him in private audience and showed him so much reverence, that he did not allow him to kneel down in front of him, as was usual. Some weeks later the whole Collegio Romano gathered in the presence of Galileo to officially celebrate his discoveries. At the same time, Galileo met all the Roman intellectuals, and one of the most famous among them, Prince Federico des Cesi, asked him to become the sixth member of the Accademia dei Lincei (academy of the Lynxes), which he had founded.[39]

Galileo's first written statement in favor of the Copernican system, his *Letters on Sunspots*, was met with much approval and no critical voice was heard. Among the cardinals who congratulated Galileo was Cardinal Barberini, the later Pope Urban VIII, who would sentence him in 1633.[40] In 1615 an accusation against Galileo was filed but denied by the Court of Inquisition. From 1615 till 1632 Galileo enjoyed the friendship of many cardinals and the different Popes.[41]

[34.] A. Mudry, *op. cit.*, 29.

[35.] A. Koestler, *op. cit.*, 457-459. Koestler shows that in Galileo's time many books were put on the "Index" without any disadvantages for the authors. He proves that even books from the cardinals and censors judging Galileo were on the "Index."

[36.] J. Hemleben, *op. cit.*, 167.

[37.] A. Koestler, *op. cit.*, 426.

[38.] *ibid.*; cf. 426-428; cf. about the visit E. Wohlwill, *op. cit.*, 1:366-392.

[39.] J. P. Maury, *op. cit.*, 96. Totally wrong is the outlook of H. C. Freiesleben, *op. cit.*, 8, who writes on the time after 1610: "From this time on Galileo tried to get the Copernican system to be acknowledged especially by representatives of the Church. Unfortunately he had the opposite result."

[40.] A. Koestler, *op. cit.*, 431, 432.

[41.] *ibid.*, 442, 443.

3. The battle against Galileo was not started by Catholic officials, but by Galileo's colleagues and scientists, who were afraid to lose their position.

The representatives of the church were much more open to the Copernican system than the scientists and Galileo's colleagues. Galileo did avoid and delay an open confession in favor of the Copernican system in fear of his immediate and other colleagues, not in fear of any part of the Church.[42]

This was already true of Copernicus himself. Gerhard Prause summarizes the situation:

> Not in fear of those above him in the Church — as often is wrongly stated — but because he was afraid to be "laughed at and to be hissed off the stage"— as he formulated it himself — by the university professor, did he refuse to publish his work "De revolutionibus orbium coelestium" for more than 38 years. Only after several Church officials, especially Pope Clemens VII, had requested it, did Copernicus finally decided to publish his work.[43]

Only few scientists living in Galileo's time confessed publicly that they followed Copernicus. Some did it so secretly, but most denied the Copernican system.[44]

> Thus, while the poets were celebrating Galileo's discoveries which had become the talk of the world, the scholars in his own country were, with a few exceptions, hostile or sceptical. The first, and for some time the only, scholarly voice raised in public in defence of Galileo, was Johannes Kepler's.[45]

Beside this, the church represented not only the interests of theologians but also the interests of those scientists who were part of the orders of the church. The Order of the Jesuits, which was behind the trial against Galileo, included the leading scientists of that day.

Galileo's case confronts us with the heaviness and clumsiness of scientific changes due to the social habits of the scientific community, which Thomas Kuhn has described in his famous book *The Structure of Scientific Revolutions*. More than once, it was not the church withholding scientific progress but the scientific community!

4. Galileo was a very obstinate, sensitive, and aggressive scientist, who created many deadly enemies by his harsh polemics even among those who no longer followed the Ptolemaic worldview.

Galileo had already earned the nickname "the wrangler"[46]during his student days. Koestler repeatedly demonstrates that this personal aspect of

---

[42.] So especially G. Prause, *Niemand hat Kolumbus ausgelacht, op. cit.*, 182-183.

[43.] G. Prause, "Galileo Galilei war kein Märtyrer," *op. cit.*, 78.

[44.] cf. D. F. Siemens, "Letter to the Editor," *Science* 1965, 8-9. His authority is B. Barber, "Resistance of Scientist to Scientific Discovery," *Science*, 1961, 596; cf. A. C. Custance, *op. cit.*, 157. The best argument for this thesis can be found in E. Wohlwill, *op. cit.*, vol. 1.

[45.] A. Koestler, *op. cit.*, 369-370.

[46.] E. Schmutzer, W. Schütz, *op. cit.*, 28.

many of Galileo's battles made it impossible for other scientists to work with him.[47]

Koestler writes about Galileo's answer to the critics of his *Messenger from the Stars*:

> Galileo had a rare gift of provoking enmity; not the affection alternating with rage which Tycho aroused, but the cold, unrelenting hostility which genius plus arrogance minus humility creates among mediocrities. Without the personal background, the controversy which followed the publication of the *Sidereus Nuncius*[48] would remain incomprehensible.[49]

A. Koestler adds more generally:

> His method was to make a laughing stock of his opponent — in which he invariably succeeded, whether he happened to be in the right or in the wrong.... It was an excellent method to score a moment's triumph, and make a lifelong enemy.[50]

Z. Solle states it similarly:

> Galileo was not afraid of personal attacks and mockery against others, but this was the easiest way to create enemies.[51]

Koestler comments on an immoderate answer by Galileo against an anti-Ptolemaic writing of the leading Jesuit astronomer Horatio Grassi:

> When Galileo read the treatise, he had an outburst of fury. He covered its margin with exclamations like "piece of asinity," "elephantine," "buffoon," "evil poltroon," and "ungrateful villain". The ingratitude consisted in the fact that the treatise did not mention Galileo's name — whose only contribution to the theory of comets has been a casual endorsement of Tycho's views in the *Letters on Sunspots*.[52]

K. Fischer comments on the same event:

> It is hard to decide what the most remarkable side of this debate is: the open proceeding of the Jesuits against the Aristotelian physics of the heavens, the almost devoted bowing of Horatio Grassis before Galileo's authority, Galileo's measureless aggressiveness, which destroyed everything that Grassi ever had said, or Galileo's genial rhetoric, which he used with a great skill against Grassi and Brahe, so that especially Grassi seemed to be a pitiable figure, who did not know what he was talking about ....[53]

Koestler writes on a vile and vulgar writing by Galileo against B. Capra:

[47.] cf. beside the quotations in the text further examples for Galileo's fury in A. Koestler, *op. cit.*, 431-436, 362-363.

[48.] "Messenger from the Stars."

[49.] *ibid.*, 368.

[50.] *ibid.*, 452.

[51.] Z. Solle, *op. cit.*, 9.

[52.] A. Koestler, *op. cit.*, 467.

[53.] K. Fischer, *op. cit.*, 128-129; cf. Thesis 10 on this battle.

In his later polemical writings, Galileo's style progressed from coarse invective to satire, which was sometimes cheap, often subtle, always effective. He changed from the cudgel to the rapier, and achieved a rare mastery at it ....[54]

A. C. Custance mentions as an example for Galileo's oversensibility his reaction against the rumor that a seventy-year-old Dominican had cast doubts on his thesis in a private conversation. Galileo wrote a harsh letter and called him to account. The Dominican answered that he was too old and would not have enough knowledge to judge Galileo's thesis, and that he only had made some private remarks in a conversation in order not to be called ignorant. Galileo still felt that he had been "attacked."[55]

The Tuscan ambassador in Rome, under whose protection Galileo lived, characterized Galileo in a letter to the Prince of Tuscany:

> He is passionately involved in this quarrel, as if it were his own business, and he does not see and sense what it would comport; so that he will be snared in it, and will get himself into danger, together with anyone who seconds him .... For he is vehement and is totally fixed and impassioned in this affair, so that it is impossible, if you have him around, to escape from his hands. And this business is not a joke but may become of great consequence, and this man is here under our protection and responsibility ....[56]

5. Galileo ignored all other researchers, did not inform them about his discoveries, and believed that he alone made scientifically relevant discoveries. As a result, some of Galileo's condemned teachings were already out of date, especially because of the progress made by Kepler's writings.

> Judging by Galileo's correspondence and other records of his opinion of himself, he was fantastically selfish intellectually and almost unbelievably conceited. As an illustration of the former there is the now well-known fact that he refused to share with his colleagues or with acquaintances as Kepler any of his own findings or insights; he actually claimed to be the only one who ever would make any new discovery! In writing to an acquaintance he expressed himself as follows: "You cannot help it, Mr. Sarsi, that is was granted to me alone to discover all the new phenomena in the sky and nothing to anybody else. This is the truth which neither malice nor envy can suppress."[57]

Galileo's relationship to Johannes Kepler is a good example for this thesis (as well as an example for Thesis 4). Galileo had shared his belief in the Copernican system with Kepler at an early stage of their acquaintance and Kepler had blindly, without proofs, accepted Galileo's book *Messenger from*

[54.] A. Koestler, *op. cit.*, 363.

[55.] A. C. Custance, *op. cit.*, 153.

[56.] A. Koestler, *op. cit.*, 452-453; cf. the quotation of the Tuscan ambassador in the quotation from Anna Mudry (with footnote 9).

[57.] A. C. Custance, *op. cit.*, 153.

the Stars.[58] But Galileo refused to give Kepler one of his telescopes, although he gave them to many political heads of the world.[59] Kepler could only use a Galilean telescope after the Duke of Bavaria lent him one.[60] Galileo wrote his discoveries to Kepler only in anagrams, so that Kepler could not understand them but Galileo later could prove that these were his discoveries.[61] After this, Galileo broke off all further contact with Kepler. He totally ignored Kepler's famous book *Astronomia Nova* even though it was only a further development of Copernicus' and of Galileo's discoveries[62] (cf. Thesis 10).

> For it must be remembered that the system which Galileo advocated was the orthodox Copernican system, designed by the Canon himself, nearly a century before Kepler threw out the epicycles and transformed the abstruse paper-construction into a workable mechanical model. Incapable of acknowledging that any of his contemporaries had a share in the progress of astronomy, Galileo blindly and indeed suicidally ignored Kepler's work to the end, persisting in the futile attempt to bludgeon the world into accepting a Ferris wheel with forty-eight epicycles as "rigorously demonstrated" physical reality.[63]

6. Galileo contradicted himself not only during the trial. In oral discussion he denied the Copernican system, which he had defended in earlier writings.

A. Koestler writes on the trial and on Galileo's defense:

> To pretend, in the teeth of the evidence of the printed pages of his books, that it said the opposite of what it did, was suicidal folly. Yet Galileo had had several month's respite in which to prepare his defence. The explanation can only be sought in the quasi-pathological contempt Galileo felt for his contemporaries. The pretence that the *Dialogue* was written in refutation of Copernicus was so patently dishonest that his case would have been lost in any court.[64]

> If it had been the Inquisition's intention to break Galileo, this obviously was the moment to confront him with the copious extracts from his books — which were in the files in front of the judge — to quote to him what he had said about the sub-human morons and pygmies who were opposing Copernicus, and to convict him of perjury. Instead, immediately following Galileo's last answer, the minutes of the trial say: "And as nothing further could be done in execution of the decree, his signature was obtained to his deposition and he was sent back." Both the judges and the defendant knew that he was lying, both the judge and he

---

[58.] A. Koestler, *op. cit.*, 370.
[59.] *ibid.*, 375.
[60.] *ibid.*, 378.
[61.] *ibid.*, 376-377.
[62.] K. Fischer, *op. cit.*, 169.
[63.] A. Koestler, *op. cit.*, 438; cf. the next paragraph 438-439.
[64.] A. Koestler, *op. cit.*, 485.

knew that the threat of torture (*territio verbalis*) was merely a ritual formula, which could not be carried out ....[65]

But these discrepancies and even hypocrisy can be found during the whole of Galileo's life. In the beginning, about the years 1604-1605, when a highly visible supernova soon became weaker and it was not possible to show a parallax any longer, Galileo sometimes even doubted the Copernican system himself.[66] In 1613, in his fiftieth year, Galileo for the first time stated in print his conviction that it was true. But in 1597 he had stated the same in a private letter to Kepler. For sixteen years "in his lectures he not only taught the old astronomy of Ptolemy, but denied Copernicus explicitly."[67] This was the case even though there would have been no danger at all in presenting the Copernican system.[68] He confessed his belief in Copernicus in private discussions and letters only. Several authors have correctly explained this by his fear from mockery of other scientists. Only after Galileo had become famous through his discoveries in the area of mechanics, dynamics and optics, did he admit his Copernican position in print.

K. Fischer occasionally indicates that Galileo could write things contrary to his own opinion,[69] namely in order to harm other people.

7. Galileo was not a strictly experimental scientist.

K. Fischer writes on Galileo's book *De Motu* (*On Motion*):

> One can doubt whether Galileo had made many experiments to prove his theories. If that been the case, it is hard to understand why he never changed his position that light objects are accelerated faster in the beginning of their natural motion than heavier ones. According to Galileo's own understanding, such tests were neither necessary to prove his theory nor enough to disprove it. His proceeding was axiomatically orientated.[70]

Koestler refers to Professor Burtt, who assumes that it was mainly those who stressed empirical research who did not follow the new teaching because of its lack of proof (cf. Thesis 8):

> Contemporary empiricists, had they lived in the sixteenth century, would have been the first to scoff out of court the new philosophy of the universe.[71]

---

65. *ibid.*, 492.
66. K. Fischer, *op. cit.*, 94.
67. A. Koestler, *op. cit.*, 357-358; cf. 431.
68. *ibid.*; cf. Thesis 1.
69. *e.g.* K. Fischer, *op. cit.*, 138.
70. K. Fischer, *op. cit.*, 53.
71. quoted by A. Koestler, *op. cit.*, 461.

8. Galileo did not and could not have proofs for his theory, as the first real proofs were found fifty to one hundred years later. But Galileo always acted, as if he had all proofs, but did not present them, as he said, because no one else was intelligent enough to understand them.

Koestler writes:

> He employs his usual tactics of refuting his opponent's thesis without proving his own.[72]

As Galileo did not work empirically (cf. Thesis 7), but regarded the Copernican system as an axiom, he did not feel the need for proofs. Not until he was put under pressure because he presented the Copernican system as proven, did he get into difficulties.

When Cardinal Bellarmine, who was responsible for the Court of Inquisition, asked Galileo in a friendly way for his proofs, so that he could accept his theory as proven fact, and asked him to otherwise present his Copernican theory as hypothesis only, Galileo answered in a harsh letter, that he was not willing to present his evidence, because no one could really understand it. Koestler comments on this:

> How can he refuse to produce proof and at the same time demand that the matter should be treated as if proven? The solution of the dilemma was to pretend that he had the proof, but to refuse to produce it, on the grounds that his opponents were too stupid, anyway, to understand.[73]

Galileo reacted in a similar way after the Pope himself asked for proofs.[74]

Koestler writes about an earlier letter from 1613:

> But Galileo did not want to bear the burden of proof; for the crux of the matter is, as will be seen, that he had no proof.[75]

Virtually all researchers agree that Galileo had no physical proof for his theory.[76] Some parts of Galileo's theory could not be proven at all because they were wrong and already outdated by Kepler's research (cf. Theses 10 and 5).

Fischer summarizes:

> He did not have really convincing proofs such as the parallax shift or Foucault's pendulum.[77]

---

72. A. Koestler, *op. cit.*, 478.
73. *ibid.*, 449; cf. 445-451, especially 449-450 for the whole debate.
74. K. Fischer, *op. cit.*, 148.
75. A. Koestler, *op. cit.*, 436.
76. cf. K. Fischer, *op. cit.*, 123; cf. A. C. Custance, *op. cit.*, 157, 154-155.
77. K. Fischer, *op. cit.*, 122.

One must not forget that the Copernican hypothesis itself was never denied by the Inquisition, but that it only was not allowed to be presented as proven scientific theory or as truth.

> In fact, however, there never had been any question of condemning the Copernican system as a working hypothesis.[78]

The Copernican system was just "an officially tolerated working hypothesis, awaiting proof."[79]

As Galileo came under pressure more and more, he finally invented a "secret weapon,"[80] the totally erroneous theory that the tides were caused by the turning of the earth. This easily disprovable theory was said to be the absolute secure proof of the Copernican system![81]

> The whole idea was in such glaring contradiction to fact, and so absurd as a mechanical theory — the field of Galileo's own immortal achievements — that its conception can only be explained in psychological terms.[82]

William A. Wallace used recently discovered manuscripts to show[83] that Galileo knew exactly that the final proof for the Copernican system was lacking and that he was covering this under his rhetoric. Jean Dietz Moss has done research on this kind of rhetoric[84] and makes clear how Galileo's own texts show that Galileo knew that he had to fill the missing evidence with rhetoric.

9. In Galileo's time, science no longer had to decide between Ptolemy and Copernicus. Ptolemy was no longer a real option. Rather it is important, "that the choice now lay between Copernicus and Brahe,"[85] because all believed that the earth moves around the sun. The question was, whether or not the earth was moving itself or was staying in the center of the universe.

> Nearly no expert believed in Ptolemaic astronomy any longer. The conflict was between Tycho Brahe and Copernicus.[86]

Tycho Brahe, predecessor of Kepler as German Imperial Court astronomer, held to the central position of the earth, while at the same time integrating the observation of the earth moving around the sun.

---

78. A. Koestler, *ibid.*, 437.
79. *ibid.*; cf. the whole paragraph.
80. *ibid.*, 464.
81. *ibid.*, 464-467; cf. Thesis 10 on the tidal theory.
82. *ibid.*, 454.
83. W. A. Wallace, *loc. cit.*
84. J. D. Moss, "The Rhetoric of Proof in Galileo's Writings on the Copernican System," in ed. G. V. Coyne, M. Heller, J. Zycinski, *op. cit.*, 41-65.
85. A. Koestler, *op. cit.*, 427.
86. K. Fischer, *op. cit.*, 139; cf. 123.

The arguments and observations which Galileo referred to, were acknowledged, but they denied only the Ptolemaic system, but did not favor in the same way the Copernican system. They were compatible with the Tychonian system, which had the advantage that the central position of the earth was maintained.[87]

Galileo never took a position on this issue nor presented arguments against Tycho Brahe with the exception of his polemical and totally distorted description of Brahe's system in his work against Horation Grassi.[88]

10. Galileo fought very stubbornly not only for the Copernican system but also for several hypotheses, which, compared to those of other scientists of his time, were out of date and a relapse into the old system.

This thesis was already contained in Theses 5, 8 and 9. Galileo defended the "epizycloids" of Copernicus, even though Kepler already had presented a much better theory.[89]

His already mentioned erroneous explanation of the tides was used as his major proof for the Copernican system, even though it was untenable and Kepler had discovered the real cause of the tides in the power of attraction of the moon.[90]

In 1618, Galileo explained some visible comets in a fiery work as reflections of light, so that nobody believed the Jesuit astronomer Grassi, who realized that the comets are flying bodies.[91]

Many further examples have been discussed by A. Koestler and K. Fischer.[92]

11. Under Pope Urban's (VIII) predecessor and his successor, no trial against Galileo would have taken place.

The arguments for this thesis can be found under Theses 3 and 16. We should not forget that in 1615 a first trial against Galileo before the Court of Inquisition was decided in favor of Galileo because of benevolent expert evidence of the leading Jesuit astronomers.[93]

12. Galileo was the victim of the politics of Pope Urban VIII, who had been very much in favor of him earlier. This was due to the political situation as well as to Galileo's personal attacks on the Pope, never to

---

[87.] *ibid.*, 121.

[88.] *ibid.*, 128-129; see the quotation from this section under Thesis 4; cf. A. Koestler, *op. cit.*, 467-468.

[89.] To expand Thesis 5, cf. A. Koestler, *op. cit.*, 378 and A. C. Custance, *op. cit.*, 154.

[90.] A. Koestler, *op. cit.*, 464-467, 453-454.

[91.] Z. Solle, *op. cit.*, 14; cf. A. Koestler, *op. cit.*, 467.

[92.] A. Koestler, *op. cit.*; K. Fischer, *Galileo Galilei, op. cit.*

[93.] A. Koestler, *op. cit.*, 441-442.

religious reasons. The Pope had initiated the proceedings, while the Court of Inquisition calmed the whole matter down instead of "stirring up the flames."

Thesis 12 discusses the personal aspect, Thesis 13 the political one, although it is not easy to distinguish between them.

Galileo's process took place under a ruthless and cruel Pope. A dictionary on the Popes says:

> Within the Church the pontificate of Urban was burdened with unlimited nepotism. Urban VIII was a tragic figure on the Papal throne. His reign was full of failures, for which he was himself responsible.[94]

Koestler writes at the end of his description of Pope Urban VIII, the former Cardinal Barberini, who for Koestler was "cynical, vainglorious, and lusting for secular power."[95] He

> was the first Pope to allow a monument to be erected to him in his lifetime. His vanity was indeed monumental, and conspicuous even in an age which had little use for the virtue of modesty. His famous statement that he "knew better than all the Cardinals put together" was only equalled by Galileo's that he alone had discovered everything new in the sky. They both considered themselves supermen and started on as basis of mutual adulation — a type of relationship which, as a rule, comes to a bitter end.[96]

This Pope also was a danger to science:

> The Pope paralysed scientific life in Italy. The center of the new research came to the Protestant countries in the North.[97]

Thus the Galileo affair was mainly an intra-Roman Catholic and intra-Italian problem, but surely no gigantic battle between Christianity as such and science as such. The Court of Inquisition did not accuse Galileo of teaching against the Bible, but disobeying a Papal degree.

Urban VIII had favored Galileo as Cardinal (cf. Thesis 1) and even had written an ode to Galileo. After he had become Pope in 1623 his love for Galileo even increased.[98]

Only a short time before the trial, Urban's friendship turned into hatred. This derived not only from the political situation (cf. Thesis 13), but from Galileo's personal carelessness, not to say insults. Galileo obtained the right to print his major work *Dialogue* from the Pope personally in case some minor corrections were to be made. Galileo cleverly circumvented this censorship, and put Urban's main argument for the Copernican system (!)

[94.] R. Fischer-Wollpert, *Lexikon der Päpste* (Regensburg, 1985), 118.
[95.] A. Koestler, *op. cit.*, 471.
[96.] *ibid.*; similarly K. Fischer, *op. cit.*, 145-146.
[97.] Z. Solle, *op. cit.*, 58.
[98.] A. Koestler, *op. cit.*, 472.

into the mouth of the fool "Simplicio," who, in the *Dialogue* of three scientists, always asks the silly questions and defends the Ptolemaic view of the world.

> But it did not require much Jesuit cunning to turn Urban's perilous adulation into the fury of the betrayed lover. Not only had Galileo gone, in letter and spirit, against the agreement to treat Copernicus strictly as a hypothesis, not only had he obtained the imprimatur by methods resembling sharp practice, but Urban's favorite argument was only mentioned briefly at the very end of the book, and put into the mouth of the simpleton who on any other point was invariably proved wrong. Urban even suspected that Simplicius was intended as a caricature of his own person. This, of course, was untrue; but Urban's suspicion persisted long after his fury had abated ....[99]

L. Pastor, a defender of Papal infallibility, has tried to show that the Pope only played a minor role in Galileo's trial and that the (anonymous) Inquisition judged harsher than the Pope, as a good friend of Galileo's, would have liked it to do.[100] Z. Solle has given convinceable proofs that, in reality, it was just the other way round.[101] The Pope initiated the trial for personal reasons, while the Inquisitors were quite lax. Some of the ten judges seem to have been mainly interested in their own forthcoming, while others applied the brakes. In the end, the final decision lacked three signatures, at least two of them out of protest. The only cardinal who zealously pushed the trial forward was the Pope's brother.

> That the whole trial was questionable could not be hidden to insiders. There was much resistance by high Church officials and from the Jesuit party.[102]

Koestler also arrives to the conclusion that the Pope initiated the process:

> There is little doubt that the decision to instigate proceedings was Urban VIII's, who felt that Galileo had played a confidence trick on him.[103]

13. Galileo was the victim of the politics of Pope Urban VIII, whose tactics in the Thirty Years' War were totally confused, who tried to bring the Italian cities under his control, who fought against all opposition within the Roman Catholic Church, and who failed in all of this in 1644, although he had made some progress in the beginning.

The situation for the Holy See was totally dependent on the political battles of the times. Z. Solle writes:

---

[99] *ibid.*, 483.

[100] according to Z. Solle, *op. cit.*, 38-39.

[101] *ibid.*, 64 and *passim*; cf. Thesis 6.

[102] K. Fischer, *op. cit.*, 126 (with additional literature).

[103] A. Koestler, *op. cit.*, 482.

The council of the General-Inquisitors became a reflection of the battles between the different parties within the Church. Neither under Borgia nor under Urban, was the issue astronomy or the faith of the Church, but always politics.[104]

We have to return to the political situation in Rome, which lead to the transformation of an unpolitical astronomer into a criminal.[105]

Fischer holds a similar viewpoint:

Now the care for the people's souls surely was not the only motive for the Church's actions. The Thirty Years' War had begun in 1618 and finished the time of verbal debate. The Church found itself in the hardest battle over its existence since its earliest history.[106]

In the beginning, Pope Urban VIII supported the Roman Catholic German emperor, but switched over to Roman Catholic France and Protestant Sweden after the two had become allies. He took as an example the ruthless French Cardinal Richelieu and was responsible for the prolongment of the war.

In 1627-1630 Italy underwent the additional Mantuan War of Succession. At the same time the two Roman powers, Spain and France, which both were allies of the Pope, started to fight each other. The head of the Spanish opposition to the Holy See, Cardinal Borgia, came into conflict with the Pope over political topics in 1632, because a peace treaty was in view, while the Pope wanted the war to go on.[107] A tumult among the Cardinals resulted, after which the Pope began a great political purge in the Vatican, which more or less by chance struck all those favorable to Galileo.[108] The Pope initiated many trials by the Inquisition and became an increasingly cruel ruler.

The following connections probably became fateful to Galileo, because they were in opposition to those of the Pope:

The close connection to the family of the Medicis, from which the Tuscan prince came, and which, together with Venice,[109] fought against the Pope and were only rehabilitated after his death in 1644;[110]

The connection with Austria[111] and Emperor Rudolf II through Kepler, as the Pope together with France and Sweden fought against the Roman Catholic German emperor. The Prince of Tuscany and the German emperor were close friends.[112]

[104.] Nach Z. Solle, *op. cit.*, 45.
[105.] *ibid.*, 22.
[106.] K. Fischer, *op. cit.*, 144.
[107.] Z. Solle, *op. cit.*, 25; cf. K. Fischer, *op. cit.*, 144.
[108.] Z. Solle, *op. cit.*, 26-27.
[109.] About the open resistance of Venice cf. K. Fischer, *op. cit.*, 144.
[110.] Z. Solle, *op. cit.*, 54.
[111.] *ibid.*, 55.
[112.] *ibid.*, 57.

Z. Solle has shown in detail that it was the beginning of "modern" nationalism, which left Galileo between the fronts of the nationalistic Pope, the Italian cities, and the parties of the Thirty Years' War:[113]

> Thus it was not the shadow of a dying and dark night, which put pressure on the scientist (*i.e.* Galileo) ... but the beginning of modern times."[114]

J. Hemleben, who favors Galileo, has argued, that he would not have had to undergo any trial, if moved from Padua to Florence, since Padua depended on Venice, but Florence on Rome.[115] Padua allowed great freedom for scientific research, because Venice was independent of Rome.[116] Even Protestants studied there,[117] a comfort impossible in Florence. One of Galileo's best friends, Giovanni Francesco Sagredo (1571-1620), had already warned Galileo in 1611 against moving to Florence, because there he would be dependent on international politics and on the Jesuits.[118] But Galileo ignored this and all later warnings.

14. Galileo died in 1642, two years before the death of his great enemy, Pope Urban VIII, in 1644. In 1644 the whole situation in Italy changed and the family of the Medicis came back to honor. Galileo would surely have been rehabilitated[119] (cf. Thesis 13).

15. Galileo was not a non-Christian scientist of the Enlightenment, but a convinced Roman Catholic.[120] It was indeed his endeavor to show the compatibility of his teachings with the Bible, which among other things brought him into conflicts with the Roman Catholic establishment.

Galileo's thoughts on the relation of faith and science can be seen in the quotations cited by K. Fischer under Thesis 7. Solle adds:

> As a deeply believing scientist, Galileo could not live with a discrepancy between science and faith, which seemed to arise when he started to interpret the Bible. As layman, he experienced much resistance by theologians .... His attempts to interpret the Bible were one of the reasons which led to the trial. Another reason was his attempt to popularize the Copernican system.[121]

[113.] *ibid.*, 64, 65.

[114.] *ibid.*, 65.

[115.] J. Hemleben, *op. cit.*, 62-64 u. a.

[116.] *ibid.*, 62.

[117.] *ibid.*, 32.

[118.] *ibid.*, 63-64.

[119.] Z. Solle, *op. cit.*, 64-71.

[120.] This has been proved most clearly by O. Pedersen. "Galileo's Religion," in ed. G. V. Coyne, M. Heller, J. Zycinski, *op. cit.*, 75-102, especially 88-92 on Galileo's faith in God and 92-100 on his Roman Catholic faith and his rejection of all non-Catholic "heresies."

[121.] Z. Solle, *op. cit.*, 9.; cf. the judgment by K. Fischer, *op. cit.*, 114-115, quoted in the explanation to Thesis 7.

Because Galileo interpreted the Bible as a layman and wrote his books in everyday Italian, and thus was a forerunner of Italian nationalism (cf. Thesis 15), he experienced the same resistance Martin Luther had experienced one hundred years earlier when he started to use German in his theological writings.

The preface of his major work *Dialogue* contains clear statements that Galileo did not want to stand in opposition to the Bible[122] or to the Roman Catholic Church. Albrecht Fölsing writes:

> Many of Galileo's admirers in the nineteenth and twentieth centuries could understand this preface only as a concession to censorship. Some interpreted it as a roguish by-passing of the Decree, others as unworthy submission, again others as a mockery of the authority of the Church .... We, on the other hand, want to suggest this text to be an authentic expression of Galileo's intention under the existing conditions. The content is more or less the same as in the introduction to the letter to Ignoli in 1624, which needed no approval from a censor, as it was not written for print, but which was intended to test how much freedom for scientific discussion the Pope and the Roman See would allow. Even if one takes into account those tactical aspects of these texts (the letter of 1624 and the preface to the *Dialogue*) there is no reason to doubt the honest intentions of the faithful Catholic, Galileo.[123]

As a defender of Papal infallibility, L. Pastor has stated that the Pope saw a Protestant danger in Galileo, but others have doubted this.[124] On the one hand, one of Galileo's first critics was a Protestant pastor from Bohemia.[125] Conversely, Galileo's writings were published and printed in Protestant states and thus became known. Besides, Galileo himself was a declared enemy of Protestantism.[126]

16. Result: Galileo was not a scientist who denied any metaphysics or favored the separation of faith and science (cf. Thesis 15).

Discussing a quotation in Galileo's *Letters on Sunspots,* Fischer speaks in more general terms:

> In those last sentences, one can hear a somewhat different Galileo from the picture of Galileo which the traditional interpretation paints. The main line of the historiographs of science from Wohlwill to Drake presents Galileo as anti-meta-physician and anti-philosopher, as the initiator of a physics based on experiment and observation, as the

---

[122.] cf. on the positive attitude of Galileo to Scripture E. Wohlwill, *op. cit.*, 1: 485-524, 542-555, especially 543.

[123.] A. Fölsing, *Galileo Galilei, Prozess ohne Ende: Eine Biographie* (Munic, 1983), 414; cf. also 414-415.

[124.] Following Z. Solle, *op. cit.*, 38.

[125.] *ibid.*, 7.

[126.] E. Wohlwill, *op. cit.*, 1:552-555; O. Pedersen. "Galileo's Religion," *op. cit.*, 92-100.

defender of science against the illegitimate demands of religion, as the promoter of a separation of faith and science. And now we hear a confession of love to the great Creator being the final goal of all our work, thus including our scientific work! Science as perception of God's truth! ... The ruling historiography of science cannot be freed from the reproach that they have read Galileo's writings too selectively.[127]

A little later Fischer writes about the misinterpretation of Galileo's work:

This misinterpretation led to the inability to evaluate correctly Galileo's early writings (*Juvenilia*), to ignoring many sections with speculative and metaphysical content scattered all over Galileo's writings, yea, even to a misinterpretation of Galileo's understanding of the relationship between science and faith ....[128]

Dr. Thomas Schirrmacher lives in Bonn, Germany. He teaches at a seminary, is editor of a theological magazine, is in charge of a German theological education extension program, and directs a small publishing house.

[127.] K. Fischer, *op. cit.*, 114.
[128.] *ibid.*, 115.

Why Christians Need to Understand Economics

Stephen C. Perks

The kingdom of Man is the Kingdom of the Creature, and it flourishes both in this world and in the after-life at one and the same time. Its pretensions are common to both and rise and fall together.

This means that the idealist must have a politically controlled reality, not a free market economy. The Bible says, concerning the creation of man, that he was created out of the dust of the earth (the dust having been previously made by God), and that man is tied to the dust and returns to it. To accept this fact about ourselves means that we accept also the fact that our economics, like all our lives, are [sic] tied to material realities, not as a penalty but as their normal and natural circumstance. Instead of rebelling against it, we recognize that life means precisely that for us, and life is good.

Economics thus is a barometer. Interest in it marks a sound eschatology, normally. Disinterest in it means an element of neoplatonism or Manichaean thinking.

R. J. Rushdoony, *God's Plan for Victory*

The Not-So-Dismal Science

Economics has been called the "dismal science." This is in a sense odd, since dismal it is not — it affects us all in the most direct and pervasive manner and as a result arouses some of the most heated arguments and angry emotions that modern man experiences — and it has no claim to be a science, at least not in the modern sense — *i.e.*, an exact science. Nonetheless, it is not difficult to understand why the subject has attracted this opprobrious appellation, which is so universally affirmed by the general population. In spite of the fact that economics affects us all vitally and is thus of the very greatest concern to us in every detail of our lives, the subject has suffered badly at the hands of professional economists. It seems always to be hedged about with ideas and arguments that seem difficult to understand and that professional economists seem reluctant to explain in clear terms — assuming of course that they understand the arguments themselves and are not just repeating in parrot-fashion the ideas of the latest school of economic mumbo-jumbo. And whenever one hears economists talking on the radio or television or reads about the subject in the paper or textbooks, one is faced with an endless and bewildering mass of statistics, equations and arguments — or perhaps just assertions masquerading as arguments — that are hard to make sense of or to follow. It is, therefore, to some extent what economists have done to economics that has turned it into a dismal science. Moreover, economics seems inevitably to be linked with politics, and hence with the

tedious and inane propaganda put out by politicians who seem utterly unable
to answer a simple question in a direct manner. I am convinced that it is the
association of economics with this latter fact as much as anything else that has
rendered the subject so odious to the general population. Politicians so often
hide behind a misleading screen of economic "doublespeak" when they know
that to answer their critics honestly would make them unpopular and possibly
even unelectable. Economics is thus abused by politicians and misunderstood
by the general public.

But why do Christians, of all people, need to understand how the economy
works and how it should be reformed?

Economics is Relevant

There are a number of answers to these questions: First, as already stated,
economics affects us all. What goes on in the economy, how politicians
manipulate it for their own ends, or for political expediency permit other
privileged groups to manipulate it, affects us all in the most pronounced
manner, whether we find the subject interesting or not. The condition of the
economy determines a great part of our lives, from where we can afford to go
on vacation to whether we can get the kind of medical treatment we need or
want when we are ill; from how much we can afford to give to charity and
thereby help those less fortunate than ourselves to how much we can afford
to give to church and thereby help to build the kingdom of God; from where
we live to how we travel to work, or indeed whether we have any work at all.
It affects how we raise and educate our children, and it affects not only
whether they will be educated in private or state schools, but what kind and
level of service is provided in both systems, and it affects how we provide for
ourselves and how our children provide for us in retirement and old age. All
these, and many more, are vitally important matters. How we respond to them
will be determined by the extent of our knowledge — or ignorance — of
economics. A better understanding of the economic realities on which our
lives depend would affect the way most people act economically in these
areas, and this would have a significant effect on the economy. Indeed,
knowledge is probably the most vital element in any form of entrepreneurial
activity or business enterprise.

Economics is Not Neutral

Second, economics is not a subject that is religiously neutral. Moral
judgments are not irrelevant in economic matters. The way our economy
works is intimately bound up with the fundamental issue of right and wrong
and thus the answers to the questions that the present state of our economy
poses cannot be neutral from a religious point of view since what one judges
to be right or wrong is itself intimately bound up with one's religious

perspective. The economy concerns Christians urgently today since it is an area where vital issues of right and wrong and the consequences of society's response to those issues are played out.

Economics is Addressed Biblically

Third, the Bible itself directly addresses this subject in the most uncompromising terms. Economics is an area of concern to God since he has, in his revealed word, given specific and abiding rules about how man is to behave economically. To be ignorant of at least the basic principles of economics is to some extent to cut oneself off from an important area of divine revelation and thus to be ignorant of God's will for man in an area in which he has commanded man's obedience. It is the calling and duty of the church to address *all* areas in which God has revealed ethical norms for human behavior. Not to do so is to ignore God's law, God's will for man. This is so in economic matters just as much as in any other area. Immoral economic behavior must be addressed and challenged by the church no less than immoral sexual behavior. God has revealed laws governing both realms of human activity. It is thus important that the church should teach God's laws for economic behavior and call society back to obedience to those laws when it departs from them. It is necessary therefore that the church bring the moral teaching of the Bible to bear on the economic issues that face us today. If Christians are to do this effectively, however, they must be informed. Ignorance of the economic realities on which so much of our life depends will vitiate the church's ability to speak prophetically in this area and to call the present generation back to faithfulness to God's word.

Economics Affects Culture and Civilization

Fourth, the future of our culture and of our civilization is vitally affected by economic issues. An economic system that systematically penalizes the kinds of economic activity that lead to capitalization and economic growth will have far-reaching effects not only on the general standard of living enjoyed by society but also on the long-term future of a civilization by effectively making the civilizing process itself impossible to sustain on a scale that would support the kind of culture and welfare that we have come to expect in the West generally today. The effect of unleashing such a system on a culture can be seen from the history of the Soviet Union. Not until the latter part of the 1950s did the peasants of Soviet Russia attain the standard of living they had enjoyed under the Tzars prior to the Russian Revolution — and this is no apologetic for tsarism. The systematic enforcing of socialist economics in Russia led to a drastic decrease in the standard of living, and this in spite of the massive Western aid that was poured into Russia after the Revolution. Socialist economics, to put the matter succinctly, cripples economic growth and retards the technological advancement of civilization, which on the physical level is made possible only by capitalization (*i.e.*, economic growth) on the scale that we have seen it in Western Christendom. And of course such capitalization was itself, historically, made possible in the West only because of the adoption of a Christian worldview and moral ethic and the subsequent rationalization of economic activity in accordance with that ethic. As our culture increasingly moves away from the kind of economic system that made our modern civilization possible to a system that has already proven not only its inability to advance civilization but its inevitable link with economic crisis and decapitalization, our society will begin to decline economically. Indeed, this has already happened in many ways. In spite of the progress made by the Thatcher government in the 1980s, the British nation is now intimately involved with and committed to membership in a pan-European super-state that is socialist throughout and, in order to achieve its goals, is strangling our nation economically and reducing it to economic servitude by means of bureaucratic legislation passed in Brussels to which our government must yield.

What is not so obvious, however, is the fact that as the worldview that in the West has made cultural advancement possible — that is, the *Christian* worldview — declines, the *kind* of culture that has characterized our society will also disappear. In other words, we shall enter a period of transition from one culture to another. The result will be the loss not only of economic power but also of all those ideals and principles that our nation has for so long taken for granted — *e.g.,* justice, the rule of law, the right of private ownership, freedom of movement and, ultimately, freedom to practise a *Christian* way of life in its fulness.

That this prognosis is no mere piece of scaremongering is amply borne out by the course of Soviet history. It may take longer for the West to arrive at the same result, and the process may be dressed up in apparel more familiar to Western man, but the outcome will inevitably be the same in substance. Our society has already embarked on this ruinous course, though few have understood its ultimate consequences. If we are to change the course of events and avert the ruin of our civilization, and, by God's grace, experience a renewal rather than the demise of our culture, it is vital that Christians understand the issues and address them decisively from a Christian perspective. A Christian perspective on the economic issues facing the nation today is thus vital for the renewal of our culture. Of course, economics is one issue among many, but it is an important issue and it must be addressed if we are to be delivered from the dark age that, without a revival of Christian civilization in our land, looms large before us.

A Brief History

Before we can determine where we need to go, however, we need to understand where we are, where we have come from, and how we got here. In this respect the modern church faces a number of problems: First, there is among Christians generally an apathy toward such matters. When a colleague of mine put forward in discussion with another professing Christian the possibility that our society may very well soon experience a period of economic decline on a significant scale as divine judgment on our nation for its abandonment of God's law, he was faced with the response, "As long as it doesn't happen in my lifetime!" Unfortunately, this attitude is all too common, and is indicative, of course, of an intensely un-Christian, indeed pagan, frame of mind. One would have expected this kind of comment from a non-believer, and such sentiments have not characterized the Christian worldview throughout its long history — not until the twentieth century, that is. This is because in the twentieth century, more than at any other time in the church's history, Christians have utterly compromised themselves in their acceptance of the world's philosophy of life — *e.g.,* existentialism, nihilism, hedonism, man at the center of his own world. In other words, the church in our age is probably more *humanistic* than at any other period of its history. Where once non-Christians thought and behaved like Christians, today Christians think and behave like non-Christians. The church is radically compromised and thus utterly ineffective in its calling to challenge the non-believing world. Christianity is a future-oriented Faith, offering hope to a desperate world. Very little of such a Faith is reflected in the church's attitude to some important social issues, however. Our culture is, as a consequence, without vision and without hope. One could hardly envisage the apostle Paul, faced with the prospect of the destruction of Jerusalem, exclaiming, "As long as it doesn't happen in my lifetime!" On the contrary, he wrote, "I could wish that myself were accursed from Christ for my brethren, my kinsmen according to the flesh" (Rom. 9:3). Such an attitude is diametrically opposed to the apathy and escapism that characterizes the modern church. The Christian religion has turned the world upside down, or rather right-side up — *i.e.,* from depravity to righteousness — wherever and whenever it has been in the ascendancy.

Economic Pietism

Second, among some Christian groups and churches — one is tempted to say "cults," since this term describes many such churches far more accurately — the problem is much more serious than this, more pathological in nature. Pietism, which sees the Christian Faith purely in personal terms, that is, which sees it as relevant only to one's private life and perhaps one's family — though even this is usually restricted considerably — and which views the corporate or public aspect of the Faith as being confined purely to the church as an institution, has provided a theological rationale in the twentieth century for the apathy mentioned above. Such apathy, for those who embrace pietism, is not only an acceptable attitude to "worldly" matters, it is the *only* acceptable attitude in their view. Pietists are convinced, it would seem, that their pietistic perspective has been the norm throughout the history of Christendom. This is peculiar, since all of Christian history points to the opposite conclusion.

Throughout the two millennia of its history, the Christian church has testified to the fact that the Christian Faith is a culture- and nation-transforming, indeed world-transforming, religion that addresses every aspect of man's life, both individual and corporate. The prominent, peculiar blindness to the facts of Christian history is easily explained, however, for the church of the twentieth century, by and large, has abandoned the study and appreciation of Christian history. Yet the problem amounts to more than ignorance of Christian history.[1] Such ignorance in our day is part of a much larger problem, namely, the church's failure to understand its calling in the world. Pietism has rendered the church of the twentieth century impotent and irrelevant at a time when the Christian gospel in its fulness — that is to say, the whole counsel or word of God, not simply the truncated message peddled by modern evangelical pietists — needs to be heard desperately. The church's failure in this century to articulate and proclaim the comprehensive claims of the Christian Faith to a society gripped by a revival of paganism more virulent than it has been for over a millennium is itself a major cause of the decline of Western culture and, as part of that general decline, of Western economies also. A pietistic imitation of the Christian Faith may have seemed attractive to many in the genteel culture of a largely Christianized Victorian England, but it is no match for the resurgent paganism that threatens to destroy Christendom today. For that, the real thing is needed.

The Injurious Effects of Pietism

This pietism is pathological for another reason. In spite of the aloofness that pietists try to create in their personal lives, the results of pietism are anything

---

[1.] By "Christian history" I do not mean *church* history, though the latter is encompassed by the former. The study of church history is a well-established and popular field in academic circles and beyond, but the study of the history of the Christian West as a Christian civilization is much less common among historians. The secular universities of the West are, of course, busily promoting "revisionist" history, which from a religious perspective means history without reference to Christianity or in which Christianity is vilified as the cause of the individual's and society's gravest problems. This we can expect from humanists, but it is a sad indication of the apathy, indeed apostasy, of the modern church that it has acquiesced in such revisionist ideas and sat idly by while Christianity, which has been the single most important influence on the development of our civilization, has been largely written out of our history.

but unrelated to the world of everyday affairs. Pietists seek to be otherworldly to such an extent that they are not concerned with "banal" and "unspiritual" subjects such as economics — about which God as so much to say. They see no need to develop a Biblical perspective on social issues because these are "worldly," whereas the Faith, so they think, is above the world and unrelated to such issues. But this attitude succeeds only in creating a vacuum. Even pietists must live in the real world and think about and act in terms of the everyday social, economic and political issues that face us all. Hence, without a well thought-out *Christian* perspective on these issues, pietists unwittingly imbibe the *truly* worldly attitudes around them. Because they believe these issues are neutral from a religious perspective, they do not stop to consider whether their views are Biblical, whether or not they conform to Christian truth. They simply imbibe the views of the world around them unthinkingly, ignorantly. In so doing they become perpetrators of the very worldliness they think and claim they have escaped by devotion to a purely personal or church-oriented faith. Thus it is that the church, by its apathy and pietism, has become an avenue by which our culture has been repaganized, since wherever the church leaves a vacuum, some ideology will surface to fill that vacuum, for non-believers and believers alike. That ideology in our day has been a godless humanism that has prepared the way for the repaganizing of Western society. But the problem does not stop here.

Humanism Masquerading in the Church

Third, when the church is then challenged about its apathy, it so often responds by merely regurgitating the latest humanistic sentiments in the dress of Christian language, thereby baptizing utterly un-Biblical and un-Christian ideals. Thus, in our day the church, because it has not developed a Biblical perspective on economic and social issues, has regurgitated socialist ideals and principles and insisted that they are Christian ideals and principles simply because good *intentions* have been imputed — though often incorrectly — to those who espouse such ideals. But good intentions do not guarantee that one will hold to *Biblical* teaching. Had this kind of sloppy thinking been adopted with regard to the doctrine of the atonement, the church would have abandoned a distinctively Christian (*i.e.,* Biblical) theory of the atonement long ago and adopted instead Unitarianism and universalism *en masse.* The Christian Faith demands, though, as vigorous an application of Biblical principles to social, economic and political issues as it does to narrowly theological issues such as the atonement, since only as this is done will the church be able to articulate a distinctively *Christian* voice on these issues as opposed to the old and worn-out humanistic answers dressed up to look Christian.

The Economics Task

The task before us, therefore, is to develop a Biblical perspective on these issues and thereby help to revive our nation's Christian heritage. The first step in this process is to pursue understanding. With regard to the economy, we must understand how it works and how Biblical teachings apply to it. If the church is to address the vitally important issues of morality that bear on man's economic behavior, it must have a clearer vision of where we are, how we got here, and what we should do if the economy is to conform to Christian — *i.e.,* Biblical — instruction.

Stephen C. Perks is the Founder and Director of the Foundation for Christian Reconstruction and Director of the Institute of Christian Political Thought in England.

The Law of God

Herbert W. Titus

It is a modern heresy that holds that the law of God has no meaning nor any binding force for man today. It is an aspect of the influence of humanistic and evolutionary thought on the church, and it posits an evolving and developing god. This "dispensational" god expressed himself in law in an earlier age, then later expressed himself by grace alone, and is now perhaps to express himself in still another way. But this is not the God of Scripture, whose grace and law remain the same in every age, because He, as the sovereign and absolute Lord, changes not, nor does He need to change. The strength of man is the absoluteness of his God.

R. J. Rushdoony, *The Institutes of Biblical Law*

Introduction

In 1973, when R. J. Rushdoony published these words in the Introduction to his monumental *The Institutes of Biblical Law,* I was teaching law at the University of Oregon. Having had no Christian upbringing, I had no idea that my evolutionary philosophy of law had its roots in a theological dispute over the God of the Bible.

All I knew was what I had been taught at Harvard Law School. The teaching there had long been under the tutelage of men like Roscoe Pound who had discarded the fixed law of God in favor of an ever-changing and increasingly complex set of rules devised by men.[1]

In 1975 — just two years after the publication of the *Institutes* — by God's providence on my conversion to Christ, my pastor introduced me to Rushdoony's works. Together with the Holy Scriptures, and under the guidance of the Holy Spirit, I learned the law.

I remember well one of my first lessons. For many years, as an evolutionist and a teacher of criminal law, I wrestled with the question of individual criminal liability. How could anyone be held responsible for making a wrong choice if his acts were determined by his genes and environment in a time-and-chance universe?

It was Rushdoony's exposition of Dt. 24:16 that first alerted me to "the Biblical doctrine ... of individual responsibility," tracing its origin to the law of the Creator and to the fact that man had been created in God's image.[2] It was that discovery that also led me to find that America's law had been founded on the Biblical creation account of the law of individual fault.[3]

[1.] See Titus, "God, Evolution, Legal Education and Law," *Journal of Christian Jurisprudence* (Tulsa, OK, 1980), 11.

[2.] R. J. Rushdoony, *The Institutes of Biblical Law* (The Craig Press, 1973), 269-270.

[3.] Herbert Titus, *God, Man and Law: The Biblical Principles* (Oak Brook, IL, 1994), 137-199.

Soon after making this discovery, I determined to impart this Biblical wisdom to my students at the University of Oregon. This teaching was not well-received.

On one occasion, I proposed to my students that they could not begin to understand the history of criminal law, if they did not take into account that the architects of that law believed what Jesus Christ taught about mankind in Mk. 7:15, 21:

> There is nothing from without a man, that entering into him can defile him; but the things which come out of him, those are they that defile the man .... For from within, out of the heart of men, proceed evil thoughts, adulteries, fornications, murders ....[4]

What ensued was not an academic discussion, but a protest. Invoking the "constitutional doctrine of the separation of church and state," several students shouted that it was illegitimate for me to quote from the Bible in a state law school.

Later, I was told by some accrediting authorities in the American Bar Association that it was also illegitimate for a private Christian law school to teach law on the premise that the Bible as the word of God is both true and relevant to the study of law in pluralist America.

I had been prepared intellectually for both of these challenges by another truth that Rushdoony taught in his *Institutes*:

> Because law governs man and society, because it establishes and declares the meaning of justice and righteousness, law is inescapably religious, in that it establishes in practical fashion the ultimate concerns of a culture. Accordingly, a fundamental and necessary premise in any and every study of law must be, first, a recognition of this religious nature of law.[5]

I had also been prepared for the spiritual battle in which I found myself by Rushdoony's astute observation that "there can be no tolerance in a law-system for another religion." And I was prepared emotionally by Rushdoony's insightful forewarning:

> Legal positivism, a humanistic faith, has been savage in its hostility to the Biblical law-system ....[6]

What I learned, then, about the law of God through my study of Rushdoony's *Institutes* was not only what to teach my students about the nature of law, but how to live lawfully in lawless times. Through the twenty years now of my Christian walk, I have met a number of students who have also learned the same lessons.

[4.] See Rushdoony's treatment of this teaching in the *Institutes*, 709.
[5.] *ibid.*, 4.
[6.] *ibid.*, 5.

In fact, during those twenty years, I have encountered with increasing frequency young people who have read Rushdoony and been influenced by him. Coming from a broad range of denominational backgrounds, and embracing a variety of expressions of a vital Christian Faith, I have been encouraged by this growth in knowledge of the law of God within the body of Christ.

Rushdoony's impact, however, has not been limited to the church. He has influenced a number of people who do not make a profession of Christian Faith to nonetheless reconsider "the historic power and vitality [of] Biblical faith and law" as the best hope for the future of America as a nation.

And what is it that Biblical law offers to a nation that no other system of law can match? Rushdoony has claimed that apart from God's revelation, covenant, and dominion mandate there can be no law.[7]

In other words, any nation that attempts to build a civil legal system on any other foundation than the law of God is doomed to fail.[8] Rushdoony is right.

Law is Revelation

In the academic year of 1921 Roscoe Pound delivered a series of lectures on the philosophy of law at Yale. Near the beginning of his remarks, Pound made a startling confession:

> From the time when lawgivers gave over the attempt to maintain the general security by belief that particular bodies of human law had been divinely dictated or divinely revealed or divinely sanctioned, they have had to wrestle with the problem of proving to mankind that the law was something fixed and settled, whose authority was beyond question, while at the same time enabling it to make constant readjustments and occasional radical changes under the pressure of infinite and variable human desires.[9]

What Pound discovered remains true today. No nation is able to establish a system of law apart from God's revelation because law, by its nature, must be fixed as to time, uniform as to person or situation, and universal as to place.[10]

By definition, finite and fallen man cannot be the source of law.[11] Only the infinite and omniscient Creator God of the Scriptures — "the self-existent and absolute one" as Rushdoony puts it in the *Institutes* — can be that source. All other sources are, by definition, limited by time, circumstance, and space.[12]

---

7. *ibid.*, 4-9.
8. *ibid.*, 4.
9. Pound, *Introduction to the Philosophy of Law* (New Haven, CT, 1954), 3.
10. See Blackstone, *Commentaries on the Laws of England* (Oxford 1765), I: 38-41.
11. *ibid.*, I: 41-42.
12. Rushdoony, *op. cit.*, 15-18.

Without God's revelation, law ceases to be objective. Instead, it becomes a pragmatic tool for those in power to manipulate men and the social order for their own purposes.[13]

The Pharisees were particularly adept at this, elevating their traditions over the law of God.[14] In order to preserve their place in the Roman Empire, the Pharisees set aside the law of God and sought the death of Jesus.[15] Forty years later, in 70 A. D., the Romans destroyed the Temple and with it the Jewish nation, dispersing them throughout the Mediterranean.[16]

Today, legal scholars, lawyers and judges justify abortion for the good of society, even though abortion is condemned by the Sixth Commandment.[17] They promote sex outside the marriage covenant as a positive good, even though forbidden by the Seventh Commandment.[18]

As was true of the Pharisees before them, these modern-day pragmatists will discover that violating the law of God will bring destruction to the nation.[19]

In the nation's early history, however, America's leaders knew better. They adhered to a common law system that rested squarely upon God's revelation. Sir William Blackstone, the great expositor of our nation's English common law heritage, defined law in relation to the law of the Creator:

> ... [N]o human laws are of any validity, if contrary to this; and such of them as are valid derive all their force, and all their authority, mediately or immediately, from this original.[20]

American lawyers — like Jesse Root of Connecticut — while affirming this revelational principle, endeavored to correct the errors of their English ancestors through a more consistent submission to the written revelation in the Bible. Thus, Root wrote in 1798 that the common law of Connecticut was "most clearly made known and delineated in the book of divine revelations":

> [H]eaven and earth may pass away and all the systems and works of man sink into oblivion, but not one jot or tittle of this law shall ever fall ....
>
> This is the Magna Charta of all our natural and religious rights and liberties — the only solid basis of our civil constitution and privileges ....[21]

---

13. *ibid.*, 17.

14. *ibid.*, 706-709.

15. John 11:47-53.

16. Durant, *Caesar and Christ* (New York, NY, 1944), 542-549.

17. Rushdoony, *op. cit.*, 263-269.

18. *ibid.*, 392-401.

19. *ibid.*, 515, 522.

20. Blackstone, *op. cit.*, I: 41.

21. Jesse Root, *The Origin of Government and Laws in Connecticut* (1798), reprinted in Miller, ed., *The Legal Mind in America* (Ithaca, NY, 1962), 35-36.

Rushdoony in our day — like Jesse Root in his — is calling America back to the God of revelation and to his law. In doing so he is also calling the nation back to its original covenant.

The Law is Covenant

In *This Independent Republic*, Rushdoony reminds his reader that America's "origins are Christian and Augustinian, deeply rooted in Reformation, medieval and patristic history."[22]

In a brilliant chapter entitled, "The Right to Emigrate," Rushdoony lays down the nation's covenant legacy. While he focuses on New England, and especially the Massachusetts Bay Colony, Rushdoony posits that the "idea of a covenant people... was common to the colonies and to their English background." [23]

This covenant principle, Rushdoony claims, originated with "the emigrant Abraham, and the emigrant people under Moses who left Egypt, the house of bondage, for Canaan, the land of promise."[24] As was the case with Abraham and Moses, so it was with the American colonists. By exercising their right to emigrate, they were duty-bound "to establish a godly society and institutions in terms of that faith."[25]

The first American covenants were the English colonial charters. Even before the Massachusetts Bay Charter of 1629, the original Virginia Charter of 1606 provides ample evidence that Rushdoony's view is correct.

First, the Virginia charter proclaims that the land under its jurisdiction is not "possessed by any Christian Prince or People." Then, it states the purpose of the Virginia colony to be the "propagating of Christian Religion to such People, as yet live in Darkness and miserable Ignorance to the true Knowledge and Worship of God, and ... to bring [them] ... to human Civility, and to a settled and quiet Government ...."[26]

This purpose — to evangelize a lost people — was recited (or implied) in every subsequent English colonial charter. The means chosen to establish a godly civil order was likewise reflected in every subsequent charter. And by what authority did the English colonists claim this purpose and this means? It was the Great Commission from Jesus Christ who alone has all authority in heaven and earth.[27]

[22.] Rushdoony, *This Independent Republic* (Fairfax, VA, 1978), vii.
[23.] *ibid.*, 43.
[24.] *ibid.*
[25.] *ibid.*, 44.
[26.] *The First Charter of Virginia* reprinted in Perry, ed., *Sources of Our Liberties* (Chicago, IL, 1978), 39-40.
[27.] Herbert Titus, "The First Charter of Virginia: Seedbed for the Nation," *The Forecast* (Virginia Beach, VA, 1994), Vol. I, No. 14.

Not surprisingly, the heart of the newly established civil orders was the covenant. As Richard Perry of the American Bar Foundation has written about one of these charters, the Mayflower Compact:

> The document represents the application to the affairs of civil government of the philosophy of the church covenant which was the basis of Puritan theology. This theology found in the Scriptures the right of men to associate and covenant to form a church and civil government and choose their own officers to administer both religious and civil affairs.[28]

From these charters came domestic political constitutions, the first promulgated in 1639 by the people of Connecticut.[29] That document's preamble stated the civil covenant in unmistakably Biblical terms:

> ...[W]ell knowing where a people are gathered to gather the word of God requires that to mayntayn the peace and union of such a people there should be an orderly and decent Government established according to God, to order and dispose of the affayres of the people ... [we] doe therefore assotiate and conjoyne our selves to be as one Publike State... for our selves and our Successors and such as shall be adjoyned to us att any tyme hereafter ....[30]

This Connecticut Constitution continued to be the form of government for the people of that State even after the American Revolution.[31] This continuity with America's early Christian covenant history, even after the formation of the nation, is the kind of evidence that gives support to Rushdoony's thesis that the American Revolution was, in fact, a counter-revolution to preserve the covenant rule of law. [32]

It is in this sense that Rushdoony refers to the early American constitutions as having established Christian civil orders, not secular states. At the heart of such orders was the legal and political enforcement of a limited civil jurisdiction, so that the individual, the family, and the church might flourish in covenant relation to God. [33]

Rushdoony's emphasis on the law as covenant, then, is not only to establish and maintain lawful authority, but to restore true liberty. Most significantly, he has called for the return of the covenant law of the family as a buffer to the totalitarian reach of the modern state. In doing so he has summoned the return of the law of dominion under God.

[28.] Perry, ed., *op cit.*, 57.
[29.] *ibid.*, 115.
[30.] *Fundamental Orders of Connecticut* (1639) reprinted in Perry, *Sources*, 120.
[31.] Perry, *op. cit.*, 310.
[32.] Rushdoony, *This Independent Republic*, 9-32.
[33.] *idem.*, *The Nature of the American System* (Fairfax, VA, 1965), 1-23.

The Law is Dominion Under God

"All kinds of reasons are assigned for the decline of the family," Rushdoony wrote in 1977, but "one important cause is commonly left out":

> This cause for the breakdown of the family is the attack on and the decline of the freedom of private property.[34]

With this observation, Rushdoony rightfully points out that four of the Ten Commandments are designed to protect the family and private property. And he sounds the alarm against communism and all other forms of state socialism as attacks not only on private property, but on the family. [35]

What is at stake in this battle is whether the family or the state is to be "the central institution in law and in society." "Historically and Biblically," Rushdoony contends, it is the family.[36]

As the family has deteriorated in American society, so has life, liberty, and property. This has come about because the State has usurped the family's authority and responsibility to educate the children and to make economic provision for its members.[37] But this was not true in the early history of our nation.

America's common law of private property was rooted in Genesis 1:26-28 and its historical account of family free enterprise from Adam and Eve to the families of Israel in the promised land.[38] The common law generally was designed "to foster and protect the family, not only through rules protecting property ownership... but also through criminal sanctions prohibiting adultery, fornication, sodomy, and bigamy." [39]

Since the Darwinian revolution, however, this common-law legacy has been replaced by New Deal entitlement programs that have undermined the responsibility of parents for their children and children for their parents. In addition, the civil authorities have not only failed to enforce the common law rules against sexual immorality, but many have promoted sexual promiscuity as a "constitutional right."[40]

These are the root causes of the economic crisis that the United States faces as a nation. Yet both Republicans and Democrats have placed the "social issues" on the back burner so that they can cut taxes and balance the budget.

---

[34] *idem.*, *Law and Liberty* (Fairfax, VA, 1977), 68.
[35] *ibid.*, 68-77.
[36] *ibid.*, 78.
[37] *idem.*, *The Nature of the American System*, 17-22.
[38] Herbert Titus, "God's Revelation: Foundation for the Common Law," *Regent University Law Review* (Virginia Beach, VA, 1994), 4:17-26.
[39] *ibid.*, 27.
[40] *e.g.*, Tribe, *American Constitutional Law* (Mineola, NY, 1988, 2d ed.), 1421-1435.

Until the family is restored, there will be no resolution of the economic ills of America. Central to this restoration is obedience to the dominion mandate, as Rushdoony wrote in his *Institutes*:

> Genesis 1:27-30 makes clear that God created man to subdue the earth and to exercise dominion over it under God ... [T]he creation mandate is plainly spoken to man in his married estate, and with the creation of woman in mind. Thus, essential to the function of the family under God, and to the role of the man as the head of the household, is the call to subdue the earth and exercise dominion over it. This gives the family a possessive function .... The earth was created "very good" but it was as yet undeveloped in terms of subjugation and possession by man, God's appointed governor. This government is particularly the calling of the man as husband and father, and of the family as an institution.[41]

Equally important is Rushdoony's teachings on the relationship between men and women under the dominion mandate. He uncovers the error of the English and early American common law which subjugated women as servants of their husbands. At the same time he critiques the modern feminist solution as having "put women into competition with men."[42]

Biblical law, in contrast, instructs that the woman, as her husband's "help-meet," is joined together with her husband "in the covenant ... to subdue the earth and exercise dominion over it."[43] She is, as Proverbs 31 demonstrates, a "businessman" in her own right and quite capable of taking over all the business affairs of the family "so that her husband can assume public office as a civil magistrate ...."[44]

Conclusion

In his Introduction to the *Institutes,* Rushdoony proclaimed that his purpose was to reverse the present trend in America away from Biblical law that she might be restored as a land of liberty and justice for all.

Rushdoony's legacy to America is like that of the prophet, Hosea, to Israel and Judah. Like Hosea, he has sounded the warning:

> My people are destroyed for lack of knowledge: because thou hast rejected knowledge, I will also reject thee, that thou shalt be no priest to me: seeing that thou hast forgotten the law of thy God, I will also forget thy children.[45]

And, like Hosea, he has reminded us of the sovereignty and lovingkindnesses of God:

[41.] Rushdoony, *Institutes*, 163.
[42.] *ibid.*, 349-351.
[43.] *ibid.*, 353.
[44.] *ibid.*, 351-352.
[45.] Hosea 4:6.

Come, and let us return unto the Lord: for he hath torn, and he will heal us; he hath smitten, and he will bind us up. [46]

Herbert W. Titus is President of Forecast Foundation and Editor and Publisher of the monthly journal, The Forecast. *An educator, he is the author of the book,* God, Man and Law: The Biblical Principles, *and numerous articles on law and public policy. He is also a practicing attorney, specializing in constitutional litigation. He holds the B. S. degree in Political Science from the University of Oregon and the J. D. from Harvard.*

[46.] Hosea 6:1.

The State Reduced to its Biblical Limits

Owen Fourie

Christianity was no sooner a recognized religion than its orthodox thinkers began to push back the claims of the state. The state was seen as the ministry of justice ... it could not claim to be the ultimate or comprehending order. Man, as God's creature, transcended the state by virtue of his citizenship in God's eternal Kingdom.

R. J. Rushdoony, *The Foundations of Social Order*

The Prevalence of Statist Slavery

The twentieth century will pass with one predominant characteristic that will become its hallmark in the annals of history. That hallmark is statist slavery. Had Shakespeare been alive to witness it, he might have written, "All the world's a state, and all the men and women merely statist slaves." Perhaps the most discerning contemporary Christian exposure of statism and man's enslavement has come from the pen of R. J. Rushdoony. He has defined the issue clearly:

> ... apart from Christianity, we will have slavery. If men will not serve God, they will become the slaves of men .... It has been a statist encouraged illusion of the twentieth century that slavery is on the wane. It has never been more prevalent. The progress of statist slavery has been accompanied by statist self-praise for the liberation of slaves, but in virtually every nation today, statist slavery is advancing or has accomplished its goal. Every increase in security provisions by the state is an increase in slavery .... Slavery increases as orthodox Christianity recedes .... In dealing with the fact of slavery, it is not enough to treat the symptoms alone; the cause must be dealt with, and the basic cause of statist slavery in our day, as always, is religious. The myth of man's autonomy from God is the source of man's slavery to man in the form of the state. The state, as the free order, has absorbed man's freedom. God, as the free and absolutely sovereign Person, is the only ground of man's true freedom, because God's control and predestination ... are in fulfillment of man's being. Under God, we are free to be ourselves; it is no violence to our being that we are what we are: this is God's predestination. The state, as an intruder on the scene, and the would-be-re-creator of man, can only predestinate by a continuing situation of coercion.[1]

Given the innate human desire for freedom and this fact of protracted statist slavery, it is not surprising to find that in the concluding years of this century, voices are being raised, particularly in the United States of America, to curb statism. But these voices are by and large political, not theological.

[1.] R J. Rushdoony, *The Politics of Guilt and Pity* (Nutley, NJ, 1970), 360-362.

Many Christians readily identify themselves with so–called political conservatism, but to trust in a political ideology will prove to be as futile as Hezekiah's trust in Egypt in the face of the Assyrian threat (2 Kin. 18:21). Political conservatism is also a "staff... on which if a man lean, it will go into his hand, and pierce it."

As Rushdoony has pointed out,

> "The conservatives attempt to retain the political forms of the Christian West with no belief in Biblical Christianity. Apart from vague affirmations of liberty, they cannot defend their position philosophically. The conservatives therefore become fact-finders; they try to oppose the humanists by documenting their cruelty, corruption, and abuse of office. If the facts carry any conviction to the people, they lead them only to exchange one set of radical humanists for reforming radical humanists. It is never their faith in the system which is shaken, but only in a form or representative of that system."[2]

In other words, the best that the conservatives can do is to offer a political answer and futile political salvation.

The problem of statism and statist slavery cannot be solved politically. It requires a theological solution because it is a theological issue. That theological solution requires a return to the Biblical and creedal foundations of the Christian West. Those Christian creedal foundations — the Nicene Creed, the Athanasian Creed, the Definition of Chalcedon, *et al.* — are rooted in God's inscriptured word.

The Roots of Statism

Statism has its roots in man's fall into sin. The essence of the fall was the sinful and rebellious desire of man to be as God. In Adam's transgression, man denied the Creator–creature distinction, and the course of the history of fallen man was set for strong delusion — the religious belief in the deification of the state. In ancient Egypt, the Pharaoh represented the point at which humanity met divinity. In ancient Rome, the state and its emperors were regarded as the link between humanity and divinity. This is no less the case in the modern political state, notwithstanding its profession of neutrality concerning religion. Rushdoony puts the matter this way:

> In pagan antiquity as today, the state was seen as a divine-human order, and as the over-all lord and sovereign. In such a view, all things have their being within the jurisdiction and only with the approval of the sovereign state. Religion, art, family, school, and all things else are departments of state and cannot be allowed to exist in independence of it. The state thus usurps the over-lordship of God and becomes god on earth. No area of freedom can exist outside the state: freedom becomes a privilege granted by the state and subject to its conditions.[3]

[2] *idem., The Foundations of Social Order* (Phillipsburg, NJ [1968], 1972), 225-226.
[3] *idem., Law and Society: Volume II of The Institutes of Biblical Law* (Vallecito, CA, 1982), 70.

The modern political state, sustained by its humanistic religion, has become the ultimate and comprehending order of life today. As such, it has supplanted God in the minds of fallen men. Therefore, it has become the transcendental reference point and the all-absorbing unity from which every part of life must derive its meaning. In its light, every detail of life must be interpreted.

We are bedeviled by the sovereignty of the state, albeit a pseudo–sovereignty. To this sovereign, all other gods must bow, even our God and his Christ and all who worship him. Before statist sovereignty, all religions must be equalized so that the state might be lord over all. There is no place for the uniqueness and deity and sovereign lordship of Jesus Christ in such an agenda.

There was a time in American history when sovereignty was equated with the triune God and ascribed to him alone. The idea of human sovereignty was regarded with horror. But, as Rushdoony has observed, "the modern state claims to be an incarnate god .... Sovereignty means lordship, and the pagan and anti-Christian state has always claimed sovereignty."[4]

Sovereignty, in this context, simply means the total jurisdiction of one party or another over all of life. Claims to sovereignty over the same territory must lead to an inevitable and inescapable conflict in which there is no neutral ground. To cite Rushdoony again:

> Sovereignty can be either transcendental or immanent, resting either in God or being an attribute of man and his order. Basically, the two conflicting concepts are between God's sovereignty and the claimed sovereignty of the state. If God is sovereign, then He is the creator and governor of all things, and his law overarches, controls, judges and assesses all things; nothing can exist or have being apart from Him. If the state is sovereign, then the state must exercise total control and judgment over all things in its world, or its sovereignty is limited and negated. The state seeks, in terms of its claim to sovereignty, to become the determining and over-arching power over every domain; no sphere is allowed to function except by permission of the state. The earth, air, water, sky all belong to the state, are used only under the law and tax of the state and are potentially or actually subject to repossession by the state. The state has assumed that ultimacy over man's life which properly belongs only to God. The creed of the state therefore requires holy warfare against the Christian creed and faith.[5]

With such assertions of sovereignty, it is a short step to claiming the position of messiah and savior, and to fallen man this is certainly the role of the state. Salvation is sought in the state; not an ethical salvation, but a participation in the divinity of the state. Rushdoony puts it succinctly:

[4.] *idem.*, *Christianity and the State* (Vallecito, CA, 1986), 45.
[5.] *idem.*, *The Foundations of Social Order*, 221.

In the state and its cradle-to-grave security man will find his salvation. The state has unlimited jurisdiction, because it is that order in which man realizes himself, the order in which man expresses his collective divinity: vox populi, vox dei, the voice of the people is the voice of God in this collective or democratic consensus.[6]

Such political salvation is no salvation at all, for it does not deliver man from the guilt of his transgression against the law of God. As Rushdoony observes,

> ... political saviors are more often interested in perpetuating sin than in eliminating it. Sin is an important and major instrument of political power .... [S]in is politically encouraged and subsidized....The religion of the state must be a religion of moralism. It must make sin socially reprehensible without liberating men from it .... [T]he power state has a stake in perpetuating sin because guilty men are slaves.[7]

The Christian Response

In the light of such an exposure of statism from pagan antiquity to the present, what should be the Christian response? It is tragic that "... God's jurisdiction has been handed over to the world by all too many churchmen, and any idea that Jesus Christ has crown rights over all things, over every area of life and thought, sounds strange in their ears. Christ's jurisdiction is limited to the church, and to the soul of man, and very feebly in both places."[8] Such was not the response of the Christians who lived in the days of the persecuting Roman empire.

> The Church of King Jesus faced ... a major threat from the divine kings of imperial Rome .... The empire was ready to grant "religious freedom" to the church *provided* the church recognized the right of the state to grant that freedom, which meant a recognition of the state as the principle of order. But it was precisely this which the church fought in pagan Rome in refusing to participate in "emperor worship." The Christians were never asked to worship Rome's pagan gods; they were simply asked to recognize the religious primacy of the state and the emperor as the divine-human order.[9]

This they steadfastly refused to do, and they suffered for their refusal: "Christianity, by asserting the supreme lordship of Christ over Caesar and all other human institutions, reduced the state to its Biblical dimensions, as a ministry of justice (Rom. 13:1-6)."[10] These early Christians, while prepared to render godly obedience to the state in its God-ordained role as a ministry

---

6. *idem.*, *The Politics of Guilt and Pity*, 309.
7. *idem.*, *The Foundations of Social Order*, 198-199.
8. *idem.*, "Jurisdiction: by Christ or by Caesar?", Chalcedon Position Paper No.7 in *The Roots of Reconstruction* (Vallecito, CA, 1991), 32.
9. *idem.*, *The Politics of Guilt and Pity*, 304.
10. *idem.*, *Law and Society: Volume II of The Institutes of Biblical Law* , 70.

of justice, resisted the claims of statist deity and sovereignty by holding tenaciously to the revealed tenets of their Faith.

As citizens of God's eternal kingdom, they knew that the ultimate and comprehending order was to be found in God who had revealed himself to be the sovereign creator of all things, the predestinator of all that comes to pass, the first cause, lawgiver, and eternal judge. In the omnipresence of the Almighty, there could be no place for usurpation by the state. In the supreme revelation of Jesus Christ as the incarnate God, they witnessed God's covenant grace at work for the redemption and justification of his elect people. In terms of this Faith there could be no place for concurrence with the pseudo–savior, the messianic state. Indeed, as God's creatures, made in his image, and with responsibility under God for self–government according to his law, and as dependent second causes, once fallen, now redeemed, regenerated, justified, adopted, and sanctified for obedience as citizens of the kingdom of God, they knew that their course was set for liberty under God's law. They were God's freemen. In such a condition, there was no place for a life of bondage to a statist power that exceeded its bounds as God's servant to assert the sovereignty and jurisdiction which it was not lawful to arrogate.

Creeds and Freedom

As the early centuries of the Christian Faith began to unfold, and heresies relating to the person and natures of Christ arose by divine appointment, Christian theologians were compelled to define the Faith and to give it its creedal basis. In those theological definitions we find the crucial points for the solution to the problem of statism and the enslavement of men then and now. Orthodox Christian thinking reduced the state to its Biblical limits.

Studies in the creeds and councils of the early church, such as Rushdoony's *The Foundations of Social Order*, reveal many points that have direct bearing on the problem of statism and its solution. Three of these crucial points warrant particular mention, and there is a fourth, drawn more from the emphasis of the Protestant Reformation than the ancient creeds.

First, there is the fact of the two perfect natures, the divine and the human, in the one divine person of Jesus Christ. The definition of Chalcedon, formulated in A. D. 451, became a touchstone of orthodoxy. It taught men to acknowledge "one and the same Son, our Lord Jesus Christ, at once complete in Godhead and complete in manhood, truly God and truly man, ... one and the same Christ, Son, Lord, Only-begotten, recognized *in two natures*, *without confusion, without division, without separation*; the distinction of natures being in no way annulled by the union, but rather the characteristics of each nature being preserved and coming together to form one person and subsistence, not as parted or separated into two persons, but one and the same Son and Only-begotten God the Word, Lord Jesus Christ ...."

Of crucial importance in this statement is the fact that although in the one divine person of Jesus Christ there is a perfect union of the divine and human natures, those two natures remain distinct; the human nature does not become divine, nor does the divine nature envelop and absorb the human nature. Since this is true of the only mediator between God and men, it is certainly true of all human institutions, including the state. It is therefore a fact that the state cannot become divine. The state cannot claim divinity. The state cannot be Lord. Moreover, the state cannot absorb its citizens into an all-embracing unity that negates their individuality.

Second, as the Athanasian Creed declares, "… the Father is God, the Son is God, and the Holy Ghost is God. And yet they are not three Gods, but one God …. And in this Trinity none is before or after other; none is greater or less than another; But the whole three Persons are co-eternal together and co-equal …" Rushdoony comments:

> Orthodox Christianity has always held to the full-orbed trinitarian faith, and the Athanasian Creed is the classic expression of this doctrine. Every heresy in the church has been subordinationist in some form or another. If, for example, by God, the Almighty Creator, the Father is meant exclusively, and the Son and the Spirit are seen as some kind of junior gods at best, the consequence has been the priority of natural order to revealed order …. In such heresies, the state becomes man's basic order …. The true vicar of God in such a situation is the state and its head, and the state comes to be man's saving order, the Kingdom of God on earth."[11]

The fact that Jesus Christ is fully and completely God as the Father is God and the Holy Spirit is God, means there is no subordination of his person and being. He rightfully claims to be our unique Lord and Savior. Therefore the pretensions of the messianic state are false. The state cannot be the savior of men from the cradle to the grave.

Third, in the doctrine of the Trinity is revealed there is one God and three Persons; or, to put it another way, one God and many Persons. Indeed, in the Trinity, we have the equally ultimate one and many, the equally ultimate Unity and Particularity or Individuality: "The oneness of God is not more ultimate than his three Persons, nor his three Persons more ultimate than his oneness …."[12] Since man is made in the image of God, he is a reflection of his Creator — in the metaphysical sense, not the ethical sense, after the fall and without Christ. Similarly, the whole of God's creation reflects the principle of the one and the many:

> The temporal one and many … are created by God, and He is the law of their creation. As a result, the temporal order must see a similar relationship between the one and the many as exists in the Eternal One-

---

[11] *idem., The Foundations of Social Order*, 93.
[12] *ibid.*, 91.

and-Many. Non-Christian philosophy veers from an emphasis on the one to the many, from, to state it politically, totalitarianism to anarchism, from an insistence that unity is truth to an insistence that individuality is the true order. It is thus in constant conflict: the state or man. ...Orthodox Christianity, by its doctrine of the Trinity, avoids this basic problem of philosophy. The state is not more important than the citizen, nor the citizen than the state; both are equally basic to God's order and equally established in His law ....[13]

The state is a part of God's created order. It is under the authority of the eternal triune God as part of the temporal order. It is without ground for any claim to be the ultimate unity into which the citizens are absorbed with the consequent loss of the validity of their individuality. The state cannot be the all-embracing unity that interprets life and gives it its meaning.

Fourth, the doctrine of justification, which includes the forgiveness of sins, is indispensable to our freedom from statist slavery: "The forgiveness of sins is the liberation of man from God's judgment, and from the sentence of his own heart. It is the restoration of man into his calling as man, to be priest, prophet, and king under God."[14] Men who are judicially and legally accounted and accepted as righteous by God for Christ's sake are men who are called to exercise righteous dominion in every area of life under God. Guilty men cannot do this because they are slaves to the messianic state. They are under the dominion of the state. They cannot exercise righteous dominion over the earth.

This righteous dominion requires that each area of life — family, church, school, state, business, and so forth — should function with limited authority in its own sphere, and in interdependence on the other spheres, under God. Rushdoony notes that "Calvin's conception of justification led inevitably to the concept of sphere sovereignty."[15] The proper exercise of sphere sovereignty under God is always ministerial and never messianic. Consequently, this reduces the state to its Biblical limits as God's servant or minister of justice.

Conclusion

Christians must return to their Biblical and creedal roots, and give the theological solution to the theological, not political, problem of statism. There is hope.

Consider that the humanism of the twentieth century is, to a great extent, the product and expression of the works of men who labored in the centuries since the Protestant Reformation. The names of Descartes, Locke, Berkeley, Voltaire, Rousseau, Hume, Kant, Schleiermacher, Hegel, Darwin, Marx,

---

[13] *ibid.*, 92.
[14] *ibid.*, 201.
[15] *idem.*, *The Politics of Guilt and Pity*, 282.

Wellhausen, Dewey, Freud, Keynes, and Kierkegaard come to mind. Their works have influenced the curricula of educational institutions in this century. The modern political state owes much to the thinking of many of these men. But the death throes of statism are evident, and humanism, which sustains it, is intellectually bankrupt.

Consider therefore that, in the providence of Almighty God, the writings of other men, men of a different Spirit, the freemen of Christ, will become the substance of the curricula of an era of Christian excellence. The product and expression of such teaching will be a day of manifest expansion for the kingdom of God with the knowledge of the glory of the Lord filling the earth as the waters cover the sea (Hab. 2:14). It will be an age in which the state will be reduced to its Biblical limits, not by political revolution, but by the preaching of God's word, the work of the Holy Spirit, regeneration, faith, repentance, and obedience to God's law in every area of life.

Surely, Rushdoony's works will prove to be a major contribution of our century to a Christian era that will have as one of its hallmarks the Biblically reduced and limited state:

> The modern state is "a god that failed." When Christians again see the total crown rights of Christ the King, the threat of the state will collapse.[16]

Owen Fourie is Headmaster of Dominion Academy, a ministry of First Presbyterian Church of Rowlett, Texas. He was born and educated in South Africa where he was ordained as a minister of the Church of England in 1972.

[16.] *idem.*, *Christianity and the State*, 160.

Christianity and Business

Ian Hodge

We depersonalize the world; we find it easier to treat people impersonally. We speak of "labor" problems and "management" problems, when we should be talking about people created in God's image. To do so, i.e., to see them as people, gives a religious dimension to the situation, not a scientific one. It requires us to view economics from a Biblical perspective, and to see all of life as God requires us to see it. We have devalued life and people, and we need again to see all things in terms of the Lord and His law-word.

R. J. Rushdoony — *Journal of Christian Reconstruction*, Vol. 10., No. 2, *Symposium on Christianity and Business*

Introduction

The work of R. J. Rushdoony and his colleagues at the Chalcedon Foundation have had a world-wide impact. This essay is written by an Australian who, in the late 1970s, came into contact with the writings of R. J. Rushdoony. Reading the works of Rushdoony can lead to a significant "paradigm shift." In this essay, the explanation of that paradigm shift is confined to the area of business.

It is a fair question to ask how the writings of Rushdoony have had some kind of impact, if any, on business. Of all the writings of Rushdoony and publications through the Chalcedon Foundation, only a single volume has been devoted to business, *The Journal of Christian Reconstruction*, Vol. 10, No. 2., "Symposium on Christianity and Business." Others associated with Chalcedon have carried on a ministry to business, such as Joseph McAuliffe with his former newsletter, *BusinessGram*, and R. E. McMaster in the financial area with his advisory services and newsletter, *The Reaper*. Does this mean that business plays a minor position in the thought of Rushdoony? The answer to that cannot be "yes," for it is not just the overt writings that indicate the place of business in the thought of R. J. Rushdoony, but the often unstated implications of the overall perspective that he has taught for more than half a century.

All of life, Rushdoony has argued, is to be thought of in terms of Christian Faith. "The gospel," he says, "is for all of life: the good news is precisely that the whole of life is restored and fulfilled through Jesus Christ, that, in the counsel of God, the kingdom is destined to triumph in every sphere of life."[1] This is not simply an esoteric idea that results in a repetition of religious mumbo jumbo. Rather, it means that every thought and action is to be

---

[1] R. J. Rushdoony, *By What Standard?* (Philadelphia, PA, 1965), 176.

governed by specific teachings of Scripture, where applicable. This is the thought expressed in Scripture in 2 Cor. 10:5, "Casting down imaginations, and every high thing that exalteth itself against the knowledge of God, and bringing into captivity every thought to the obedience of Christ." It is this "bringing into captivity every thought to the obedience of Christ" that leads us directly to an application of Scripture to the world of business.

Faith *vs.* Rational Planning

Often the most significant issues are not the obvious ones. Rushdoony's emphasis on the meaning of faith is very important. Too often faith is loaded with connotations of spirituality that are far from its true meaning in the Bible. Rushdoony's concept that faith is a total reliance on, acceptance of, belief in, and obedience to every word that is contained in the word of God makes Biblical Faith far more objective than many people wish to recognize.[2] Some of the current concepts of faith are more closely related to some idea of mysticism than they are to Biblical Faith, and it has been a very important emphasis in the work of Rushdoony to ensure a proper definition of faith.

More than that, however, is Rushdoony's emphasis on a proper understanding of the doctrine of God. In his system of thought, Rushdoony begins with God, not man. In particular is the emphasis on the practical outworking of the doctrine of the Trinity: one God, three Persons. For Rushdoony this means not an escape into mysticism and irrationality, but the exact opposite. "The effect of the Spirit," he says in relation to the Holy Spirit, "is not unreason and confusion but power and clarity." Furthermore, Rushdoony argues, "two of the earliest references to the person of the Spirit speak of Him as the source of practical knowledge and workmanship."[3]

The implications of this concept of the Christian life are quite profound, for they place a necessity on man not to live on his mystical experiences, real though these might be, but on the objective standard of Scripture. This objective standard leads, in turn, to rational action: an increase in wisdom and knowledge, and an application of that wisdom and knowledge to the real world. This is almost the opposite of what many today teach as Biblical faith and true spirituality. For example, consider a farmer who is a Christian. He can prepare the soil and plant the crop. Thereafter, he could, like many, spend his time sitting on the porch with his Bible in his lap, reading the Scriptures and praying that God will give him a good crop. Maybe he could spend time in town witnessing, attending missionary rallies — and generally ignoring the farm. Another farmer, also a Christian, might appear less spiritual, and

---

[2.] *idem.*, audio-tape lectures through Romans, especially chapter one, verse 16, "The just shall live by faith."

[3.] *idem.*, *Systematic Theology* (Vallecito, CA, 1994), I: 203-204. See Ex. 31:2-5 and Ex. 35:30-35.

instead of sitting on the porch with his Bible in study and prayer, spends most of his time tending the crop, removing the weeds, ensuring there is sufficient water, and keeping out the scavengers and other animals that might destroy or ruin his crop.

Now there are very few Christians who believe it is one or the other of these two illustrations, and that proper Christian Faith combines the practices of both men. But it is strange and curious behavior that when the Christian businessman steps off the land and begins a manufacturing or service-type business, the concept of applying proven business methods is ignored and he begins to act as if God will mysteriously bless his failure to apply proper business practices.

There are too many well-meaning people who like the idea of going into business but do not have the least idea of how a business should run and be operated. They are like the first farmer; they go so far in their business practices then get "religious" and hope and pray that somehow God will overcome their inability to run the business with proper administrative and financial management.

There are times when God does overcome our limitations. Many times we are blessed, and there may be no correlation between our labors and the blessings we receive: "A man's heart deviseth his way: but the LORD directeth his steps" (Pr. 16:9). The Bible does not, however, allow us to use this passage as an excuse continually to ignore the ordinary means of blessing that God has ordained for us, for elsewhere God has said, "He becometh poor that dealeth with a slack hand: but the hand of the diligent maketh rich" (Pr. 10:4). This "diligence" is the ordinary means of proper business practices and procedures, just as for the farmer they are the most appropriate farming methods available at the time.[4]

To be sure, all these practices, whether on the land or in the city, are to be governed by Biblical teaching. Thus farmers are increasingly aware of the damage that artificial fertilizers do to the soil. God's methods of farming (*e.g.* resting the land every seventh year) need to be recognized and applied. So, too, do God's instructions for manufacturing and service-oriented businesses.

This means, among other things, the establishment of rational business methods and practices. This would begin with a proper business plan which, in turn, contains a budget with revenue and expenditure estimates. The

---

[4.] Courts in Australia apply the test of "due diligence," a hang-over from Christian common law origins, to ensure directors and management of public companies act responsibly. On common law origins see "Our English Heritage" by Greg Booth, in Graham McLennan, ed., *Understanding Our Christian Heritage* (Christian History Research Institute, 81 Woodward Street, Orange, NSW 2800 Australia); also "Origins of the Australian System" by Rev David Mitchell, in Ian Hodge, ed., *Is This the End of Religious Liberty?* (Homebush, NSW, 1993), 24-31; Stephen C. Perks, *Christianity and Law: An Enquiry into the Influence of Christianity on the Development of English Common Law* (Whitby, England, 1993).

business plan would also lay out concrete objectives together with strategies to achieve those objectives. The strategies would be broken down into shorter-term activities so that a measured response to them can be established. For example, an objective for a company might be to achieve a minimum of ten-percent return on investment so that this money can be given to various mission programs. A business would normally have more objectives than this, but this could be one of a number of options. In order to achieve this objective, a certain level of sales at a particular price might be necessary. If the business is already charging the right price, then it needs to ensure it has the necessary sales to achieve the objective. Once broken down into shorter-term goals, (*e.g.*, *x* number of sales per month over the year), then monthly (or more frequent) review meetings can be used to ascertain if the strategies being used to achieve the objective are successful.

It is at this point that many raise a voice in protest: "If God is in control of whatsoever comes to pass, then how can a business set sales goals and targets?" The question assumes there is a conflict between God's eternal purposes and rational business planning, and when this discord occurs it is very easy to deny business planning and accept whatever comes our way. Is this a proper response, however, for the Christian businessman or woman? The answer is both "yes" and "no." In the Bible we see many examples where man's plans and objectives are thwarted. The plans that are put into place are not achieved. But we also see that this is primarily (but not exclusively) what happens to those who are covenant-breakers rather than covenant-keepers.[5]

The question that should be asked is what are the *ordinary* means that God has ordained for businesses to operate. The answer is rather clear, not only from the Bible but also from experience. God's ordinary means are that we plan our work and use the intelligence he has given us in order to achieve the goals we believe he has set for us. If a child has a God-given gift as a violinist, he will almost certainly fail to develop this gift if he does not practice daily. If a person has a calling in life to sell widgets,[6] he will almost certainly fail if he does not find some way to advertise or promote his product to the buying public. In short, he must *sell* them, and the selling process requires the finding of prospective customers, putting the product in front of them (or a description of it), and asking them to buy. These are examples of the ordinary means God has ordained for developing a business.

When David heard that Goliath was making fun of the Israelites and their God, he could have called a prayer-meeting to call on God to remove the problem. But the Scriptures do not tell us he did this. Instead, David tried the weapons of warfare, and when he found that his lack of experience with them would hinder him in his task, he set out to get rid of the problem (*i.e.* Goliath)

[5.] See Dt. chapter 28.

[6.] A widget is a non-existent product that economists like to use to illustrate a point in their argument.

with a sling. And when he selected the stones for his purpose, he did not select just any old stone, but smooth stones, stones that would fly true when he aimed at the target. This is rational planning. And while it is true that God sometimes gives us results when we have no plans or when we have poor plans, this is not an excuse to live without planning.

Work in Christian Perspective

Business cannot be considered apart from of the general concept of work. In this area, Rushdoony has contributed timely reminders that work is intimately connected to our vocation or calling, and our callings, in turn, are connected to the unique gifts and abilities that God gives each of us. At the heart of our topic, then, is the concept of man's purpose on earth, and Rushdoony has called to our attention that the first chapter of Genesis sets the framework for man's purposes on earth.[7] Man is called to have dominion, to work, to subdue everything to the purposes of God. This is especially so after the fall, where man's general calling is made more difficult by the curse that resulted from the sin of our first parents.

"Work," Rushdoony reminds is, "is eschatological in meaning. It has a goal, the Kingdom of God."[8] This indicates that work is more than a means of putting food on the table. It also explains why men put such energy into work even when they do have enough food and shelter. It is inherent in the nature of man that he work and that his work contribute to God's purposes for his creation.[9]

Banfield also called attention to the eschatological nature of work in his sociological study on the nature and future of what he called the urban crisis. In this work Banfield argued "that each class subculture is characterized as having a distinctive psychological orientation toward providing for a more or less distant future."[10] This involved not only the ability to imagine a future, but included the "ability to discipline oneself to sacrifice present for future satisfaction."[11] Upper-class socio-economic groups are more future oriented, whereas the lower class is evident by its lack of ability to be future-oriented. Most salesmen learn this fact early in their career. Selling to lower socio-economic groups can be easy. But if the sale requires the person to pay a premium at a date in the future, there is a poor likelihood of that occurring. Insurance sales people, for example, tend to keep out of the lower socio-economic groups when their commissions can be reclaimed if renewal premiums are not forthcoming.

[7.] R. J. Rushdoony, *Systematic Theology*, II: 1019ff.

[8.] *ibid.*, II: 1020.

[9.] *idem.*, *Revolt Against Maturity* (Fairfax, VA, 1977), 17-21.

[10.] Edward C. Banfield, *The Unheavenly City* (Boston, MA, 1970), 46.

[11.] *ibid.*, 47.

Work, in addition, has a moral dimension. According to Rushdoony, "*work* is ... a moral fact, a moral statement."[12] Labor is a means of providing goods and services which can be exchanged with others for their produce. An alternative to work is living off the welfare of others, and the Bible is quite clear "that if any would not work, neither should he eat" (2 Thes. 3:10). The morality of work, therefore, is intimately connected with the eighth commandment, "Thou shalt not steal," and has both negative and positive applications. Not only does work imply the necessity to provide for one's self and family, but it also means that our work should positively benefit others. This view is expressed, for example, in the Westminster Larger Catechism (Q. 141) when it states that a duty required in the eighth commandment is "an endeavour, by all just and lawful means, to procure, preserve, and further the wealth and outward estate of others, as well as our own."

In an age that increasingly sees government redistribution of wealth as the panacea for many social ills, the Biblical emphasis on work and its moral nature is a timely reminder that God's plan of wealth redistribution is not through confiscation and redistribution but through productive labor and the exchange of goods and services.

It needs to be stressed that the Biblical concepts are not merely pie-in-the-sky ideas with little practical results. This Christian view of work and vocation has had significant effects. For example, as Christianity expanded across Europe, it brought with it an attitude towards work that was in stark contrast to the Roman civilization which it replaced. In the Roman world, work was something to be despised and reserved for slaves. Christianity, however, provided a new standard that made work something highly prized and sought after. *Laborare est orare!* — Work is worship! — became an identifying mark of the Christian monasteries that were built as the Faith expanded across Europe.[13] Whereas Rome was hostile to productive labor, Christianity positively encouraged human endeavour. The historical emphasis on work within the Christian Faith has led to changes in farming methods, warfare, and to a technological revolution that created the windmill, water power, the crank and, of course, the clock.[14] It also led to man's first recorded flight in the early eleventh century when Eilmer (or Oliver) of Malmesbury glided over 600 feet before crashing, breaking both legs in the fall. Forest land was reclaimed, rivers and streams dyked, and usable land created out of swamps and moors.[15] Education became a central activity of

---

[12.] Rushdoony, *op. cit.*, II:1041, emphasis in original.

[13.] Herbert Lüthy, *From Calvin to Rousseau* (New York [1965] 1970), 59.

[14.] See Jean Gimpel, *The Medieval Machine: The Industrial Revolution of the Middle Ages* (London, 1992, 2nd ed.); Lynn White, Jr., *Medieval Religion and Technology* (Berkeley, CA, 1986); William Carrol Bark, *Origins of the Medieval World* (Stanford, CA, 1958).

[15.] Henri Pirenne, *Medieval Cities* (Garden City, NY [1925], 1956), 57; Lynn White Jr., *Medieval Technology and Social Change* (Oxford, 1962), 72.

the monasteries that spread across Europe. By the thirteenth century, quite remarkable advances in medicine were evident, since surgery was a necessary and legitimate part of the work in a monastery.[16] This was the first industrial revolution.[17] The combination of reciprocal and rotary motions, more than any other invention at the time, provided the foundation for the second industrial revolution almost 1,000 years later.[18] This revolution has given us steam and electric power, jet travel, the motor car and the silicon chip. This is the heritage that has been left to us by a Christian emphasis on work.

Christian Stewardship

The influence of Rushdoony and Chalcedon does not stop merely with a reminder of the rightness of work. Biblical concepts can be applied to work not only in a general sense; they can be applied to business and business activities in particular. If the Bible is to be our governing document in all that we do, it is possible to take teachings from the Bible that will apply to business activities. For example, the Biblical concept of stewardship has application to business and business management. Stewardship, in its broadest context, has five ingredients. These are responsibility, accountability, planning, measurability, and authority. Let's consider each of them briefly, then make some observations to its application in modern business.

At the top of the list is *responsibility*. There can be no stewardship without the allocation of responsibilities. In Lk. 12:42 we find these words: "And the Lord said, Who then is that faithful and wise steward, whom his lord shall make ruler over his household, to give them their portion of meat in due season?" A steward is one who has responsibilities given to him. In the gospels, the steward is one to whom many important tasks are delegated, as in Mt. 20:8.

With responsibility, however, goes *accountability*. Jesus uses this concept in one of his parables: "And he said also unto his disciples, There was a certain rich man, which had a steward; and the same was accused unto him that he had wasted his goods. And he called him, and said unto him, How is it that I hear this of thee? give an account of thy stewardship; for thou mayest be no longer steward" (Lk. 16:1,2). The steward was to be held accountable for his actions; it would be determined how well he had attended to his responsibilities.

The third ingredient to stewardship is *planning*: "For which of you, intending to build a tower, sitteth not down first, and counteth the cost,

---

[16.] See Lawrence R. Brown, *The Might of the West* (New York, 1963), 520.

[17.] Jean Gimpel, *The Medieval Machine: The Industrial Revolution in the Middle Ages* (London, 1992, 2nd ed.), viii.

[18.] Lewis Mumford, *Technics and Civilization* (New York, [1934] 1963), 80. See also White, *Medieval Religion and Technology*, (Berkeley, CA, 1986), xvi.

whether he have sufficient to finish it?" (Lk. 14:28). Planning, thinking ahead, and counting the cost are all concepts tied up in this idea of planning. A man who is to build a tower needs to make up his mind before he starts if he has sufficient resources to accomplish the task. And not only does he need to consider the physical resources, he needs to think through his own psychological resources to ensure he has not commenced an activity which he will later regret or abandon because he does not have the desire to see the project to its end.

Responsibility, accountability and planning, however, require something in addition: *measurability*. It is difficult, if not impossible, to give a proper account of something if it cannot be measured. While it is not always possible to measure things in an objective sense, there is still the requirement somehow to measure activities in order to determine if the objectives are to be met. This is why planning is so important. Activities are measured against plans, and decisions can be made about many aspects of the project once the information is to hand.

None of these ingredients has much impact without *authority*. If people are to be given responsibilities, to be held accountable and measured for their activities, then it follows that they need the necessary authority to fulfil the delegated responsibilities. In contemporary business language this is called empowerment.[19]

Stewardship Applied

Consider how stewardship might be applied to modern business practice. Central to modern business practices is management theory and its application. In recent years management theory has undertaken a significant revolution. There are a number of factors driving this, most of them pragmatic rather than philosophic. But the Christian businessman or woman is in need of principles by which the ideas of the management theorists can be evaluated. And it is here that we can apply Rushdoony's ideas. If the Scriptures are to guide to life, then we can consider the concept of stewardship and apply it to business practices.

How will the owners of a business treat their staff? Is the relationship of employer-employee the same as that as master-slave? If not, then the only relationship that remains is one of free contract between employer and employee. But the contractual nature of employment indicates mutual obligations. Employers may provide facilities, machinery, equipment and remuneration. Employees, on the other hand, might contribute their labor, and in some instances provide more than this. In some cases, both parties will agree to share the risks of the business venture, with an employee's salary

---

[19.] See, *e.g.*, Peter Block, *The Empowered Manager* (San Francisco, CA, 1987).

linked to the success of the business. Both employer and employee are required to be stewards and exercise stewardship in their respective capacities.

What this means, among other things, is that a top-down bureaucratic model of business management is inappropriate; it does not fit with the concept of free contract and stewardship. Interestingly, current management theory is increasingly recognizing that management practices need overhauling.[20] Principles of Total Quality Management (TQM) have at their heart a transformation of the individual worker and his relationships and activities within the business. According to Rafael Aguayo, "the purpose of all management, the purpose of cooperation, is to bring out the best in each of us and allow each of us to contribute fully."[21] Man, as prophet, priest and king, can exercise responsibility in all areas of life, including business. Since business occupies such a large portion of our time, we could say this is true *especially* in business.

The older, military model[22] methods of business management that have served industry for so long are giving way to a new approach. Bureaucratic management is being replaced with leadership.[23] Greater responsibility is being given to workers at the lower end of the corporate chain. They are being empowered to ensure that quality is the benchmark in their activities. Thus, in some places, workers can stop the production line without reference to management in order to ensure quality.[24] In this example workers have been given the responsibility to ensure quality, authority to achieve that goal, and they will be measured and held accountable for the results.

This style of management is a contributing factor to the reduction of layers of middle management in the larger corporations.[25] No longer do the workers need management to tell them what to do and when to do it. Instead, they are empowered with greater control over their own activities within the business. The results have been intriguing. In some instances, businesses have reduced layers of management from seven or more down to three. In other places, the

[20] Peter Block. *Stewardship: Choosing Service Over Self-Interest* (San Francisco, CA, 1993); W. Edwards Deming, *Out of the Crisis* (Cambridge, MA, 1982); Stephen R. Covey, *Principle-Centered Leadership* (New York, 1990).

[21] Rafael Aguayo, Dr. Deming: *The American Who Taught the Japanese About Quality* (New York, 1990), 243. For a fascinating account of an application of this approach to business, see the unusual story of Semco company in Brazil by its owner, Ricardo Semler, *Maverick!* (London, 1993).

[22] In Australia, even the military forces are abandoning the former top-down bureaucratic method of command and introducing principles of Total Quality Management into military command procedures.

[23] Merrill J. Oster, *Vision-Driven Leadership* (San Bernadino, CA, 1991); Bob Wall, Robert S. Solum, Mark R. Sobol, *The Visionary Leader* (Rocklin, CA, 1992).

[24] Robert L. Shook, *Honda: An American Success Story* (New York, 1988).

[25] John Naisbitt and Patrician Aburdene, *Re-Inventing the Corporation* (London, 1986), 12ff.

number of staff have been significantly reduced, while at the same time quality and output have been improved.[26]

Can we say, then, that modern business practices are Christian? Not necessarily. Many of the ideas of modern management are posited in the name of New-Age philosophy, humanism, or some other non-Christian concept. But this does not mean that the Christian must disagree with everything that the non-Christians say. Rather, with the Bible in his hand, the intelligent Christian can evaluate all ideas, selecting those which do not violate his Faith, endorsing those with positive results, and recognizing that any ideas in management which prove fruitful are those which men cannot escape because they are made in the image of God. The Christian can point out that ideas are right not because they work pragmatically, even though there is a legitimate place for pragmatic testing. In the final analysis, says the Christian, ideas are right because they conform to the standards of Holy Scripture.

An Overview of Business

This analysis of business need not stop with management structures. If Biblical principles were only to apply to management and structures and personnel issues, there would be no comprehensive Biblical view of business. But we don't have to limit ourselves in an application of Christianity to business precisely, because there are no areas of life where God's word does not have some application.

Marketing

Are there Biblical guidelines for a sales and marketing campaign? If so, what are they? Clearly, God requires honesty in all our dealings with others. Truth in advertising, then, is a key ingredient for the Christian in business. So, too, are integrity and honesty in the presentation of the product. False claims as to achievements, quality, durability, etc., will be shunned. On the other hand, honest advertising will ensure prospective customers know what they are buying. It is no shame to admit that a product only has a life span of 12 months and will sell for a certain amount. Customers might well be happy with such a product provided they are not charged a price which represents, to them, unfair value. Others might prefer a product which lasts 10 years but sells at a higher price. This represents value to them, and they are prepared to pay the price tag. Honesty allows the customers to use their resources to the best of their advantage, as they apply the principles of stewardship to the possessions that God places in their hand from time to time.

[26.] Tom Peters, *Liberation Management* (London, 1992), especially 87-104, the transformation of Union Pacific Railroad.

Customer Service

Many people in business view customers as problems: "If we had no customers, we'd have no problems," is a statement frequently heard, often said seriously. Without customers there would be no business and no employment for millions. Customer service, then, should be a joy, a delight. Serving other people is a significant aspect of our calling in life. We are not here to be self-seeking and self-serving. Rather, we are to serve God, and a significant aspect of serving God is serving our fellow man, helping him achieve his calling under God. Our work activities are thus not primarily a means of making money: they are a mechanism for putting other people's needs ahead of our own. Jesus first, customers second, ourselves last, to paraphrase a popular sentiment amongst Christians.

Finance

The Bible has some relevant things to say about finance. Timely payment to creditors is a question of honesty and integrity, not of cash flow. That many businesses make it the latter is a shame, and does not help to build good working relationships with suppliers. Financing a business also has very real moral questions. Rushdoony has argued that debt, if not completely prohibited, is limited to six years with a full remission in the seventh.[27] This means that the modern practice of financing business through debt must be abolished in favor of equity financing. True participation in the success or failure of the business is required by those financing business. Becoming a financial stakeholder in the business through equity financing or joint venture rather than through loans is a more appropriate Biblical method of financing business.[28]

Research and Development

The capital-producing process requires research and development. Research and development, however, requires funding, often on a massive scale and for long periods. For this to occur, people need to forego present consumption in order that resources can be used in the future.[29] Without saving, there is no research and development, and businesses survive only if they develop a long-term view and fund their own growth and development. The modern emphasis on debt, however, is antithetical to the concept of saving. Thus, it is not surprising that for the modern business world, research and development take a lower priority, and economic progress is less than what it could be.

[27.] R. J. Rushdoony, *The Institutes of Biblical Law* (Phillipsburg, NJ, 1973), 145.

[28.] R. E. McMaster, Jr., *No Time For Slaves* (Phoenix, AZ, 1986), 137-142.

[29.] Mark Skousen, *The Structure of Production* (New York, 1990), 231ff.

A long-term view, however, is a religious phenomenon, and again Rushdoony has played an important role in returning our thoughts to a more Biblical, longer term view of the future.[30] That longer-term view will again revive business, provided it goes hand-in-hand with an abandonment of debt and a return to sound financing.

Competition

For many, modern business is likened to warfare. It seems necessary to some that business is a constant battle between employers and employees, amongst employees themselves, and between businesses. Books such as Suntzu's *The Art of War* are being read in the corporate boardroom rather than military headquarters. Competitors are seen as the enemy rather than cooperative enterprises by which the market may be expanded for all to benefit.

In this climate Christianity has a unique message. Rather than seeking power and glory for themselves, Christians should rather be seeking what is best for their fellow-man. And the concept of fellow-man includes those businesses that are in direct competition with us. This means we do not have to treat competitors as enemies but as cooperative enterprises. We are not necessarily disadvantaged by competitors, even though it is true that competitors can sometimes put us out of business. Buggy manufacturers were superseded by motor car companies, but this only indicates that it is through competition of the kind that develops new goods and services that economic progress is achieved. Christians do not have to fear progress, even though it can mean a change in employment for some. What is needed is a far wider vision for the future of mankind under God, and none of us has a claim to a perpetually unchanging business. An application of Biblical principles, therefore, will lead to greater cooperation among businesses, not a development of the "art of war."

Government Assistance

Modern business is very much affected by government assistance in various forms. This might be assistance by direct handouts, or it might be various laws that provide help and assistance to businesses, such as protection from competitors. Tariff laws, for example, are designed, ostensibly, to help local companies remain in business against foreign imports. This results in higher-priced goods that are produced locally, thus increasing the cost of living for everyone. Tariff protection also hurts foreign businesses by making it more difficult for them to enter new markets.

[30.] R. J. Rushdoony, *God's Plan For Victory* (Fairfax, VA, 1977); *The Journal of Christian Reconstruction* Vol, III, No. 2, Winter, *Symposium on the Millennium,* 1976-77.

It is a sad commentary on contemporary affairs that Western countries such as Australia have gained their economic advancement at the expense of their neighbors. By keeping cheap labor out of the Australian labor market, by keeping cheaper foreign goods away from Australian consumers, Australian workers, heavily unionized, have been able to improve their standard of living. This has been achieved primarily at the expense of those who have been denied access, as sellers, to Australian markets.[31] In the past decade or more, however, this trend has begun to reverse itself. Australian workers and manufacturers have priced themselves out of world markets; foreign goods, produced more cheaply and often of better quality, have taken over from the local product. This trend will continue until there is a more equitable comparison of prices of labor and goods between nations.[32] While this is going on, the standard of living for many Australians will reduce while that of our foreign neighbors will increase.

Centrality of Ethics

Not surprisingly, the businesses that plan well seem to survive best of all. This does not mean that planning is all that is necessary, for there are other aspects of business that need to be kept in mind. We cannot isolate one aspect of life and make it the test of everything. Business planning without consideration of other issues is inadequate. For example, a group of thieves might plan a robbery with meticulous care. Since the activity is an immoral act, we cannot expect God to bless the planning in this instance. But when our activities are legitimate and our ambitions honorable, God can and does bless the plans that we make, so we are fruitful in our labors.

While rational planning has its proper place, it cannot be the sole and central focus of business. Righteousness is what God says is important, for our Lord says those that hunger and thirst after righteousness are blessed (Mt. 5:6). "Better," says Wisdom, "is a little with righteousness than great revenues without right" (Pr. 16:8). Again, it has been a central focus of Rushdoony to point us back to a unified Bible as the standard by which we live. This means that our standards of righteousness are to be taken from both the Old and the New Testaments. But we need to remember that Rushdoony's emphasis on the Old Testament is not a simple return to the Old Testament's forms and structures. "Thus," he says, "while Col. 2:16, 17 makes clear that the *formalisms* of the Old Testament observances are ended, the essence of the law is in force and is basic to all Biblical law."[33] The task ahead is to seek

---

[31.] It has also been achieved at the expense of Australian residents who must pay higher prices for the locally produced goods.

[32.] There are already signs in some areas where the trend to foreign goods is slowing down. At one time, book publishers were using print shops in Singapore and Hong Kong. Now, publishers can have their books printed in Australia at equal or even lower costs than those supplied off shore. Printing is again becoming profitable for Australian printers.

[33.] Rushdoony, *The Institutes of Biblical Law*, 157, emphasis in original.

out teachings of both Old and New Testaments in order to maintain righteousness in business methods and practices.

Conclusion

Man's desire is to be his own god, as Gen. 3:5 indicates. This is no less true in the world of business than in any other area of life. The reconstruction of business according to Biblical teaching can be total and comprehensive. This essay has given a broad outline of how business can be affected if those running the businesses and those working in business take seriously the command to bring "into captivity every thought to the obedience of Christ" (2 Cor. 10:5). Worldly standards of success, together with improper interference in business by civil government, make it difficult and very costly for businessmen to apply Biblical teachings in the current political climate. Tax laws, for example, encourage the use of debt in business, as they do in private life, as a legal means of tax minimization. Debt, however, fuels the inflationary policy of modern governments that refuse to reign in their spending and provide balanced budgets. While individuals are in debt they are unlikely to complain about government debt, or at least they must diminish their argument against government debt.

The work of Rushdoony and Chalcedon is a timely and important reminder that businesses are not exempt from the claims of the Crown Rights of Christ the King. It remains for God's people to build Christian businesses. These will be businesses that make every effort to run all aspects of their business from a distinctly Christian perspective. They will also be businesses that create and provide goods and services that improve the welfare of others.

Rushdoony has called us into the service of the King of kings in all areas of life, including the commercial sector. It is thus a joy and privilege to serve God and our fellow-man in our business activities.

Ian Hodge is a businessman, writer and teacher living in Brisbane, Australia. He has Ph. D. degree in Christian economic thought from Whitefield Seminary. Dr. Hodge is a member of the Australian Institute of Management and is active in applying Biblical teachings to business and business management.

Reconstructing Church and Culture by the Media

Colonel V. Donor

As we all know only too well, the media (TV, radio, film and print) have served as the major change agents in American culture sine the 1920s; no force in history has so rapidly and thoroughly *de*constructed a culture. More than any other factor (surely the liberal elite would be impotent without the muscle of the media to mass propagate their humanistic occultism), television has remolded us in its image — a nation of fickle, faddish, shallow, semi-literate and apathetic boobs — living only for the next moment of gratification: Whether escapism, proffered by the "boob tube," or a myriad of tax-payer-subsidized "freebies" provided by Uncle Sam. In fact, conservative sociologist and best-selling author George Gilder asserts: "American mass entertainment is the most powerful force in global culture" (*Life After Television*, George Gilder, 33). Scary. Particularly when one pauses to contemplate what passes for "entertainment" these days.

TV is "King"

When it comes to molding not just public opinion, but core "values" — indeed even forming a worldview — television is the undisputed king, far more efficacious in seeding young minds with its masters' suppositions than fuddy-duddy public school "educators," who are largely ignored if not ridiculed by their young charges. If, in fact, an instructor of the public youth wishes to gain her pupil's ear, she will mimic the latest notion, attitude or personality popularized by the nihilists of MTV — life imitating "art." The hapless heirs of Dewey's theories of behavioral modification have been reduced to desperate attempts to be "hip" in order to "communicate" with TV: lobotomized ignoramuses.

Impotence of the Church

Meanwhile, according to various studies, the church ranks twenty-fifth (or last) in its perceived ability to influence our culture. Probably even used-car salesmen are more successful at communicating their agenda since they seem to employ a lot of media.

There are, of course, a myriad of reasons the evangelical church ranks least as a cultural force, the most obvious of which is its willful disengagement from our culture; the separatism, dualism, privatism, selfism and escapism that pietism and dispensationalism bred as they consumed the Calvinistic Puritan ethic of stewardship and left in its place a legacy of irresponsible abandonment. When evangelicals abandoned cultural engagement they, naturally, forsook interest in the arts, culture, education — and media. The secularists did not launch a blitzkrieg to capture the media; they simply walked into the institutions we abandoned, convinced as we were that the world was unsalvageable and Christ would return in "this" generation.

As evangelical pundit Cal Thomas observed: "For most of this century, the Christian Church has been in self-imposed exile. It taught that politics and the Kingdom of this world have headed in a direction opposite to the Kingdom of God." His insight is made all the more poignant by the irony that Thomas's boss at the Moral Majority, Jerry Falwell, was a vociferous prophet of precisely that view until the mid 70s — about six years before starting the (now defunct) Moral Majority.

Now that it appears their eschatological timing was badly off — prominent evangelicals who lean to (or used to) a dispensational view, like James Dobson, Jerry Falwell, and Pat Robertson, spend a lot of their time decrying the media's anti-Christian dominance and a lot of our money attempting to buy "equal time." Yet their efforts are, for the most part, spectacularly unsuccessful (other than in building an impressive fund-raising and popularity base among the already faithful). Indeed, even when their strength is combined with the ubiquitous Paul Crouch's Trinity Broadcasting Mega Network, it is clear the secular media has made superior progress at inducing Christians to buy into their worldview (consumerism, individualism, hedonism, evolutionism, antinomianism, and cultural ambivalence) rather than *vice-versa*.

A Strategy

Which brings us to the issue of the cart and horse. Which should go first? Should we attempt to use the media to reach the nation when the evangelical church has become a theological petri dish for spawning about every abomination from orthodoxy thinkable: antinomianism, dualism, neo-platonism, gnosticism, selfism, privatism, spiritualism, mysticism, legalism, escapism, separatism, cultural marginalization, individualism, self-deification, and just plain off-the-wall weirdness?

Surely our first goal in reconstructing the media should be to educate the church: Reformed, evangelical, Roman Catholic, etc. A properly educated, motivated and directed force of several tens of millions of Christians (including men of influence) could be truly effective as salt and light in restoring justice and sanity to a people on the verge of national suicide — and therefore ripe for discipling. When the church acknowledges its lawful role to disciple our nation and steward all of God's creation, the rest will follow.

Thus I submit our first priority should be to employ the media in an effective catechization of the church.

The subsequent question we must ask is who will step forward to reconstruct the media, and how can they achieve what is seemingly the impossible quest?

It is my assertion that those who have directly or indirectly been edified by three decades of Rushdoony's faithfulness to orthodoxy and his insistence on applied (rather than just discussed) Calvinism, are uniquely qualified for this challenge due to the following four factors:

First: the desire to win. It should be absurdly obvious that a belief that we are both called to battle and that victory will be ours (Christ's) is necessary to reconstruct the media, "win the culture war," "disciple the nation," or whatever metaphor one chooses for returning America to its early Christian foundation (and no, I don't mean Jefferson, *et. al.*)

Nevertheless, not one of evangelicalism's three main camps (when it comes to policies regarding cultural engagement) meets this elemental criteria. Briefly they are:

— The "Not of This Worlders." A collection of dispensationalists, pietists and anabaptists who simply don't believe it's our job to be involved — period. Dr. James Dobson recently lamented in the pages of *Christianity Today* that this attitude seemed to be the majority report amongst evangelicals.

— "Evangelical Admirers of LBJ's No-Win War Policy." This group, perhaps best represented by Dobson himself and the leading lights of the National Association of Evangelicals, believes we must fight a primarily defensive action to "keep the government off our backs," "keep our children and families safe" and to ensure "religious freedom" (pluralism). On this agenda homosexuality, pornography and abortion are in big trouble. But the thought of an all-out offensive actually to "Turn America into a Christian Nation" is perceived as impossible if not offensive. Perhaps another aborted attempt at Prohibition is as close to the kingdom of God as this group can envision.

— "Victims of Cognitive Dissonance." This group of warriors ably represented by Pat Robertson seems at first glance to be quite serious about winning. So serious in fact, Pat's willing to bankroll some of the nation's shrewdest political operatives to the tune of $20 million a year (why didn't I take that great offer from Robertson's people a couple of years back?). Trouble is, Dr. Pat appears to have a severe case of cognitive dissonance — mentally mixing two radically opposed principles or strategic constructs.

With one hand Robertson admirably invests literally hundreds of millions of dollars in what can only be thought of a long-term strategic development — a university complete with graduate and law schools, a state-of-the-art communication network, and a formidable political machine, all of which suggests the good doctor plans to be a major player in rebuilding our culture into the next millennium.

Yet, with his other hand he fills the airwaves and his fund-raising letters with nonstop financial appeals predicated on the imminence of "these last days." For a few dollars, Pat offers a special "Sign of the Times" video documenting amongst other amazing facts: "signs of the Lord's immediate return" and a "shocking new technology that could lead to the mark of the beast." While in Robertson's case, this pandering to the lowest common denominator of the evangelical market may be rationalized as simply a clever fund-raising gimmick, this cognitive dissonance is very real for most evangelical activists. The conflict caused by the polarities involved sacrificing and building for a long-term struggle *versus* fending off the enemy in the short-term until Jesus comes again breeds a deep and deadly ambivalence amongst these warriors. To win they must consciously disavow or subconsciously be inconsistent with their theological foundations.

A Reconstructionist Agenda

Happily, reconstructionists are not hindered by such double-mindedness. No one has ever accused the Reconstructionist school of being handicapped by short-term vision or strategies!

Second, reconstructionists, more than most Christian Right activists, are willing to be servants. As I pointed out in my book *The Samaritan Strategy*, the Christian Right which I once led was forced to forego serving, because in the words of one of our most prominent leaders, "We didn't have time." Such a short-term vision pressures one to assert dominance in a top-down method (which works only sporadically — and even then only temporarily reverses serving our way into leadership over the long term). Of all thinkers on the "right," Rushdoony has been the most consistent in admonishing those who would "win the culture wars" or "disciple the nation" to dominate through service. Rushdoony's formula is quite simple: First comes sin, then salvation, followed by its fruit, service.

Service, of course must spring from our obedience to God's command to love (care for) others. As we begin to reflect God's compassion and empathize with those in need of our help (not just the economically poor, the widow and the orphan, but all those in need of God's justice and love), our service flows more naturally and consistently.

When we serve, we also take on responsibility for properly fulfilling whatever we've committed ourselves to accomplish. Faithful and responsible service and stewardship are closely followed by authority. Those who are served — whether followers or leaders — give those who diligently steward their responsibilities the authority to do even more. He who serves well as club secretary is soon elevated to a higher position. She who volunteers on several community boards is an excellent candidate for the city council.

In encouraging this process, Rushdoony has painstakingly emphasized that the foundation for discipling the nation (as with the early church) is through our example — love and service, not through political diatribe — be doers of the word, not just speakers. Before godly legislation can be introduced with any effectiveness, it must be desired by a people who see that Christians are wise, compassionate stewards of God's creation, here first to serve, not to rule.

Third, reconstructionists are not influenced by gnostic or neo-platonic dualism as are the revivalists and most modernist evangelicals. We believe all of God's creation is ours to enjoy and to steward, and therefore experience no misgivings over utilizing the theatrical arts for the glorification of him who created all. Unlike John Wesley and his spiritual heirs, we do not believe the dramatic arts are to be inherently evil.

Fourth, reconstructionists have the vision requisite to such a mammoth undertaking. One does not inspire the sort of long-term commitment necessary to reconstruct media, church and nation with a plea for returning America to the Eisenhower Era which Robertson recently offered as his vision for the future. Surely, a godly and righteous society based on God's great law and providing God's love and justice to all makes for a more inspiring vision!

A New Millennium of Opportunity

Now we must ask ourselves, how is such a thing even possible? How can we even hope to offset the monopoly of the major networks and cable systems?

The good news is that these giants are slowly being rendered obsolete by the same factors that gave rise to their dominance — the incredible rate of advancement in communications technology. Through the rapidly emerging technologies of fiber optics, micro electronics and digital video, the current communications stranglehold will be totally overthrown. Within a few years, with the help of a simple video camera and computer, we will be able to broadcast our message — any message — twenty-four hours a day to anyone who has a computer. The computer will act like a TV set — except it will be interactive — with the viewer able to fully participate in the discussion.

Think of the possibilities — hundreds, even thousands of independent teachers and strategists broadcasting from their home or office to hundreds of thousands of students, pastors, activists and business professionals. As radio was to the print media and TV was to radio, the revolutionary potential of this new medium is beyond anything we can even conceive of today. Futurist George Gilder notes in his book *Life After Television*: "Through this crystal (fiber optic) web, we can reclaim our culture from the centralized influence of mass media" (Gilder, 42). Gilder prophesies further that this new media "will bring an eruption of culture unprecedented in human history" (*ibid.*, 54).

The question now is, who has the vision, commitment and long term strategy to take advantage of this emerging force? Who will step forward to channel this imminent cultural disruption?

The New Age, the secular Right and Left, for sure. For most evangelicals, it will seem a waste of time. After all, the rapture is just around the corner! That leaves the door wide open for reconstructionists to master this revolutionary force in the service of our Almighty King — first discipling the church, then the nation, then the world (Mt. 28:19-20).

Our utilization of this next wave of communication technology will be a fitting tribute to a half century of unceasing work by one of this century's great Reformed theologians, R. J. Rushdoony.

Author and lecturer, Rev. C. V. Donor, a founder of the Christian Right in the late 1970s, has spent the last decade ministering to the poor and needy as Chairman of the International Church Relief Fund. In addition to his writing and speaking schedule, he conducts seminars for men on "Rediscovering the Purpose, Passion and Power of Godly Masculinity."

The Testimony of a Reconstructionist Entrepeneur

Ellsworth E. McIntyre

My task or assignment is to testify how the ministry of R. J. Rushdoony has blessed from the viewpoint of a Christian entrepreneur. When the request came for this article, I was genuinely pleased and honored. I have had many titles conferred on me over my sixty years of life. The title or designation "entrepreneur" does not appear on my resume. Why? Because I have no need for a resume. Entrepreneurs don't have use for such things; employees such as "executives" need resumes. Owners don't even need titles or college degrees; employees do, however. I know; I used to be an employee before I became an entrepreneur.

Twenty years ago, when the title of entrepreneur entered my ear, I had visions of *Amway* or some kind of commission scheme. *Amway* and their many imitators have done a good job creating visions of the glories of financial independence, but you will learn by this article that such schemes are not entrepreneurial, at least not in the Biblical model. If you have ever attended a sales convention promoting such ideas, you will be told that hard work, enthusiasm, and following some system will bring you the fulfillment of all your dreams; but you will learn from this article that the key to successful promotion to higher levels is not hard work or such bootstrap notions and working someone's business system other than the one of the Lord's choosing for you. These are doomed to failure. After all, a thief can be self-employed and may be very successful. I suppose a thief could die of old age surrounded by the fruit of his labor. Psalm 73 and other Scriptures, however, teach that such wealth is not enjoyed in eternity and those who attempt to gain wealth through fraud or stealing or any system not of the Lord's choosing shall put their money in bags with holes. If you are called to be a businessman, and you decide to preach instead, even your preaching shall yield no eternal prize for you (Pr. 21:4). On the other hand, if you are called to own and control a business for the Lord's glory and your desire is to do that task with all of your heart, rejoice, because with R. J. Rushdoony's theology, your reward can be multiplied both on this earth and in eternity. I have received a down payment on such treasure, and it is my honor to testify how such treasure can be yours.

As I wrote above, I was honored to be asked how I was transformed from a servant to a master. No, master is not the term that captures the essence of what being an entrepreneur is all about either. An executive can be someone's master, but the executive doesn't create his own wealth. The orders and policies come down from some place higher than a mere corporate president. To those below, the president appears to be the master, but when we climb to that height, we find the president is a wage slave also. He doesn't direct his life according to his own choices. His major decision is the same as other employees. Do I quit to sell my skills and time to another or shall I stay in the hope someday to earn more?

The entrepreneur, on the other hand, owns and/or controls the capital (tools), land resources, and the laborers' contracts and arranges these to perform his personal vision of a marketable need. If he's really an entrepreneur, his vision and his arrangement (system) will "create" wealth. When the entrepreneur's system becomes a reality, everyone within his system must be wealthier, not just himself. To illustrate, I have developed a system that produces a safe environment for the care and education of children while their parents work outside the home. In order for my system to confer on me the designation "entrepreneur," I must benefit everyone touched by my system, or I will soon return to employee status. Failing to benefit the mother, the child, my employees, or my vendors (those who sell me books, food, cleaning supplies, etc.) will bring failure to me. Oh, someone will not give me a pink slip, not just one pink slip anyway. In my case, parents give me pink slips every week, but so far, more people hire me to benefit their children every day. Every day money is paid for my services and just as long as less goes out, I am an entrepreneur and not an employee. I am the head and not the tail, as the Bible describes. Someday, I hope to climb still higher. The Bible says, "You shall lend and not borrow" (Dt. 28:13, 14). I am seeking to be free indeed, because my Lord promises that if the Son shall make you free, you shall be free indeed (Jn. 8:36). The entrepreneur has more freedom than an employee. I know because I used to be less free. It's much better to have hundreds of clients to please than just one. If your only client refuses to buy your services, you are out of business. A successful business owner has time to adjust his services to please more people or advertise or find new clients to replace the ones who wish his financial death. As Dr. Stuart Crane, my college economics professor, so often lectured, "The difference between a free man and a slave is the right to own and control private property."

The entrepreneur is free to create more property. If he can create a better system to please more clients, he gets more income. To the degree that the entrepreneur can own and control his system, he can move up the ladder of freedom. Create a system that benefits all involved and you are an entrepreneur. The children who attend my schools learn to read better. It is not unusual for three-year-old children to read fluently at Grace Community Schools. Bright five-year-old kindergarten students can read at the fifth-grade level. Ordinary students usually have a two-year advantage. In other words, the student gains more from my school than the ordinary day-care center. The mother gains, because she has time to sell for a paycheck. Since 99% of mothers can't or won't teach their children to read, count, and obey at three years of age, she's made a very good trade. She's happy and she has a better child and a paycheck to boot.

I am also pleased to note that many of these single mothers are delighted their children are taught the Commandments, the Twenty-third Psalm, the Lord's Prayer, etc. Some are delighted because they see value in children learning these things. Other mothers are pleased because they see their children becoming polite and obedient. In short, the child is also benefited.

My employees are also happy that they have jobs and more freedom to teach Christian values than at ordinary schools.

Moreover, I am benefited because my soul-winning ministry is multiplied to hundreds of children instead of a handful in church. These are also hundreds of children whom no church or school would have any opportunity to convert. I am also benefited because the free market gives me a much higher income than any possible as an employee. The free market also gives me a much larger tithe and offering that I can distribute to godly ministers who don't have the benefit of being an entrepreneur. As a matter of fact, I take no salary as pastor of the Nicene Covenant Church. I prefer to earn 100% of my income from selling my services to the public. This way I can donate my pastor's salary and my entire tithe to the Lord's work. One hundred percent of our church's offering also is distributed in like manner. Our church uses one of our school classrooms for Sunday service. We have no plans to build a separate church auditorium. Our outreach is through the schools and by helping other deserving ministries.

It is common for educators to regard entrepreneurial activity as something that cannot be taught. The creative act of producing a system that creates wealth is not understood. Even those who have accomplished this mystery seem universally blind to why they succeeded while others failed. It's not just the winners who can't explain why; it's also the losers. As they look back over the events of their lives, they see only meaningless circumstances tied together only by "time and chance."

Solomon wrote in Ecclesiastes 9:11 about this blindness, "I returned, and saw under the sun, that the race is not to the swift, nor the battle to the strong ...." I once read about a comedian who quoted the above saying, "'The race is not to the swift nor the battle to the strong,' but it's always your best bet that the fastest and strongest will always win!" Yes, it is our best bet, because that's the best and most reliable information we have. We are limited by what we see, hear, teach, and taste (the empirical data). Only history is our guide. But history cannot tell us "why" one is stronger and faster than another, can it? "Why" gets into theology, and theology is out of favor in respectable, accredited, educational circles.

Solomon continues in the same verse, "... neither yet bread to the wise, nor yet riches to men of understanding, nor yet favors to men of skill; but time and chance happeneth to them all." All wise and skillful men are not wealthy business owners. Such men more often work for a pittance wage paid by superiors who obviously are not their superiors in many areas. Why?

I graduated from high school in 1953. I don't recall anyone ever suggesting to me to become an entrepreneur. I do recall talk of becoming an "executive." Executives are employees. Why didn't my teachers or my preacher or someone say, "Shoot for the top, become a business owner and don't settle for less. You'll never know if you don't try."

Well, the fact that my teachers were mere government employees and that my preacher was a church employee may have something to do with it. Maybe they thought that it would be cruel to give us dreams too high reasonably to attain. Perhaps. But they did tell us to go to college and try to become a doctor. I am certain that almost none of my classmates became doctors, and over 30% of them who followed the college dream flunked out. Colleges were tougher in those days. We were advised to get skill and worldly degrees at college in order to get more bread, riches, and respectability. You got to go to college to be someone. Solomon, the wisest born of woman, says that such nonsense can't bestow riches, and he's right. Even an average entrepreneur with a successful shop can make far more money than three college professors put together. I know, the soft-hearted among you will say, "Isn't that awful?" No, I think the average college professor is worth even less than he's paid. After all, most professors continuously bring great harm to their students with unproductive, false doctrine. The shop owner provides an honest living for his employees and their families. The pizza shop owner teaches, by example, that God's free market is the appointed means to earn for yourself and bless others. After four years as a shop employee, the employee knows how to earn a living and even become an owner himself. What's the market value of four years of college? Why, the pizza shop owner, for example, will even pay you to learn his trade while the ungodly professor will gouge you mercilessly for a diploma that has lots of prestige but value that often is less than four years' experience at nearly anything productive. In some circles, we call that "fraud" or to be more kind, "a sucker's bargain."

Well, let's suppose that it is generally agreed that becoming an independent businessman is a worthy goal, or to make a personal application to a teacher like me, let's suppose it's much better to be a private Christian school owner than a religious worker in some kind of church institution. As the owner, you can do more good for children, parents, and yourself; but Solomon has just said above that all that we can think or see cannot guarantee success. Both losers and winners at the business owner game can't tell anyone why they have succeeded. They say, "I was just in the right place at the right time." They may also offer reasons like, "hard work," "thrift," "good advice," "careful planning," and on and on. There are mountains of books with advice such as this. I know, I have in times past read a pile of them. But, once again, because it bears repeating, Solomon, under the inspiration of God, says none of these explain why some fail while others succeed.

Psalm 75 adds to Solomon's wisdom this explanation for success: "Lift not up your horn on high; speak not with a stiff neck. For promotion cometh, neither from the east nor from the west, nor from the south. But God is the judge; he putteth down one, and setteth up another."

In this passage, we are told that behind the history of events that appear only to be time and chance, works the free will of the only being with total free will — our Lord Jesus Christ. He chooses the winners. He hands out the "lucky breaks." He puts a few in the right place at the right time and he curses many to be in the wrong place at the wrong time.

So far, all readers with "Calvinistic" ideas are in agreement with me except for the possible exception of "thin-skinned" college teachers. They quit reading long ago. If you made it this far, and you are a college professor, congratulations! You are bigger than your job. Yes, Calvinists like to affirm their devotion to God's sovereignty. "Yes, praise God!" they would cry (unless they are Presbyterian who just slowly nod, while others cry out for joy). It's a rave, nonetheless, and I accept, while I still may, your applause, because what follows will divide the camp of Calvinist readers.

If God decides and all factors like strength, I.Q., influential families and friends, and sage advice from experts — if all this means nothing compared to God's favor, our means of gaining success in this world is absolutely, positively only this: We must find the way to curry favor from God. There's just no other way!

Calvinism and Wealth

For this Christian school teacher, and sometimes preacher, the "way" became open to me by the grace of God through the writings of R. J. Rushdoony. During the summer of 1974, I read this line from page four of the introduction to *The Institutes of Biblical Law*, "Man's justification is by the grace of God in Jesus Christ; man's sanctification is by means of the law of God."

I had long been a secret believer in Calvinism. Bitter experience had taught me to conceal (or soft-pedal) my Calvinism, however. I was a spy laboring in the tents of the Arminian. I lived by the advice, "Cast not your pearls before swine lest they turn again and rend you." Or "Only a fool speaketh his whole mind," or... well, you get the idea. I pretended to be one of them.

I realized when I read Rushdoony's line that while I gave "lip service" to the doctrine of the sovereignty of God, my life was not ordered by his law as much as my life was ordered by the homemade church customs, expectations, and superstitions of my peers and superiors. For example, I preached regularly in chapel with due deferment to the "invitational system." That is, I either endorsed or let stand the false, anti-Biblical idea that one could be certain of acceptance with Christ just by presuming that every sinner's prayer was answered, yes, by Christ. I had a school of 180 students at that time, all under the illusion that a life changed from obedience to sin to obedience to God's law was "best" or "wise" or "right principles for right living," but none had been taught the idea that if Christ doesn't supernaturally turn the supplicant from sin, he's not bound for heaven, but bound instead for hell! What to do? I read, "'To be spiritually minded is life and peace' (Rom. 8:6), and to be spiritually minded does not mean to be other-worldly, but to apply the mandates of the written word under the guidance of the Spirit to this world." (*Institutes*, 4). Rushdoony was applying his truth to the social order, but I could not honestly avoid applying "despiser of God's law" to myself. I believed that if I kept on endorsing by silence, this church culture of anti-law that surrounded me, I was certainly "marked for judgment."

A Remarkable Reconstructionist Story

Well, if it cost me my career, so be it, was my conclusion. I had left a high-salary, full-expense sales position six years before reading *Institutes*. Our Christian life had been grinding poverty. My wife had followed me past the eight-foot stone fireplace, over the hardwood floor, across the slate foyer, and out the door of our six-year-old brick home. We moved into a trailer in South Carolina where we added three more children to our family while I worked my way through college. We lived in that same trailer in Georgia while I worked as a Christian school teacher. In the evenings and weekends, I studied for my master's degree in education. We lived in a slum in Maryland while I finished my masters at Johns Hopkins. I was now the principal of a Baptist day school, but my salary easily made me eligible for food stamps and public assistance. What did I have to lose? I could make this much money selling brushes door to door. No, that's not right. I could make much more! This line of Rush's hurt very badly: "The social order which despises God's law places itself on death row; it is marked for judgment."

Until now, I blamed the church for keeping us in poverty and shame. The old ladies would bring us bags of second-hand clothing and various "goodies." After shuffling off with their hearts warmed by their good deeds, they fashioned in the dark criticism to undercut each other, their pastor and his staff. It was an "equal opportunity" gossip attack. But, now, I realized that I was suffering not for God but for my sin. Before my eyes were opened by hearing R. J. Rushdoony, I even "gloried" in my poverty. I fancied that the Lord would greatly reward me in the Great By and By with a heaping big pie in the sky. I lived by the lie of the Pharisees. I regarded my poverty as some sort of a "test" that if I endured to the end, I would have all tears wiped away. It was a very sad day for me to discover that I was not one of the "good guys";

I was part of the problem. No wonder I was paid low wages; I wasn't worth even the little crumbs that fell from my church master's meager table.

I took the *Institutes* to my pastor and asked his permission to use it as a teachers' in-service training manual. Before he could ask what the book contained, I told him I was going to leave a copy for his review and, "By the way," I added, "please accept the book as a gift."

"Thanks, Mac," smilingly he picked up the book, his eyes shining. He liked big, important-looking books like that. They looked very intellectual and impressive on his shelf. Well, my decision was made: if he read the book and was converted, I could keep my job until we both were fired, or if he didn't read the book and gave me permission to use it, I could delay the firing for a while. What was it that Rush had written? "... apply the mandates of the written word under the guidance of the Spirit to this world." Well, let's see what the Spirit would do. The worst thing that could happen would be losing my job and since this job was only causing me present pain and possibly even more disappointment in the future, this was the wise and lawful thing to do.

Well, in two weeks, the pastor had moved the book to the shelf to join the other "impressive" books. He said, "You're the school principal, Mac; we will follow your judgment in this matter." Outwardly, I thanked him, and inwardly, I thanked the Holy Spirit for his guidance.

I made it all the way to the chapter on the tenth commandment before the church blew the whistle. Obediently I agreed that perhaps that book was not the "best choice" for an in-service manual. (Who knows, there may be one better?) Of course, I wanted to be in subjection to the church in such matters. "Please assure the church I will drop teaching the *Institutes* this day." Everyone seemed pleased! The teachers were now thoroughly sold on the need to teach God's commandments to little children. The pastor was in a bind; he did give permission so he saw no easy way to fire me... not yet anyway. The church was reluctant to fire me for another reason. The Lord seemed magically to prosper every facet of my ministry. The student body was increasing so rapidly that the church was dreaming of building. Only ten months before, they were two steps ahead of the bill collector. Now, the school would finish the year with the first surplus in their history. For the first time, the church would not have to raise funds to keep the school above water.

I applied God's law at every opportunity, being careful to seek "guidance" from the Holy Spirit at each step. I made it an "extra credit exercise" for all Bible classes to write the Ten Commandments from memory at every Bible exam.

I started to give an invitation at every chapel service but not the usual Baptist invitation. At every chapel service, I preached that only the power to keep God's law better and better was the proof of a real born-again experience. I found endless ways to say this just as the Arminian finds endless ways to exalt man's free will. My invitation, however, exalted the Lord's freedom to bless or curse. I would say, "If you can't truthfully say that you are more obedient to the law (I would insert the lesson of the service) then while heads are bowed and eyes are closed, no one looking around, raise your hand for prayer. God sees your heart; give me the encouragement of your hand. We will pray in a moment for the grace of God to help us obey his holy Commandments. By your uplifted hand, you are saying, 'I want to know for certain that I am growing in grace. Lord help me!'"

Well, that's the form (the words varied) but what never varied was that all of my students now knew the Commandments by rote and all understood how to use them to measure genuine salvation and genuine progress in sanctification. For example, a second grade boy, the son of a school board member, asked to join the church after baptism. The custom of this G.A.R.B. (General Association of Regular Baptists) church was to interview each new church member to "listen to their testimony." This little guy was asked by the examiners if he was saved. "Yes, sir," he proudly replied, "I am sure I am saved."

His manner was so confident that one deacon asked, "Are you sure Jesus is in your heart?" The deacon expected the usual response, "Yes, because I asked Jesus to come in." This is what the thoughtful student said, but added something very new to the ears of the deacons.

"I listen to Mommy and Daddy better all the time; my grades are getting better; and I don't lie anymore!"

The pastor jumped in to explain the boy's testimony to the puzzled deacons. After some explanation, I was happy to learn they came to accept that a profession of faith backed up by a changed life was very good testimony indeed. Children can be the most powerful of witnesses in the Lord's hand.

God was very pleased with me, I thought. I got raise after raise. In six years, my student body increased from 180 students to over 750. My family and I prospered. We added two more children to make a quiver of eight. I was blessed with creative idea after creative idea: tutor class system, separate classes for girls and boys, better math techniques, better English tutor techniques — test scores went up and up. Why?

In Psalm 1, we are instructed that if one accepts the counsel of godly men like R. J. Rushdoony, meditate on the law day and night, that "whatsoever he doeth shall prosper." The Lord went before and behind. I enjoyed the "breaks" as never before.

In the next years until 1985, I was to transform another school in like fashion, and to my shock, the Lord used my witness to convert a wonderful, godly pastor, Dr. Ronald Welch. Pastor Welch led his entire church of 300 souls out of Arminianism and into a form of theology that I call "robust Rushdoony Calvinism." The Lord took my friend, Ron Welch, home to heaven after his task was complete but not before he apprenticed two men to continue his work, Rev. Thomas Clark as pastor and Rev. Paul Edgar as principal of the school. Both church and school are prospering just as Psalm 1 promises. I am, by Pastor Welch's demonstrated faith, persuaded that Rev. Dr. Welch went home to a full reward instead of disappointment.

Rushdoony's Influence

Now to the question, "How did Rushdoony's writings bless you?" When I was led to read his *Institutes*, I was already a child of God, but a child stunted in stature. Doctors who treat children would term the disorder as "failure to thrive." The enemy of our souls cannot prevent our birth in Christ. Dead men rise only by the Lord's bidding. After our rising from spiritual death, we are able to make choices. We do have to some degree free will after our new birth from above. To those born-again ones, the Bible speaks, "Honor thy father and thy mother, that thy days may be long upon the land that the Lord thy God giveth thee (Ex. 20). The sermons that the typical evangelical pastor preaches at every service contain the same message: "Ye must exercise your free will to choose Christ, so that you may go to heaven when you die."

The unspoken premise is that the sinner can save himself by the power of walking down an aisle and praying a sinner's prayer. Once the sinner humbles himself in this manner, he returns each service to be reassured again and again all his remaining days in this earthly life that all is well. Heaven is his home if he can just believe God's simple plan. Growing in grace to obey as evidence of salvation is ignored.

Rushdoony's gospel was very different. He said, "Sanctification is by means of the law." This meant to this "secret Calvinist" that unless I applied the law to myself, my family, my school, and all within my power, I had no hope. Why? Very simple! Unless there is sanctification or growth, there is no life! Unless I could honestly claim growth in grace, I had a fool's salvation. If it doesn't move, it's dead. I know I am alive, because I am moving in the direction of pulling down everything that doesn't exalt the law-word of my God, the Lord Jesus Christ. Rush planted a fearful question in my heart: "How can you be certain that heaven is your home if you are not growing in the power to obey his law?" Or in another form the same question, "How can you be sure you are alive spiritually when you hold down the truth that stabs you in the heart day and night?"

Obedience the Key

When I surrendered to seek the Lord's wisdom to apply the law to my life, I began to grow up! Now I had also solved the problem of why men like me usually qualify for poverty status. Our power is stunted, our growth is impaired, and our progress to become Christ-like, our march to claim our birthright as sons of God are robbed by our disobedience. By substituting obedience to the doctrine of a disobedient church, we disobey the doctrine of the Lord's universal church. The demons cannot rob us of our salvation, but they can rob us of our reward here on earth and also our reward in heaven (3 Jn. 7 and 8). The servants of a disobedient church preach endlessly on what the Christian has no power to perform, and they are silent on those things the Christian can by God's grace do.

The "Breaks"

Why is it that some get the "breaks" while others do not? The robust Calvinism of R. J. Rushdoony clearly had the answer for me. They are poor, blind, yet say they have need of nothing, because of disobedience to the law-word of God. They worship idols. In my case, the idol was a church that I served without caring if that church's doctrine agreed with Scripture or not. I struggled to keep my meager position, hoping to receive promotion from men. After applying Rushdoony's theology to my ministry, this Christian principal turned schools from bankruptcy to success, while others begged door-to-door selling chocolates, magazines, and trinkets. My enrollment tripled while others closed their doors. Rushdoony's Calvinism did not split Pastor Welch's church. As of this date, his church is still growing under Pastor Clark's wise leadership. I have founded six schools from scratch, while others failed even with the support of a large sponsoring church. The better answer to who wins the race is not who is the fastest and strongest, but why the winner is the fastest and the strongest? *Why* is a theological question. I was blessed, and you can be blessed, if you lay on your beds at night and fill your hours during the day with this question, "How can I apply the law of God to myself and my calling?" How can I do my task that lies at my right hand better? We must always remember that nearly all fail at their tasks. We can't do the politically correct, respectable thing and hope for anything but failure. Most people fail; therefore, don't do what most people do! Instead, apply the law of God; you can be certain that will raise you above the ordinary. Ordinary Calvinists are usually no more successful than Arminians. Why? Because ordinary Calvinists fail to use the sword of God, the word. Instead, they use tradition, sentimentality or whatever gets approval from those who control their paychecks, pensions, and honorary doctorates. I am a follower of "robust Rushdoony Calvinism." The day I applied the law to myself, my family, and my schools, I was on the road to becoming a winner! It was not just "time and chance," as Solomon writes. It was the Holy Spirit of God pointing to his law, saying, "This is the way; walk ye in it." By the Lord's grace, I stopped worrying about being my own savior, and began working on the little foxes that spoil the vines. By his grace, I began to do with all my heart what lieth at my right hand to do (Ec. 9:10). Since 1985, my wife and all of our children, their wives and husbands, and six grandchildren (so far) labor in our six Christian day care/schools and the church we founded under authority of the Tri-City Covenant Church. Our schools are named Grace Community Day Care and Schools. Our church is the Nicene Covenant Church. We rejoice that the Lord has blessed and had mercy on foolish preachers like myself. We praise the Lord for His servant, R. J. Rushdoony. We will always be in his debt.

Reverend Ellsworth E. McIntyre lives in Florida where he pastors the Nicene Covenant Church of Naples. Rev. McIntyre has a Ph. D. from Faith Theological Seminary of Avon, Indiana, an A. B. D. for a Doctorate in education from the University of Southern California, a Masters of education from Georgia Southern University, that was completed at Johns Hopkins University, and a B. S. in education begun at the University of Pittsburgh and completed at Bob Jones University.

Politics and Localism

Howard Phillips

... the presupposition that man can save himself and his society by his own works and law rests not only on the assumption that man's basic problems are environmental rather than ethical and religious, i.e., due to a fallen nature, but also on the assumption that all human differences are of degree only, and not of kind. Hence, they can be remedied or reconciled by man. Man must therefore seek relief, not from God but from himself magnified into the form of a world state. Orthodox Christianity, by its insistence on the sovereignty of God in salvation as in all things, cannot give assent to this faith.

A one world order requires a one world religion in order to be undergirded by a living fabric of faith and law. The issue will be joined, accordingly, in the arena of Christian faith rather than in political action, for the dynamics of action are in the realm of faith. For the one world order to advance, it must wage war against religion, orthodox Christianity in particular. There is thus no escaping the fact of religious warfare. Those who refuse to offer incense to the new caesars will face both hostility and persecution. But even more certainly, they will have from their faith the assurance of victory (I Jn. 5:4, 5).

R. J. Rushdoony, *The Nature of the American System*

Features of a Godly Political Order

Sovereignty, delegation, authority — these three concepts are fundamental to any understanding of a godly and just political order.

God alone is sovereign. Man exercises authority legitimately only to the extent that such authority is delegated to him. That which civil government may legitimately do is set forth in and bounded by God's word.

In a well-developed Christian civilization, the patriarch is the principal ruler. His election derives from God. Under his direction, justice is administered, the human needs of all are to be met, and children are to be taught.

The Christian, to his peril, surrenders to civil government powers and responsibilities beyond *its* intended scope and with which *he* has been entrusted. In obtaining freedom *from* responsibility, he enslaves himself and those dependent on him.

The Christian aspires to freedom *under* the laws of God. He rejects the idea of freedom as an escape from accountability to God's requirements. Those who reject the triune God either explicitly or implicitly seek escape from his law order. They think of such as freedom from care and may even acknowledge that they desire freedom from responsibility. But the inevitable consequence of such yearning, when acted on, is dependence and enslavement, rather than liberty.

America's several states could trace their origins to contracts, compacts, and charters, civil and commercial, from which they derived their authority for territorial governance:

> The states ... had their independent existence as Christian republics prior to the Revolution. They retained their prerogative here without diminution, sharing none of it with the federal government. They did, however, in varying degrees, share that prerogative with their constituent units, the counties.[1]

> ... power gravitated from the state (*i.e.*, the colony) to the local level. A large degree of autonomy was accorded to each town in Massachusetts as early as the General Court of 1635 because of the steady insistence on local self-government.[2]

This was appropriate, inasmuch as the legitimacy of civil government is properly dependent on its accountability to the propertied family elders whose consent and participation assigns it life and force.

At the same time, it is presumptuous and unlawful for us to surrender that which is not ours to give — "Thou shalt not steal." Yet all too often we suffer our political legates to give up, not only on our behalf, but for others as well, much which we never authorized nor could properly authorize them to deliver.

Localism and Jurisdiction

Trends concerning law enforcement provide a case in point. In *The Nature of the American System*, Rushdoony reinforces the fact that the county, not the state, was long recognized as the basic unit of our domestic political order:

> ... it would be a serious error to assert that the alternative to federal sovereignty is State Rights. Important as the states are, they are not the basic unit of the American system. The basic unit is clearly and without question the county.[3]

> ... criminal law was and is county law in essence. This was an important safeguard against tyranny and against the political use of criminal law. Law enforcement officers, including judges, were and are officers of the county, in the main, or of its constituent units... not too many years ago executions were also held at the county seat. Police power and criminal law are thus matters of local jurisdiction in the American system.[4]

[1.] R. J. Rushdoony, *The Nature of the American System* (Nutley, NJ, 1965), 5.
[2.] *ibid.*, 6.
[3.] *ibid.*, 8, 9.
[4.] *ibid.*, 10.

Ideally, the local administration of justice should not be subverted by federal or even state intervention. The affected community and the citizens who reside within it ought themselves be able to apprehend, judge, and punish those who have transgressed against what is, after all, their lives, liberty, and property.

> ... the citizenry (... the propertied citizenry) does not surrender its police power to the police. It is delegation without surrender.[5]

The police are subject to the authority of those who establish and subsidize the police, the contributing citizenry. Their service as law enforcers should be honored, but it must never be forgotten that professional law enforcers have only that authority which has properly been delegated to them. They must not be allowed to become a law unto themselves. Nor should we forget that their delegated law enforcement function is not necessarily exclusive or primary:

> ... Attempts to destroy the police by destroying their purely local nature are thus veiled attacks on the right of self-defense ....
>
> A slave state has no true criminal law .... The slave population have no rights to be defended, and no police power, or right of self defense, to delegate. If all are slaves of the state, there is no police power but only state power. In a free society, the citizenry can establish a local police force, exercise their own police rights, and also create private police, patrol or detective agencies to further their right of self-defense ....
>
> Moreover, the citizenry have a further right, written into the U.S. Constitution in Amendment II: "A well-regulated militia being necessary to the security of a free state, the right of the people to keep and bear arms shall not be infringed." Attempts to infringe this right and other rights are linked also to the assault on the police power.[6]

Localism and Armament

"Gun control" is an illegitimate assault on our pre-existing God-given right and responsibility to defend ourselves from unlawful evildoers, in and out of government. Insofar as the nation-state exists to safeguard the God-given rights of those who inhabit it, arms-control treaties, analogously, constitute a kind of international "gun control," the purpose of which is to make the nation-state subject to and dependent upon a "higher" authority. In that context, even as local citizens and nation-states are disarmed, supranational authorities illicitly assume "peace force" and "police" functions.

America's Declaration of Independence was a declaration of nationhood, whose framers recognized that national status was required to safeguard liberty.

---

[5] *ibid.*, 160.
[6] *ibid.*, 160, 161.

Procedure becomes policy. By an improper delegation of authority, we in fact surrender our duty as creatures of God's will to implement his principles of restitutionary justice.

There is no such thing as a value-free choice. Procedural decisions have substantive consequences.

Assaults on Localism

There are other important areas in which America faces a crisis of accountability, wherein the state, by denying its accountability to us, diminishes our capacity to be accountable to our sovereign Lord.

Increasingly, judges fancy themselves as little gods, supposedly endowed with authority to establish their own law order and overthrowing the laws of God.

Our legislative bodies are similarly presumptuous, as are regulators, bureaucrats, and officials of private organizations subsidized with our tax dollars and politically empowered to lobby, litigate, organize, propagandize, and proselytize for their particular notions of justice and equity.

Even chief executives, unsatisfied with the extraordinary powers vested in them, seek yet more power illicitly by means of executive orders and other usurpations.

The Federal Reserve is another institution which intrinsically mocks God's specifications with respect to sovereignty, delegation, accountability, and justice.

> The drive for power knows no limits; its rationale is to be as god, and hence it is itself law in its every wish. Total warfare, in and out of war, and total conspiracy have as their goal total control. This means the control of men through their minds, by means of controlled news media, schools and churches, and also control of men economically, in particular through the control of money.[7]

> The Civil War saw the banking powers working on both sides to effect a control of money, and of civil governments and people through money .... Industry, transportation, news and other centers of power rest today on the foundation of finance capitalism and are accordingly predominantly subservient to the financial powers.[8]

The predicate for all which the Fed does is debt and indenture to quasi-political overseers, rather than providence and financial independence in a godly order:

> The Federal Reserve System is a money trust, privately owned, over which the Federal Union has little control. The Federal Reserve System

---

7. *ibid.*, 148.
8. *ibid.*, 149.

issues paper money which the United States of America, on the face thereof, guarantees, not the Federal Reserve itself. When the U.S. needs money, it issues bonds for the needed amount to the Federal Reserve System, which then issues to the U. S. Government the equivalent amount in a new currency printed by the U. S. Bureau of Engraving and Printing. At no cost to itself, the Federal System issues or creates money against which the people must pay interest on bonds, and every expansion of currency is an expansion of debt. On the other hand, when the Federal Reserve System wants new currency, it simply calls for it from the Bureau of Engraving and secures it, debt-free. This fantastic system, common to most nations, is a form of slavery without manumission.[9]

A free society is one in which the civil government is dependent on the people for its money, not one where the people rely on it for theirs. The Fed is more powerful than Congress, in that when it "taxes" the people through devaluation and manipulated interest rates, those who control it need not stand for re-election.

God's word is straightforward and explicit. That is why, at one time, ignorance of the law was no excuse, when free men knew the Bible and acknowledged it as law.

Politics is not an instrument of salvation, but, when civil government fails to do its duty, it offends against God. And, of course, when it promotes evil, it condemns itself in his eyes.

Long before George Bush made the term fashionable, Rushdoony warned of a New World Order as but the most recent version of man's desire to be as God and to rule over his fellow creatures as if he were himself Creator and Lord:

> All men insofar as they are divorced from the alienating faiths of nationalism and supernatural religion, are assumed to seek peace and to desire it. Man is good, except when perverted by limited allegiances of country and faith. But idealism is one of the worst enemies of orthodox Christianity, in that it denies the doctrine of original sin and asserts that man's works and law can overcome the effects of sin and sin itself. It assumes that men's motives are good... orthodox Christianity says that men seek... death and destruction apart from Christ. "All they that hate me love death" (Pr. 8:36).[10]

The United Nations is the incarnation of anti-Christian rebellion against God's design for a social order in which his sovereignty is not challenged by human political institutions.

It constitutes a comprehensive challenge to sovereignty and accountability by seeking to exercise ultimate control over the policies and resources of its constituents.

---

9. *ibid.*, 151.
10. *ibid.*, 127.

Indeed, former assistant UN Secretary-General Robert Mueller, now retired, in his book, *My Testament to the UN, A Contribution to the 50th Anniversary of the UN*, asserts that

> "Peace is unity ruled by law .... The United Nations seeks that unity but has been denied by nations the instrument of law. At this stage in our evolution, we should be ready for world democratic government .... A New World political system must sooner or later be devised with effective legislative, executive and judicial powers."

Conversely, Rushdoony observes:

> The U. N. believes in salvation by law, but in no historic sense does it have law. The two central definitions of law are (1) the binding custom or practice of a community, or (2) the commandments or revelations of God .... In the name of defending all cultures, the U. N. is a new humanistic culture aimed at destroying all others by means of the imperialism of world law and a world police.[11]

But, as with all those mortal creatures who seek to be as God — from the Garden of Eden to the Tower of Babel to the present day, such vanity and presumption is predestined to fail.

Howard Phillips has been chairman of The Conservative Caucus (TCC) since 1974. A 1962 graduate of Harvard College, where he was twice elected president of the Harvard Student Council, Phillips is a former chairman of the Republican Party of Boston. He is founder of the U. S. Taxpayers Alliance.

---

[11] *ibid.*, 130.

Afterword: Why We Will Win

Andrew Sandlin

In a 1977 work, prior to the dissolution of the Soviet Union and Eastern Bloc, Harold O. J. Brown wrote:

> A capitalist economy may produce better than a Communistic one, but it cannot defend itself against *Communism*, because Communism is more than an economic system .... The same thing is true in the spiritual and ideological realm where values clash. The fact that a free-market economy may produce more efficiently than a state-controlled one by no means assures that people will invariably choose it in preference to state control. A free-market economy is only an economy; it does not provide the values, the moral and spiritual reasons for preferring, and if necessary struggling to keep, the free form of economic organization. Communism, by contrast, is not only an economic system: it is also an ideology, and provides the philosophical, "spiritual" values to justify its own existence.[1]

It is a grave mistake, Brown is asserting, to assume that in a head-on clash with communism, free-market economics will win. Life is more than economics, just as communism is. Certain people are willing to make the sacrifice of economic freedom communism requires because they value certain features of communism more than they do economic freedom. Communism is a life-system, while free-market economics is an economic scheme, and when communism came crashing down in the late 80s, and literally at the Berlin Wall, it was because communism is ideologically, "religiously" — and not merely economically — untenable.

The Comprehensiveness of Real Religion

Communism, to put it ironically, is today withering away. But the genus of which communism is but a single species remains. That genus is secularism, the anthropocentric religion, *i.e.*, the religion of man. This religion of man is a worldview — just as its species communism is. It involves a view of man, work, economics, education, the arts, the future, etc. It is, in other words, a *real religion*. All true sustained religions are worldviews. This is one reason they are so attractive. They have answers for most of life's questions. The answers may not be the right answers. Indeed, because of so many conflicting religions, they *cannot* all be the right answers, but religions furnish attractive, if usually inaccurate, answers nonetheless.

---

[1] Harold O. J. Brown, *The Reconstruction of the Republic* (Milford, MI [1977], 1981), 61, 62.

The Impotence of Truncated Religion

One reason historic, orthodox Christianity has lost hegemony in the West over the last three centuries, and especially since 1865 in the United States, is that it has become something other than a full world and life view, that is, it has become something less than a *real religion*. A chief culprit contributing to this truncation has been pietism,[2] the idea that godly obedience and devotion are preferable to creeds, confessions, and doctrinal precision. Pietism ultimately diminished the truth claims of Christianity and, along with revivalism,[3] ushered in liberalism,[4] which decried doctrinal and confessional controversy and stressed instead the "ethics of Jesus" and a more personalized existential religion.[5] True, liberalism's twin, modernism, wanted the Faith to apply widely in society, but the faith it applied was a shell of the true Faith — it was, indeed, another faith altogether[6] — and its ideology could not sustain its worldview.[7]

The Fundamentalist and "Neo-Evangelical" Reaction

The chief orthodox reaction to this truncated liberal religion in the United States was fundamentalism.[8] It rightly perceived in liberalism and modernism an antisupernaturalistic bias that undermined and eventually destroyed the Faith. Because of its isolation from classical orthodoxy,[9] though, fundamentalism did not see the truncated worldview these heterodox religions represented. Therefore, ironically enough, fundamentalism developed its own truncated religion — the five points of fundamentalism (a distillation of classical confessional orthodoxy), and an attendant separatistic and anabaptistic social scheme that guaranteed its own irrelevance.

The emergence of the so-called "neo-evangelicalism"[10] signalled, it was declared, an end to the fundamentalist reductionism.[11] The neo-evangelicals,

---

[2] Dale Brown, *Understanding Pietism* (Grand Rapids, 1978).

[3] Harold O. J. Brown, *Heresies: The Image of Christ in the Mirror of Heresy and Orthodoxy from the Apostles to the Present* (Garden City, NY, 1984), 422-429.

[4] See Friedrich Schleierrnacher, *On Religion: Speeches to Its Cultured Despisers,* trans. John Oman (New York, 1958).

[5] L. Harold DeWolf, *The Case for Theology in Liberal Perspective* (Philadelphia, n.d.), 137-152.

[6] J. Gresham Machen, *Christianity and Liberalism* (Grand Rapids, 1923).

[7] William R. Hutchison, *The Modernist Impulse in American Protestantism* (Cambridge, 1976).

[8] George M. Marsden, *Fundamentalism and American Culture: The Shaping of Twentieth-Century Evangelicalism, 1870-1925* (Oxford, 1980).

[9] Carl F. H. Henry, *Evangelical Responsibility in Contemporary Theology* (Grand Rapids, 1957), 32, 33.

[10] Harold J. Ockenga, "From Fundamentalism, Through New Evangelicalism, to Evangelicalism," in ed., Kenneth Kantzer, *Evangelical Roots* (Nashville, 1978), 35-46.

[11] Carl F. H. Henry, *The Uneasy Conscience of Modern Fundamentalism* (Grand Rapids, 1947).

however, in their desire for a bland evangelical ecumenicity, were pointedly unwilling to return to the form of classical Christianity that supports a comprehensive worldview.[12] The results of this unwillingness included not merely social irrelevance almost rivaling that of the fundamentalists, but also an erosion of the orthodox Faith within evangelicalism's own ranks.[13]

Applied, Orthodox Calvinism the Only Hope

The only form of Christianity which offers a full-fledged, comprehensive historic orthodoxy equipped with the interpretive views capable of applying the whole of the Bible to the whole of life and the sound expectation of earthly ideological and institutional triumph is the Reformed Faith, and the most consistent expression of the Reformed Faith is Christian Reconstructionism — of which Rousas John Rushdoony, the theme of this book, is the ideational father. It represents a return to classical Calvinism — not just confessional Calvinism, as crucial as that is, but *applied* Calvinism — and purges the lingering elements of autonomous thought in sixteenth- and seventeenth-century Reformed orthodoxy. It thereby constitutes the purest form of Christianity, a comprehensive Faith and worldview capable of meeting and defeating the forces of secularism and other rival religions (notably Islam). This success no other form of orthodox Christianity can hope to accomplish. Its very reductionism militates against its success. Not so with Reformed Reconstructionism. It wages the battle uncompromisingly on all fronts — familial, ecclesiastical, social, political, educational, economic, artistic, technological, indeed, *everywhere.*

Reconstructionists know that only comprehensive worldviews can compete with other comprehensive worldviews. You won't beat secularism with three sermonic points and a poem. You won't beat humanism with three tearful verses of "Amazing Grace" and an Arminian altar-call. You won't beat Islam with a vacation Bible school and AWANA program. You will beat all these and other rival faiths with *full-orbed, virile, Spirit-empowered, intelligent, applied Reformed Christianity.* This is what Christian Reconstructionism is.

The humanists consider us dangerous. Of *course,* we are dangerous — to humanists. They know — even if pietistic evangelicals do not — what Christian Reconstructionism embodies: a rival Faith qualified to replace the regnant secular system *in toto.* We are not merely a "shadow government"; we are a shadow society, pressing the Crown Rights of the Lord Jesus Christ and his infallible law-word in all spheres of life, expecting eventual triumph. The great Cambridge Puritan Richard Sibbes wrote in 1630, "This very belief, that faith [in the advancement of the kingdom of God] shall be victorious, is

---

[12.] Millard Erickson, *The New Evangelical Theology* (Westwood, NJ, 1968), 210-211.

[13.] James Davison Hunter, *Evangelicalism: The Coming Generation* (Chicago, 1987).

a means to make it so indeed."[14] Humanists are not troubled greatly by a whimpering, pietistic church engaged in internecine navel-contemplation. But they sit up and take notice when Christians begin to reconstruct areas of modern life by means of the infallible word of God. They realize that Christians who jettison the idea that the world is Satan's province by right and adopt in its place the Reformed view that the world belongs to the King and those to whom he assigns its use, are in fact dangerous to the humanist ideology. They possess the worldview and implements to subvert humanism. This frightens humanists. It *should* frighten them.

We reconstructionists are sometimes accused of "triumphalism"[15] in our dedication to the postmillennial notion that the kingdom of God will advance inexorably and visibly in time and history by means of the faithful preaching and application of the Bible, the infusion of the power of the Holy Spirit, and the obedience of the covenant people of God. If by "triumphalism" is meant an attitude of eschatological smugness, the charge is, one hopes at least, incorrect. If, however, by "triumphalism" one means belief that God will employ his Spirit to energize his covenant body to advance the kingdom of God in time and history in all spheres, we reconstructionists plead guilty. This is not smugness, but faith.

Victory Assured

Satan's kingdom and hosts, in alliance with humanism and other false faiths, is ripe for destruction. No human kingdom or ideology can withstand the kingdom of the Lord Jesus Christ, the stone cut without hands that becomes "a great mountain, and fill[s] the whole earth" (Dan. 2:35).[16] Of this kingdom Daniel predicts, "the saints of the most High shall take the kingdom, and possess the kingdom for ever, even for ever and ever" (7:18). Christian reconstructionists advance this kingdom by the preaching of the gospel in its purity and law in its cogency, and by applying the Biblical Faith in every sphere of life and society. We present a Biblical, Spirit-empowered comprehensive alternative to all rival faiths. Our Faith cannot but triumph. We can meet all rival faiths, point by point, issue by issue, law by law, practice by practice, and, by the grace of God, defeat each. We demand of all rival faiths unconditional surrender *in every dimension of existence* to the King of kings and Lord of lords.

This is why we will win.

[14.] Richard Sibbes, *The Bruised Reed and Smoking Flax,* in *Works of Richard Sibbes* (Edinburgh, 1973), 100.

[15.] Richard B. Gaffin, Jr., "Theonomy and Eschatology: Reflections on Postmillennialism," in ed., William S. Barker and W. Robert Godfrey, *Theonomy: A Reformed Response* (Grand Rapids, 1990), 216. For a cogent answer, see Kenneth L. Gentry, "Whose Victory in History?", in ed., Gary North, *Theonomy: An Informed Response* (Tyler, TX, 1991), 207-230.

[16.] For an exegetical defense of postmillennialism, see Marcellus Kik, *An Eschatology of Victory* (no location [Presbyterian and Reformed], 1975), and Kenneth Gentry, *He Shall Have Dominion* (Tyler, TX, 1992).

Works of R. J. Rushdoony

(* indicates pamphlet)

By What Standard? 1958

Van Til 1960 (also included in *By What Standard?*)

Intellectual Schizophrenia 1961

The Messianic Character of American Education 1963

This Independent Republic 1964

*Translation and Subversion** 1964

Freud 1965

The Nature of the American System 1965

*The Religion of Revolution** 1965

"Has the U.N. Replaced Christ as a World Religion?"
    chapter in *Your Church - Their Target* 1966

*Preparation for the Future** 1966

The Mythology of Science 1967

The Biblical Philosophy of History 1969

The Foundations of Social Order 1968

The Myth of Over-Population 1969

Bread Upon the Waters 1969

Thy Kingdom Come 1970

The Politics of Guilt and Pity 1970

The One and the Many 1971

Law and Liberty 1971

*Killing by Abortion** 1971

"The Doctrine of Man" and "The Doctrine of Marriage,"
    chapters in *Toward a Christian Marriage* 1972

The Institutes of Biblical Law 1973

Flight from Humanity 1973

The Politics of Pornography 1974

The Word of Flux 1975

"The Quest for Common Ground" and "Psychology,"
    chapters in *The Foundations of Christian Scholarship* 1976

*God's Plan for Victory** 1977

Revolt Against Maturity 1977

Infallibility: An Inescapable Concept (also in *Systematic Theology*) 1978

Necessity for a Systematic Theology (also in *Systematic Theology*) 1979

Tithing and Dominion (with Edward Powell) 1979

The Philosophy of the Christian Curriculum 1981

The Roots of Inflation 1982

Law and Society, Vol. II of the Institutes of Biblical Law 1982

Salvation and Godly Rule 1983

The "Atheism" of the Early Church 1983

Christianity and the State 1986

The Roots of Reconstruction 1991

The Great Christian Revolution
   (co-authored with Otto Scott and Mark R. Rushdoony) 1991

Systematic Theology 1994

Commentary on Romans and Galatians (in preparation)

Some unpublished works:

Commentary on Exodus

Commentary on Leviticus

Commentary on Numbers

Commentary on Deuteronomy

The Ministry of Chalcedon

CHALCEDON (kal•see•don) is a Christian educational organization devoted exclusively to research, publishing, and to cogent communication of a distinctively Christian scholarship to the world at large. It makes available a variety of services and programs, all geared to the needs of interested ministers, scholars and laymen who understand the propositions that Jesus Christ speaks to the mind as well as the heart, and that His claims extend beyond the narrow confines of the various institutional churches. We exist in order to support the efforts of all orthodox denominations and churches. Chalcedon derives its name from the great ecclesiastical Council of Chalcedon (A.D. 451), which produced the crucial Christological definition: "Therefore, following the holy Fathers, we all with one accord teach men to acknowledge one and the same Son, our Lord Jesus Christ, at once complete in Godhead and complete in manhood, truly God and truly man ...." This formula directly challenges every false claim of divinity by any human institution: state, church, cult, school, or human assembly. Christ alone is both God and man, the unique link between heaven and earth. All human power is therefore derivative: Christ alone can announce that "All power is given unto me in heaven and in earth" (Matthew: 28:18). Historically, the Chalcedonian creed is therefore the foundation of Western liberty, for it sets limits on all authoritarian human institutions by acknowledging the validity of the claims of the One who is the source of true human freedom (Galatians 5:1).

The *Chalcedon Report* is published monthly and is sent to all who request it. Your donation in support of this ministry is appreciated. All gifts to Chalcedon are tax deductible. Send contributions and correspondence to:

Chalcedon
Box 158
Vallecito, CA 95251 U.S.A.

Ross House Books

For a list of books by R. J. Rushdoony and other Christian reconstructionists, contact:

Ross House Books
Box 67
Vallecito, CA 95251 U.S.A.

Friends of Chalcedon

Friends of Chalcedon exists to assist those attempting to live out the implications of the Reformed, reconstructionist Faith. All gifts to Friends of Chalcedon are tax deductible. Send contributions and correspondence to:

Friends of Chalcedon
4960 Almaden Expressway, #172
San Jose, CA 95118 U.S.A.